AF594609

FORGOTTEN
NOVA SCOTIA

Ted Pritchard and Ingrid Bulmer

MacIntyre Purcell Publishing Inc.

MacIntyre Purcell Publishing Inc.
194 Hospital Rd.
Lunenburg, Nova Scotia
B0J 2C0
(902) 640-3350

www.macintyrepurcell.com
info@macintyrepurcell.com

Printed and bound in Canada by Friesens

Cover design: Denis Cunningham
Book design: Denis Cunningham
Author photo (Ingrid Bulmer): Axel Wirth Bulmer
Author photo (Ted Pritchard): Ingram Barss

ISBN: 978-1-77276-155-9

Library and Archives Canada Cataloguing in Publication Title: Forgotten Nova Scotia / Ted Pritchard and Ingrid Bulmer. Names: Pritchard, Ted, photographer. | Bulmer, Ingrid, photographer. Identifiers: Canadiana 20200227114 | ISBN 9781772761559 (hardcover) Subjects: LCSH: Nova Scotia—Pictorial works. | LCSH: Abandoned buildings—Nova Scotia—Pictorial works. | LCGFT: Photobooks. Classification: LCC FC2312 .P75 2020 | DDC 971.6/050222—dc23

MacIntyre Purcell Publishing Inc. would like to acknowledge the financial support of the Government of Canada and the Nova Scotia Department of Tourism, Culture and Heritage.

Funded by the Government of Canada | Canada NOVA SCOTIA

I want to dedicate this book to my late father, Jim Bulmer,
and my late husband, Christoph Wirth-Bulmer.
They were taken too soon but
we will carry them always in our hearts.

— Ingrid Bulmer

I want to dedicate this book to my lovely wife, Sandra Bulmer.
None of this would be possible without her love, support and guidance.
To have such a wonderful partner in life is truly a blessing.

— Ted Pritchard

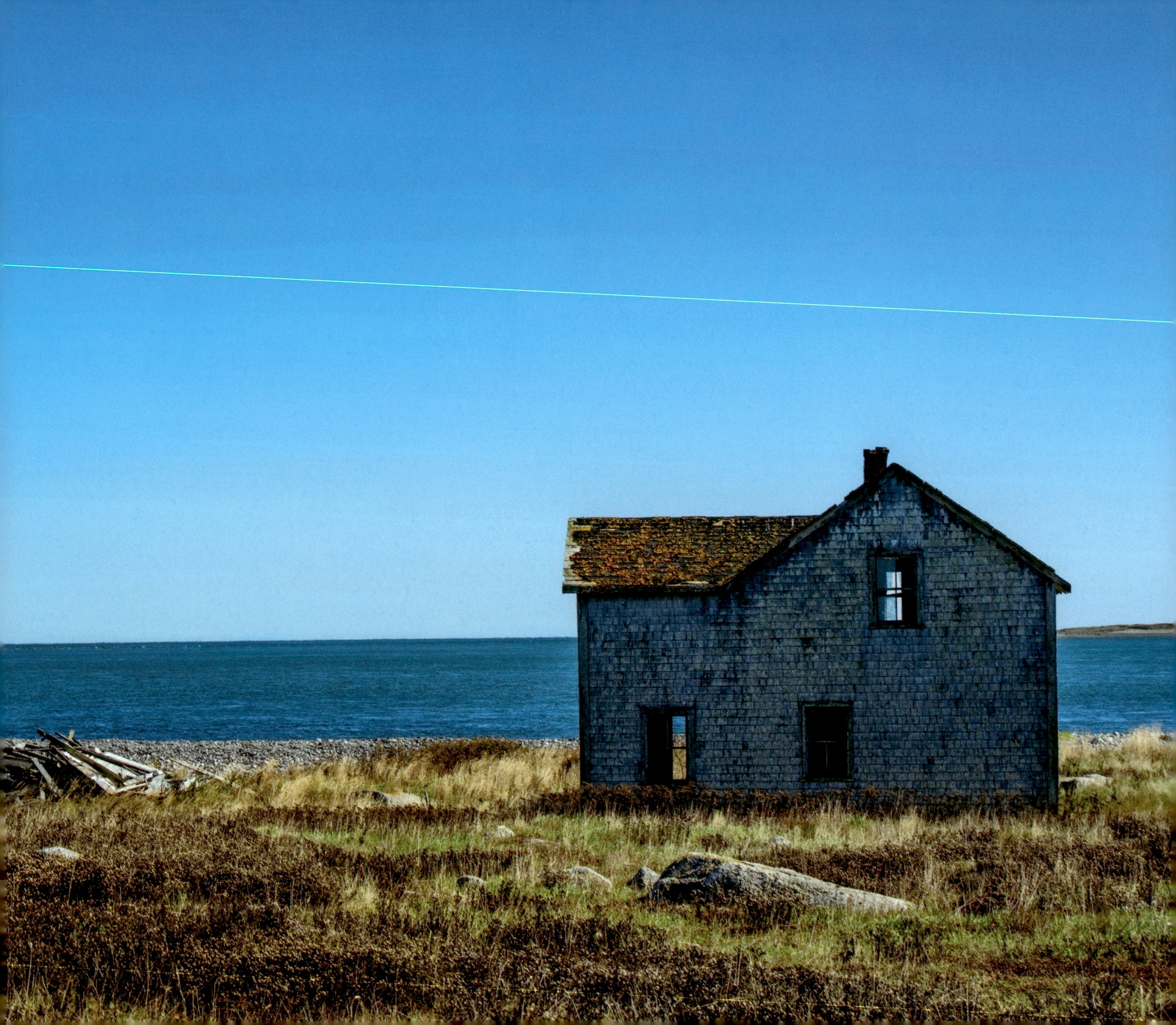

Introduction

In the summer of 2019, we set out to search for abandoned places across Nova Scotia. It didn't take long to find a treasure trove of old homes, forgotten schools, derelict churches and vehicles.

As seasons changed, we continued our journey to capture these places forsaken to the elements and document what we could outside and, if possible, inside.

Along the way we started to ask ourselves about the series of events that could lead a person or family to simply leave a home and never return. We suspected many were estate properties with nobody left to care for them. But whatever the reason, we wanted to help the reader get a closer look at what was inside these buildings, to take you on a journey to places you may not physically be able to reach for a variety of reasons.

Abandoned, forsaken, forgotten are terms used to describe anything left unattended for long periods of time. Focusing primarily on homes left to the vagaries of Nova Scotia's weather, we also wanted to explore other places and items people left behind. One such place was Seal Island, 32 kilometres off the southwestern tip of Nova Scotia. The other is Flat Island, where only one of two houses built on the two-hectare Yarmouth County retreat remains standing.

(Opposite) A house once used by fishers lies abandoned on Flat Island, more than 15 kilometres off the southern coast of Nova Scotia

These islands embody abandonment. An occasional wild sheep grazing in the high grass interrupts the quietude of lobster traps washed ashore amid a sanctuary of abandoned barns, outhouses and buoys.

Having explored the province, we realized there is beauty in isolation. Some homes were built in remote areas and those owners probably had their reasons for separating themselves from others. We went out of our way to respect these properties by not disturbing items we found inside. Everything we photographed is how we found it.

Does that mean others who were there before us exercised the same level of care? No. But we felt strongly that we should capture what was there and not create a new storyline.

We know there are endless possibilities to document forgotten places across the province, but we hope you enjoy sampling some of the homes and places we felt fortunate to find.

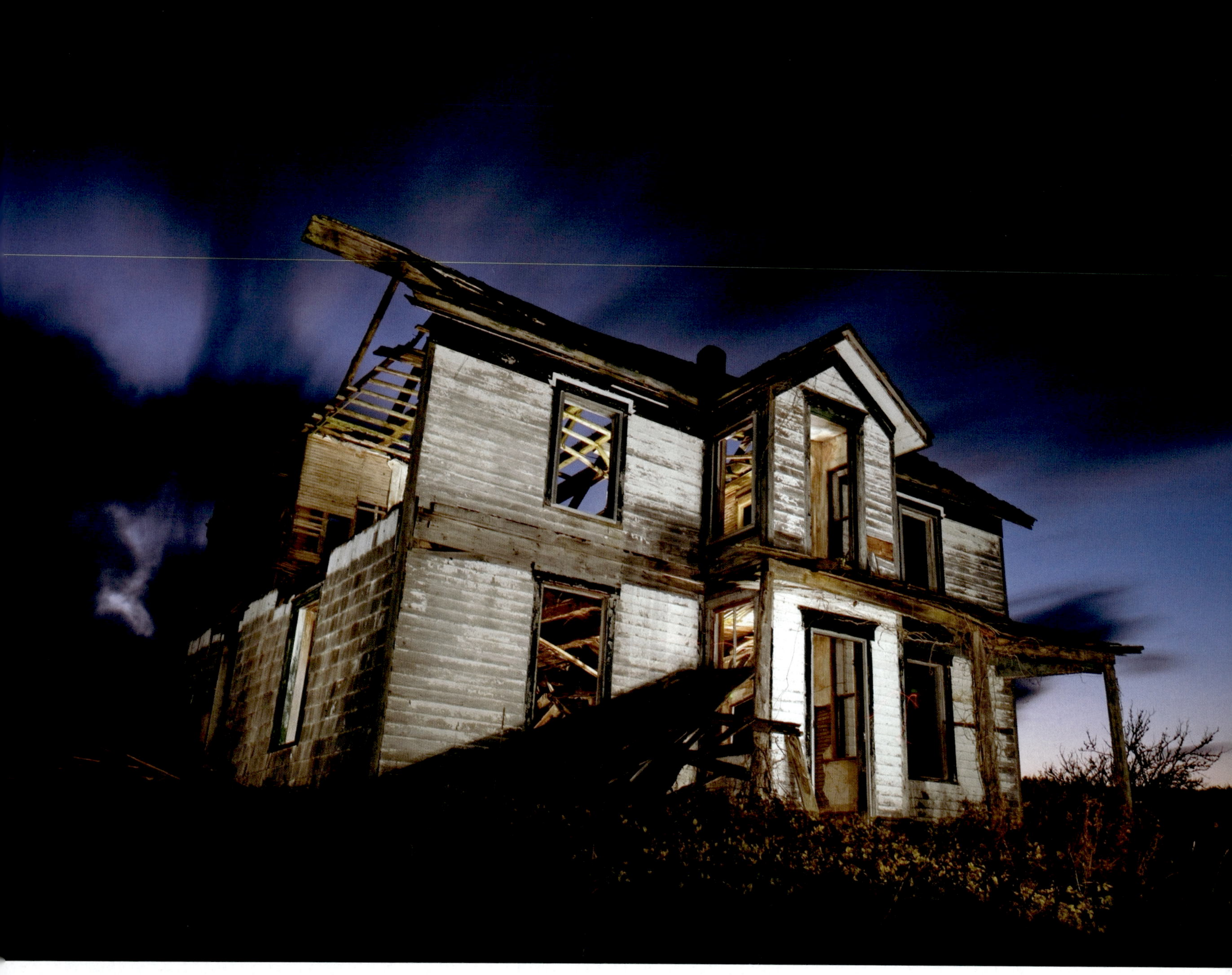

(Opposite) About 32 kilometres north of Truro, this classic structure in the rural community of Earltown, Colchester County, is a popular spot for abandoned photo enthusiasts. The elements are slowly taking a toll on this farmhouse, which was built in 1860. According to a story on CBC's *Land and Sea*, family members dubbed the house Funny Farm because of how much they would laugh together while growing up in this rural community.

(Right) A forgotten home sits under a moody sky along the road between the communities of Whitehead and Lower Whitehead in Guysborough county.

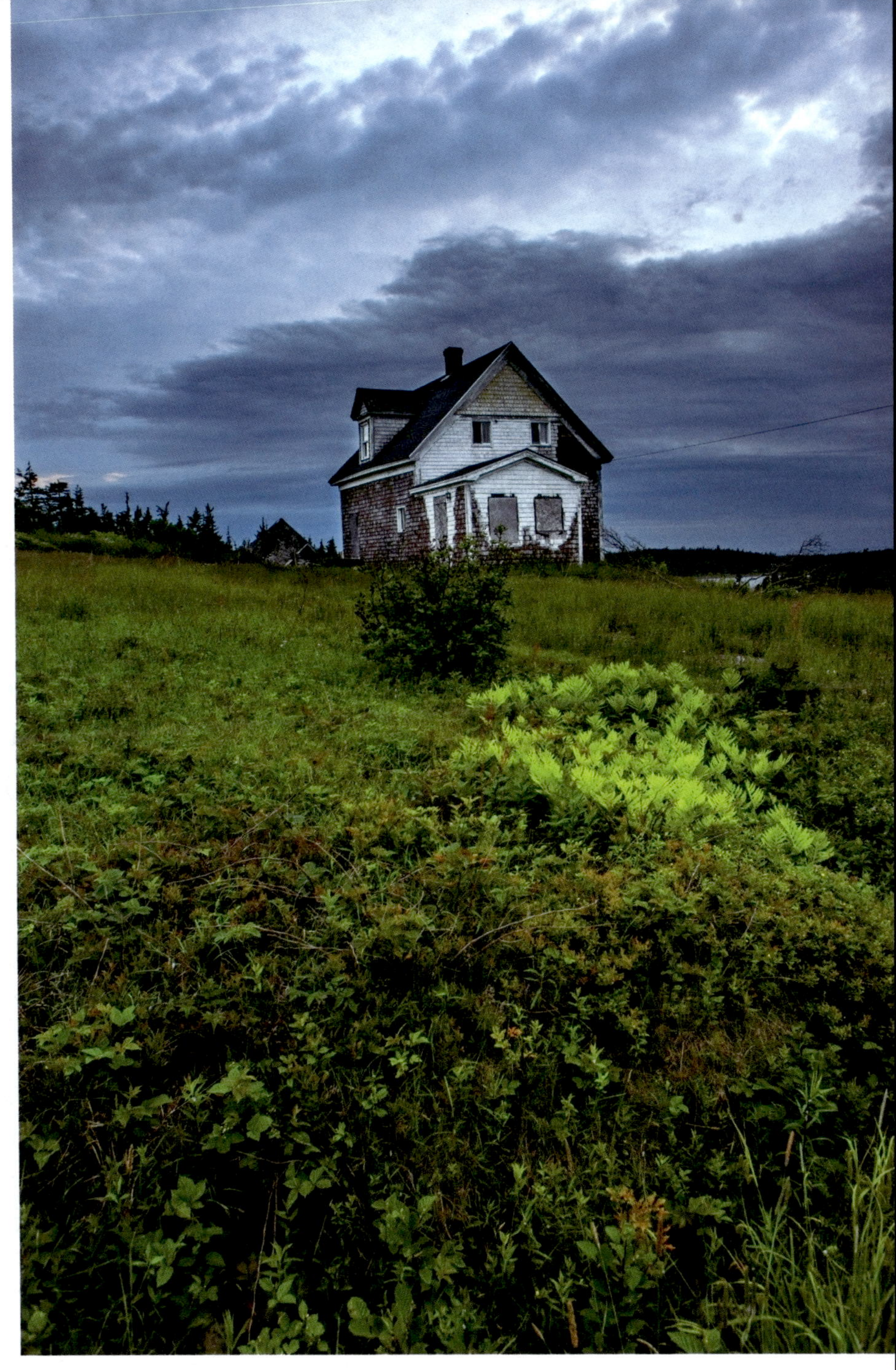

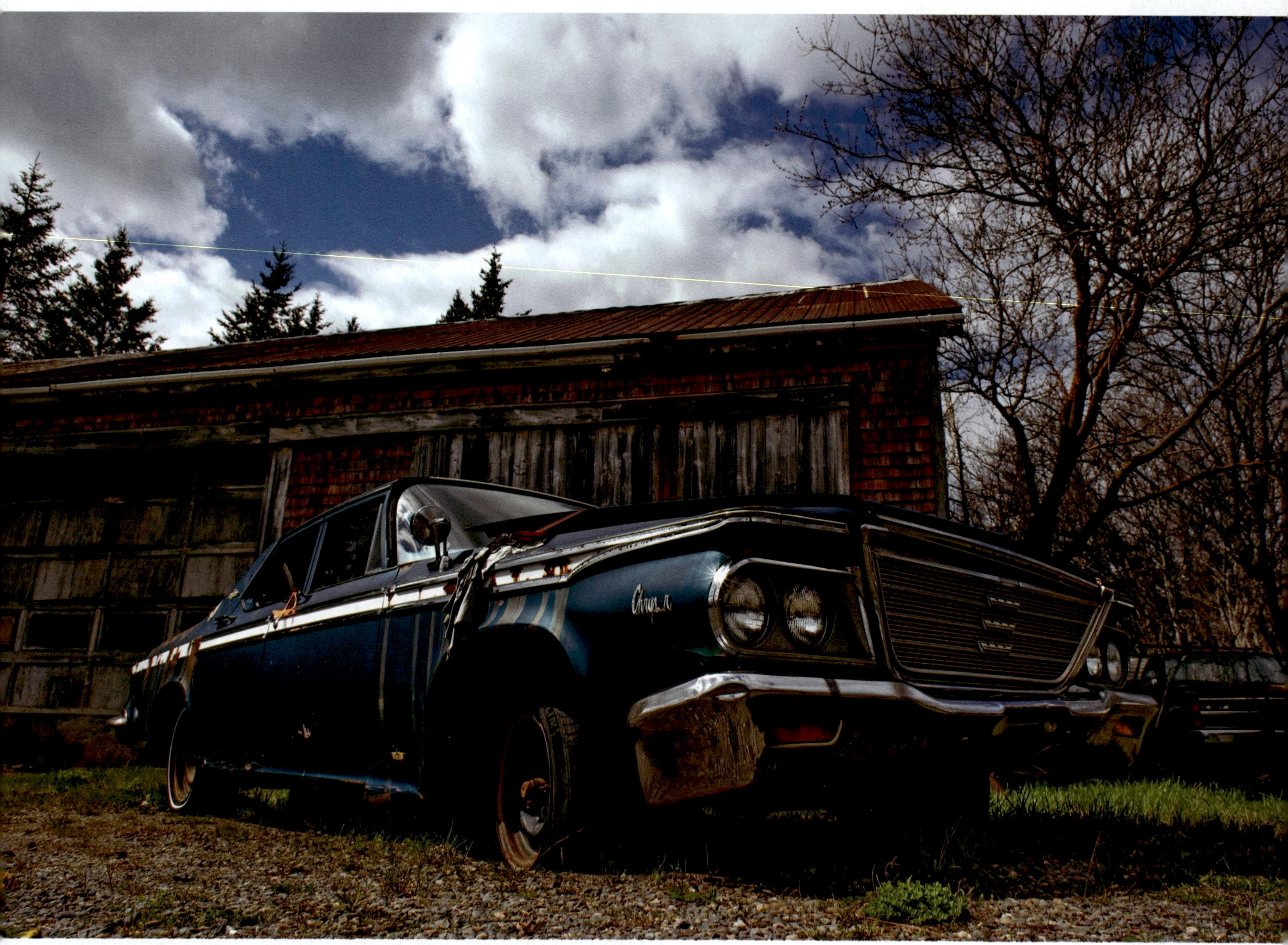

An old classic car sits rusting in a lot in Middle Musquodoboit in central Nova Scotia.

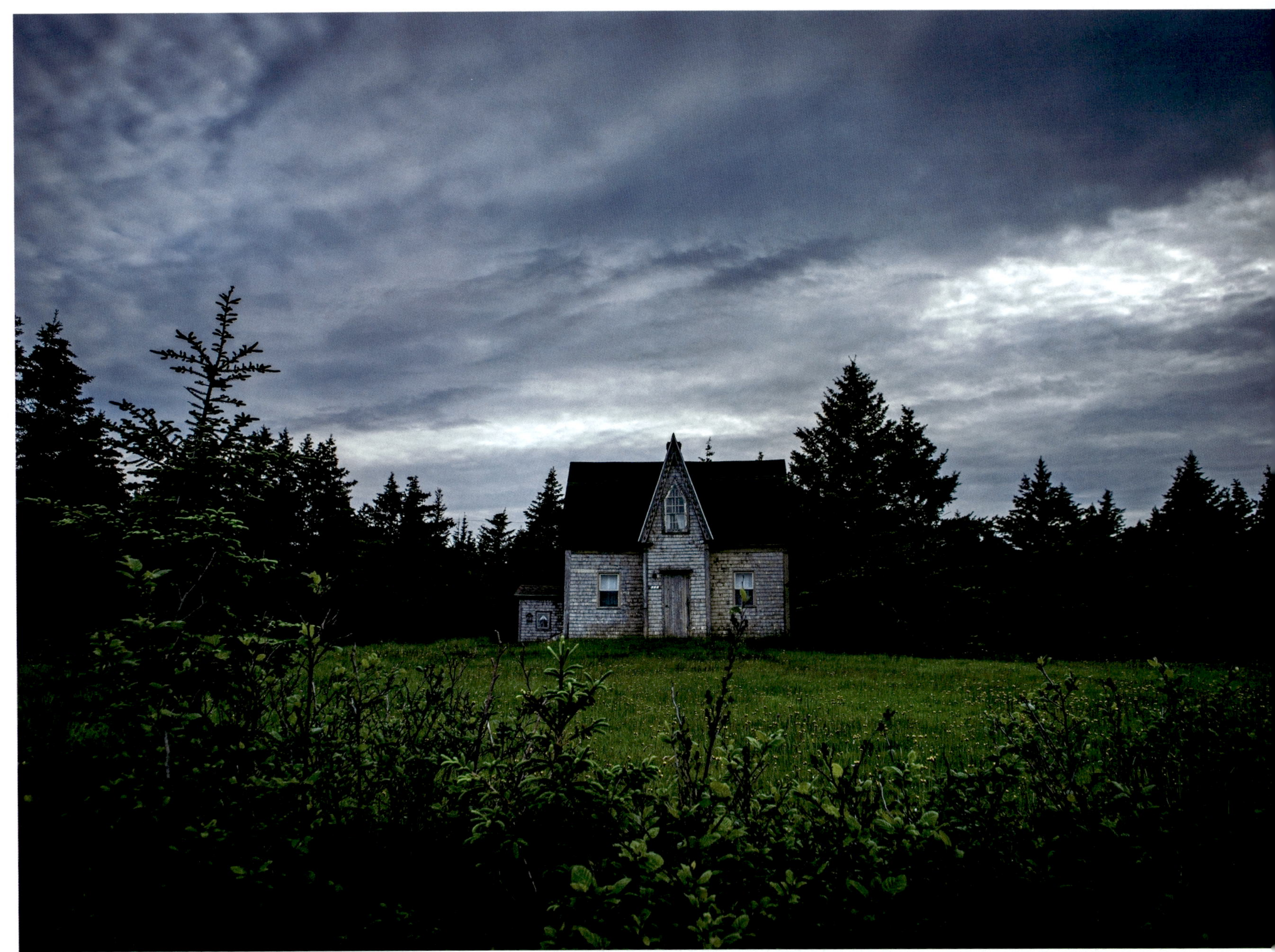

This eerie home in Lower Whitehead is located at the end of a road in Whitehead Harbour. Although it is no longer occupied, there appeared to be some upkeep of the grounds.

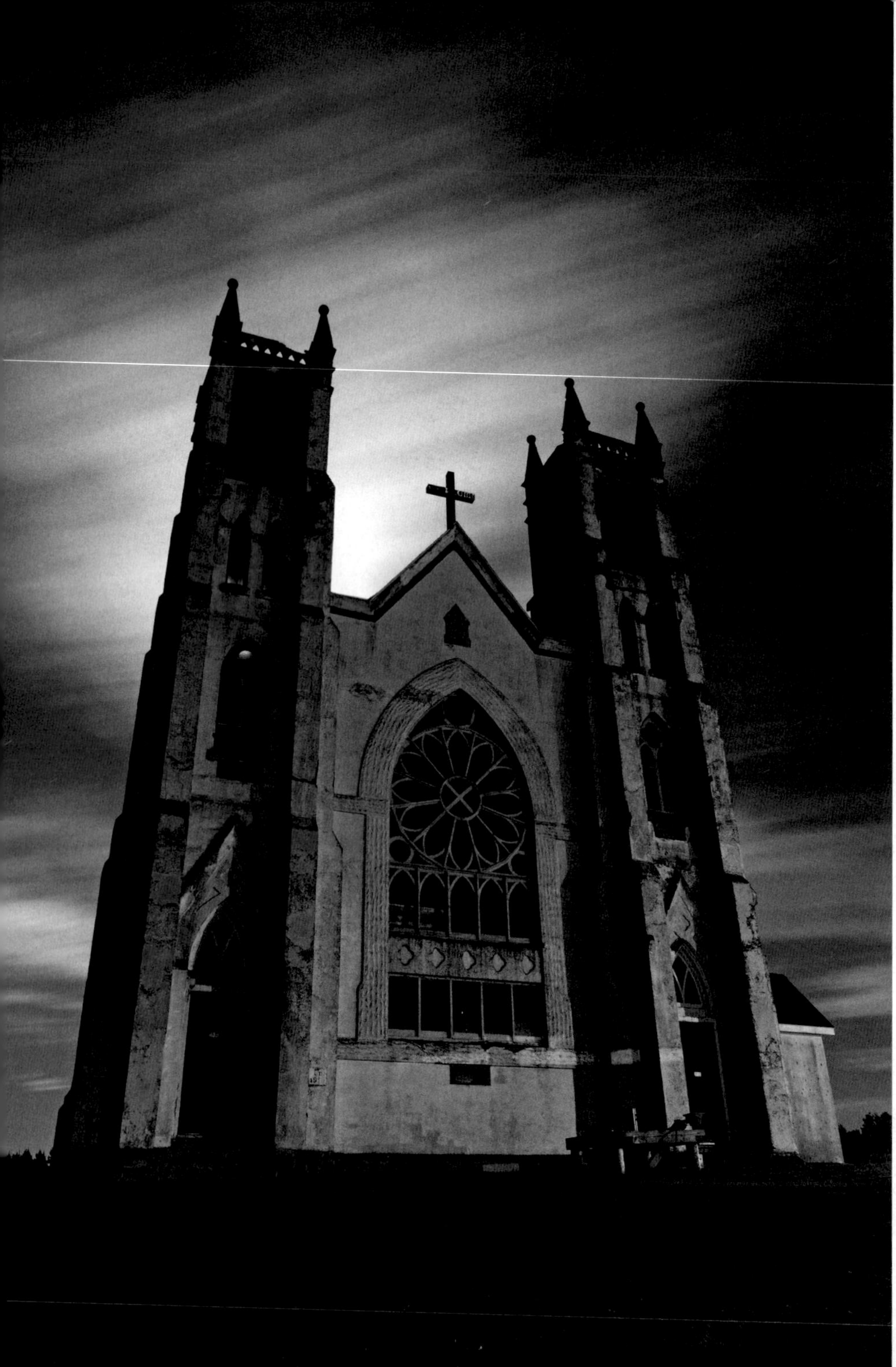

(Left) The historic and deconsecrated St. Alphonsus Church in Victoria Mines, Cape Breton, pictured in a long night exposure.

(Opposite) A dress hangs in a window of a remote, abandoned home on the South Shore.

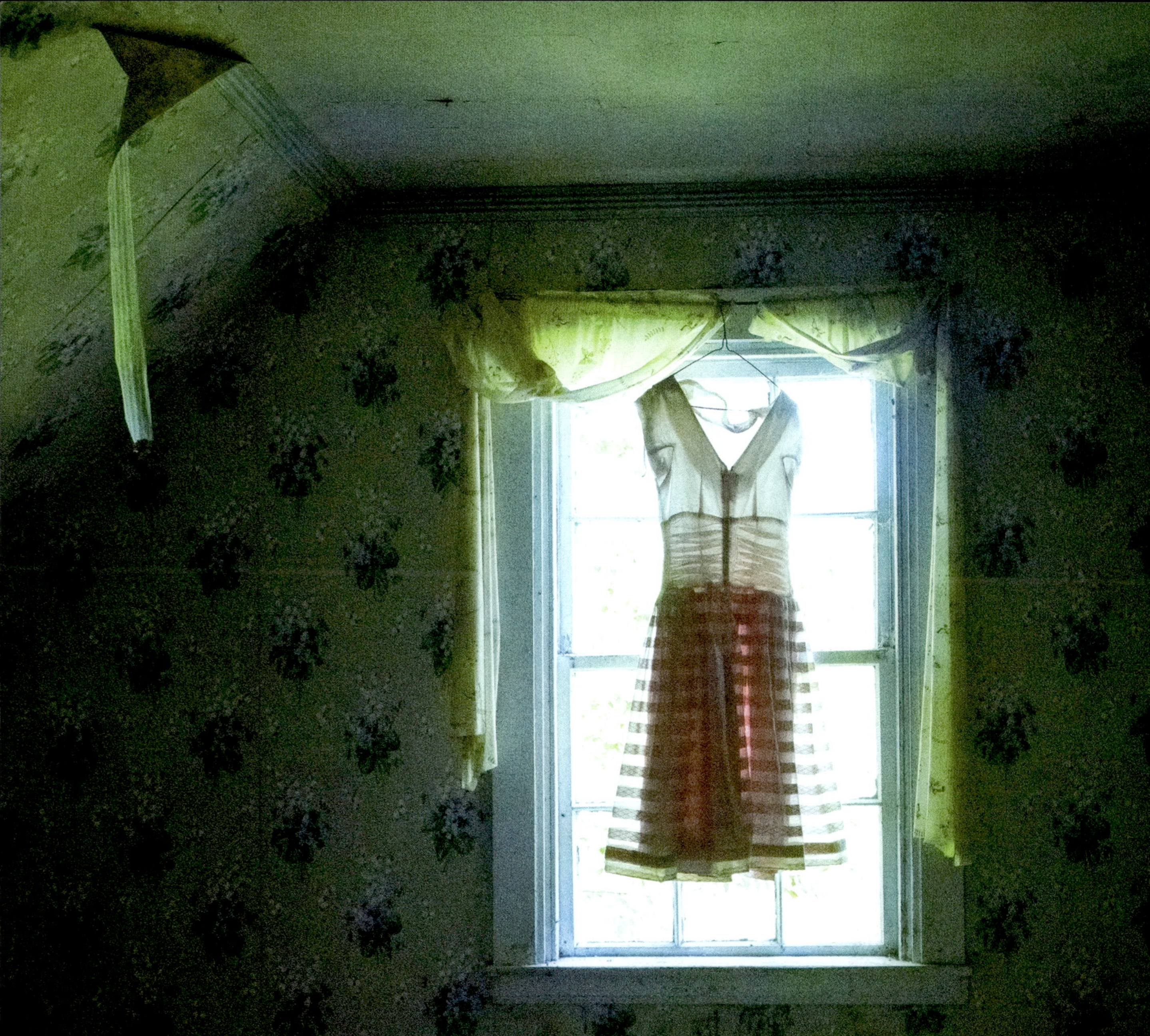

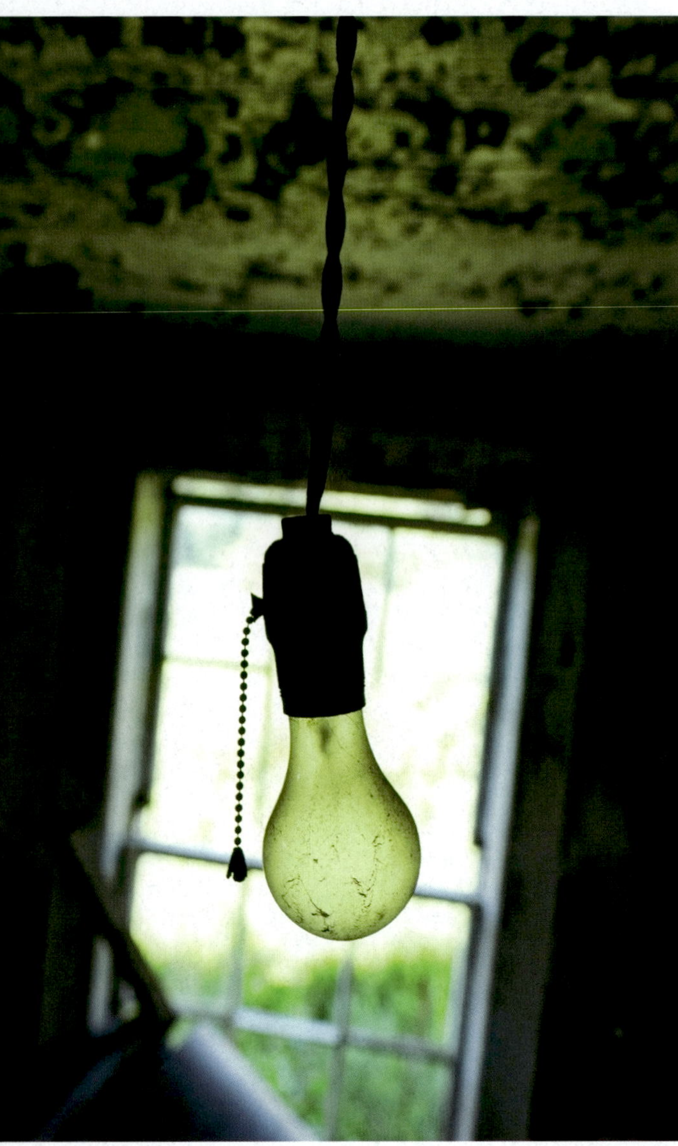

(Left) A common theme in abandoned houses is the single hanging lightbulb like this one from a home outside Antigonish. Once the roof has been breached and water is allowed to enter the home, ceilings and fixtures are often the first to go.

(Opposite) A glass door handle from a home in central Queens County on the South Shore. Isolated and set back from the road, the home was barely visible with the trees surrounding it. We don't know the age of the house but the front page of an old newspaper was dated 1934.

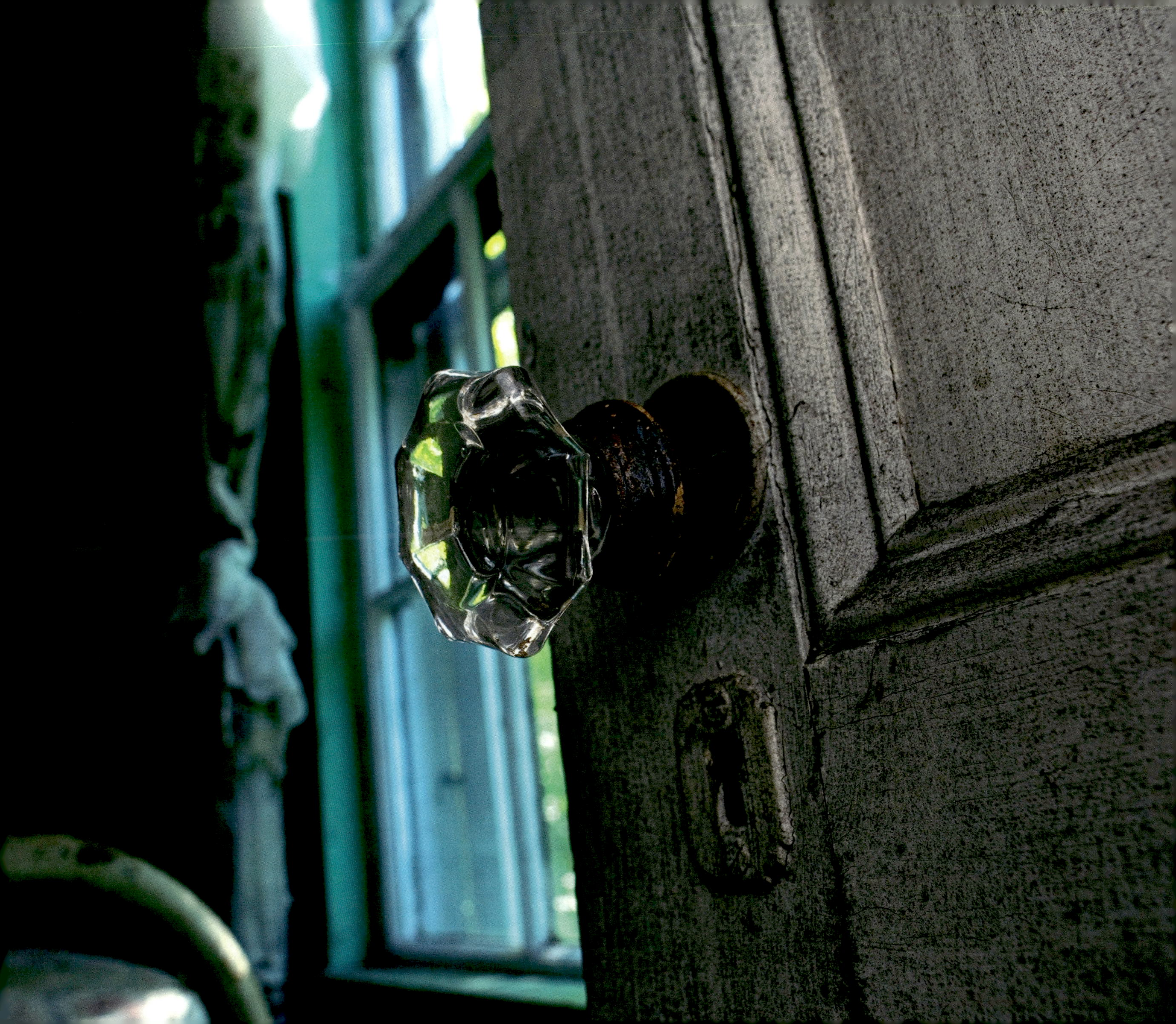

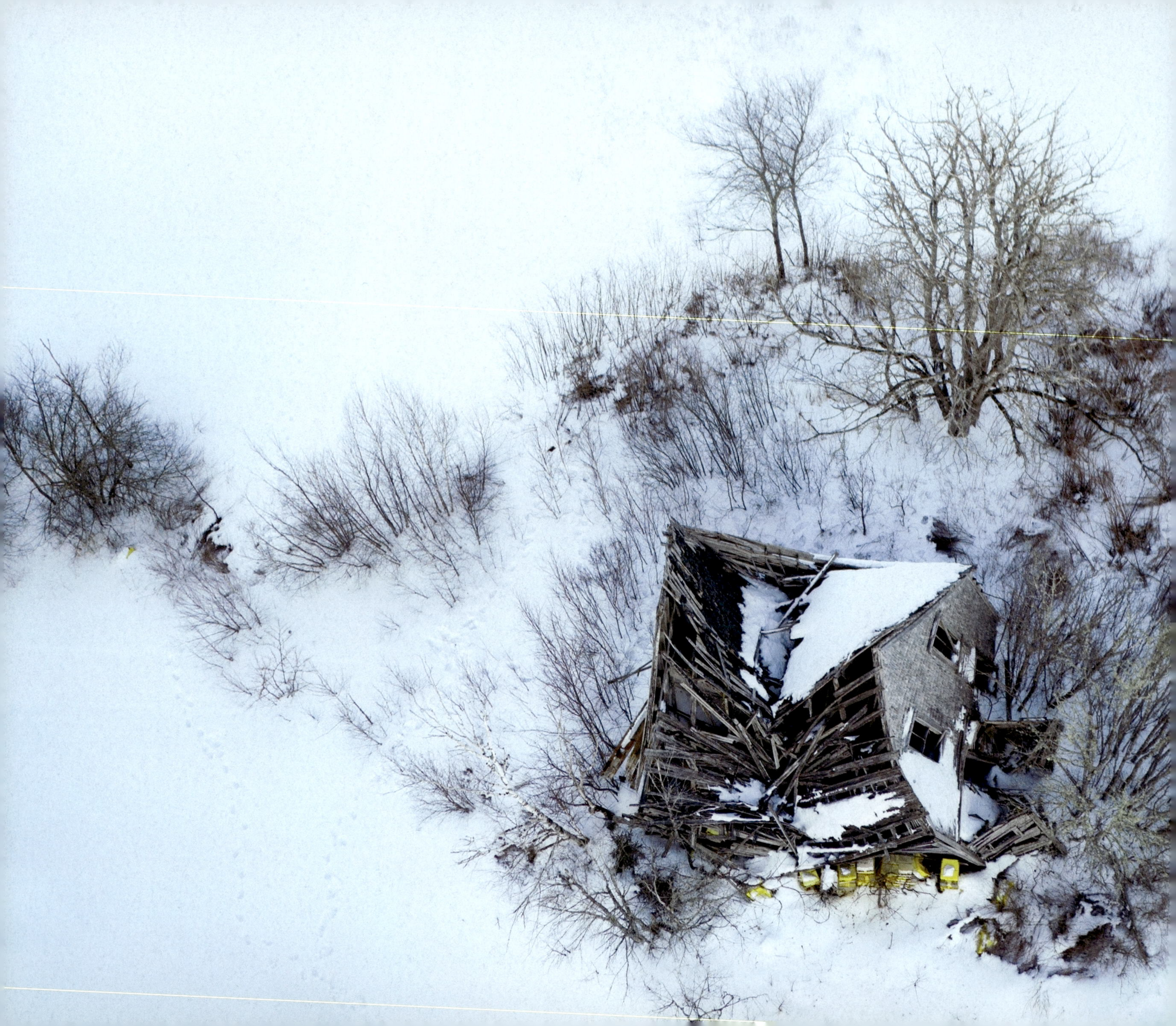

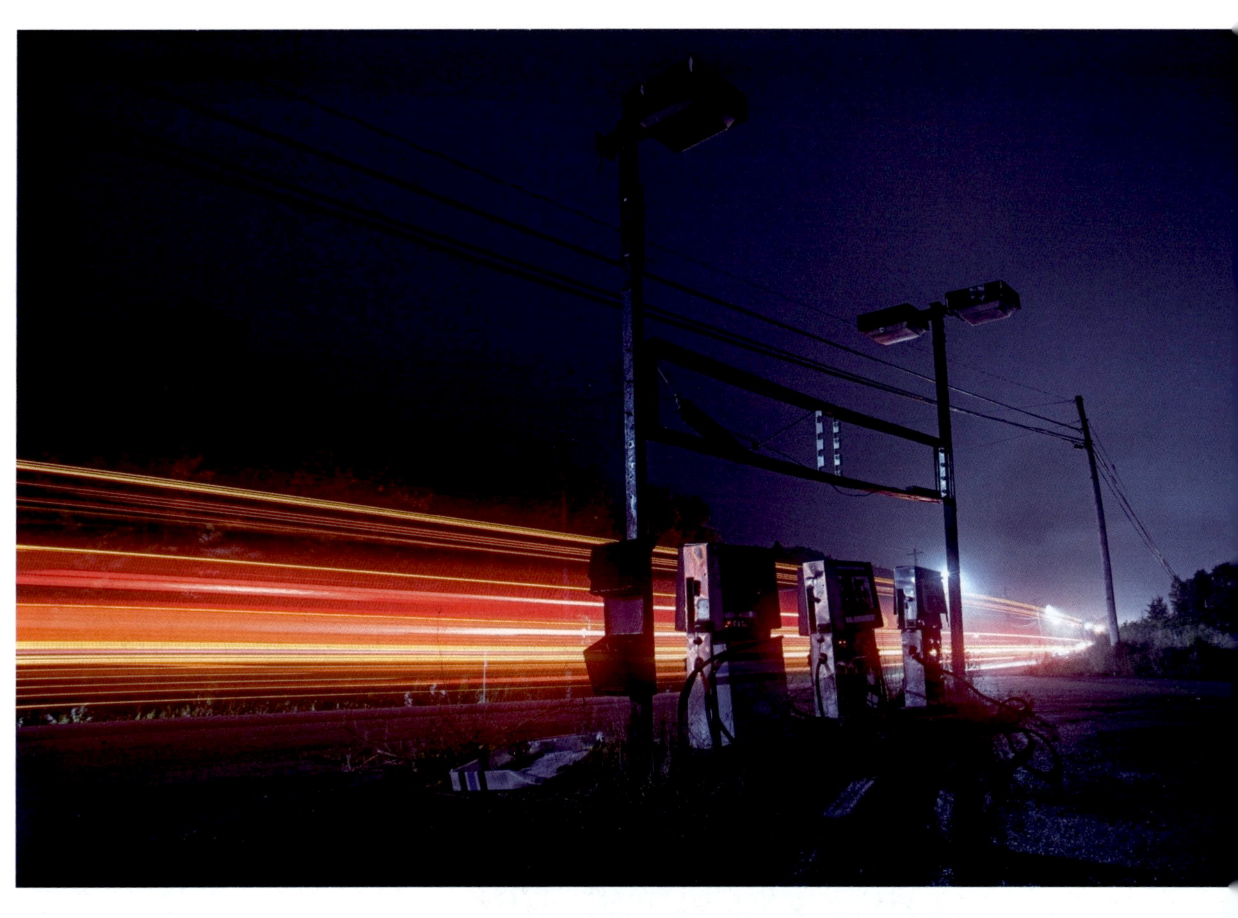

(Opposite) The collapsed structure of an abandoned home high on a hilltop in remote Cumberland County viewed from the perspective of a drone.

(Above) Long night exposure of road traffic passing derelict gas pumps. The abandoned gas station is off the Trans-Canada Highway in Whycocomagh, Cape Breton.

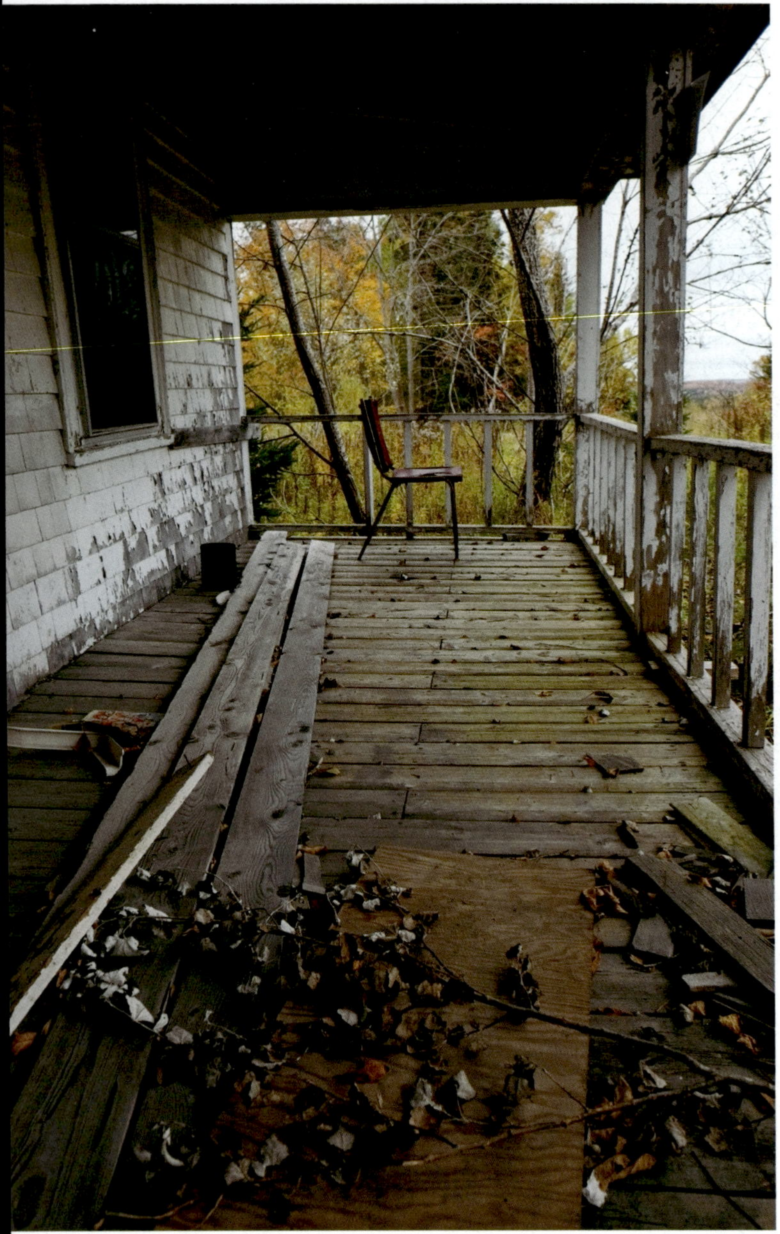

(Opposite and Left) The front facade and porch of an abandoned home tucked away in Inverness County in Cape Breton.

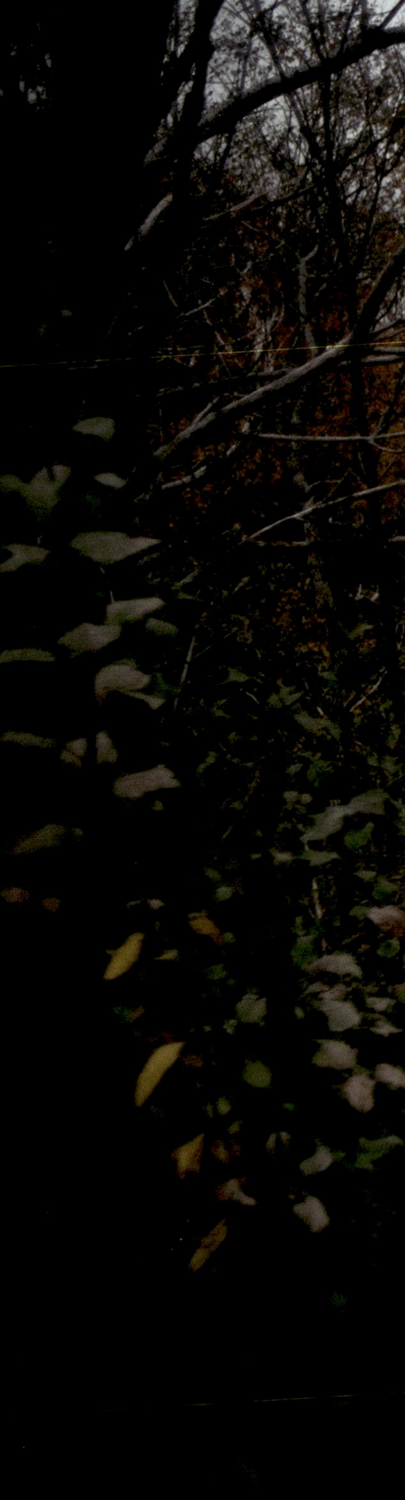

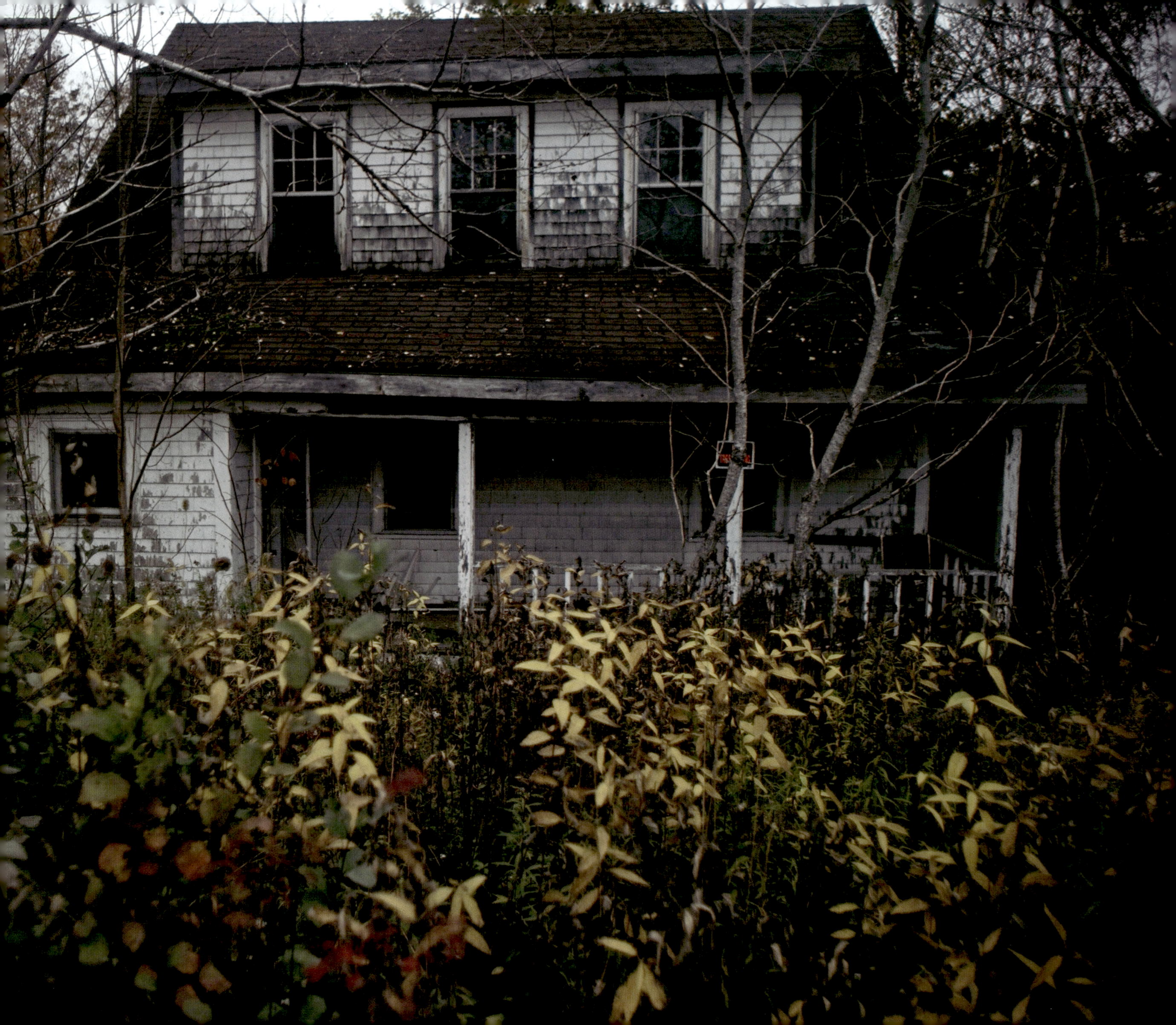

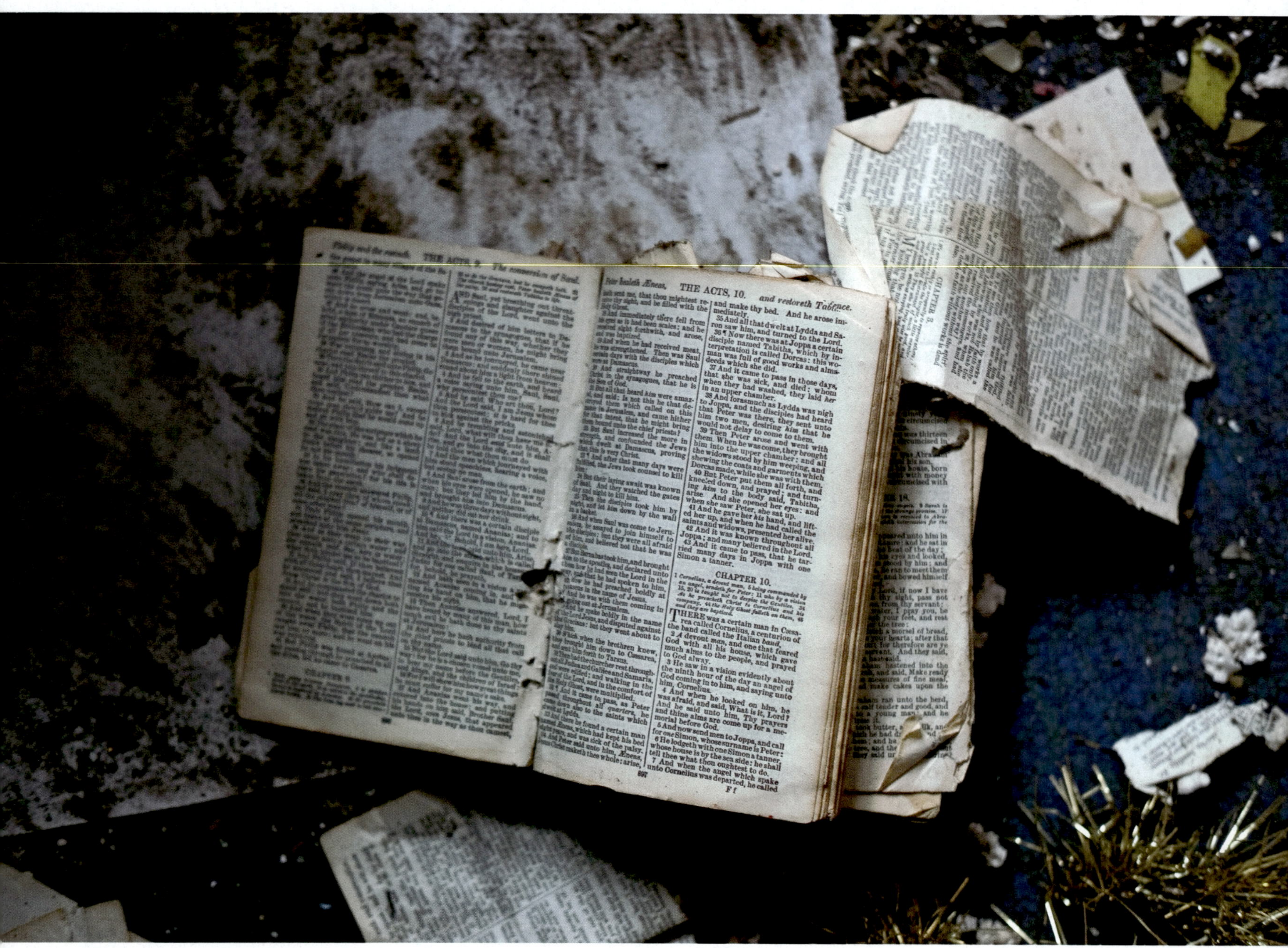

As we made our way through the Inverness home (featured on page 16 and 17), we found an open bible among the debris.

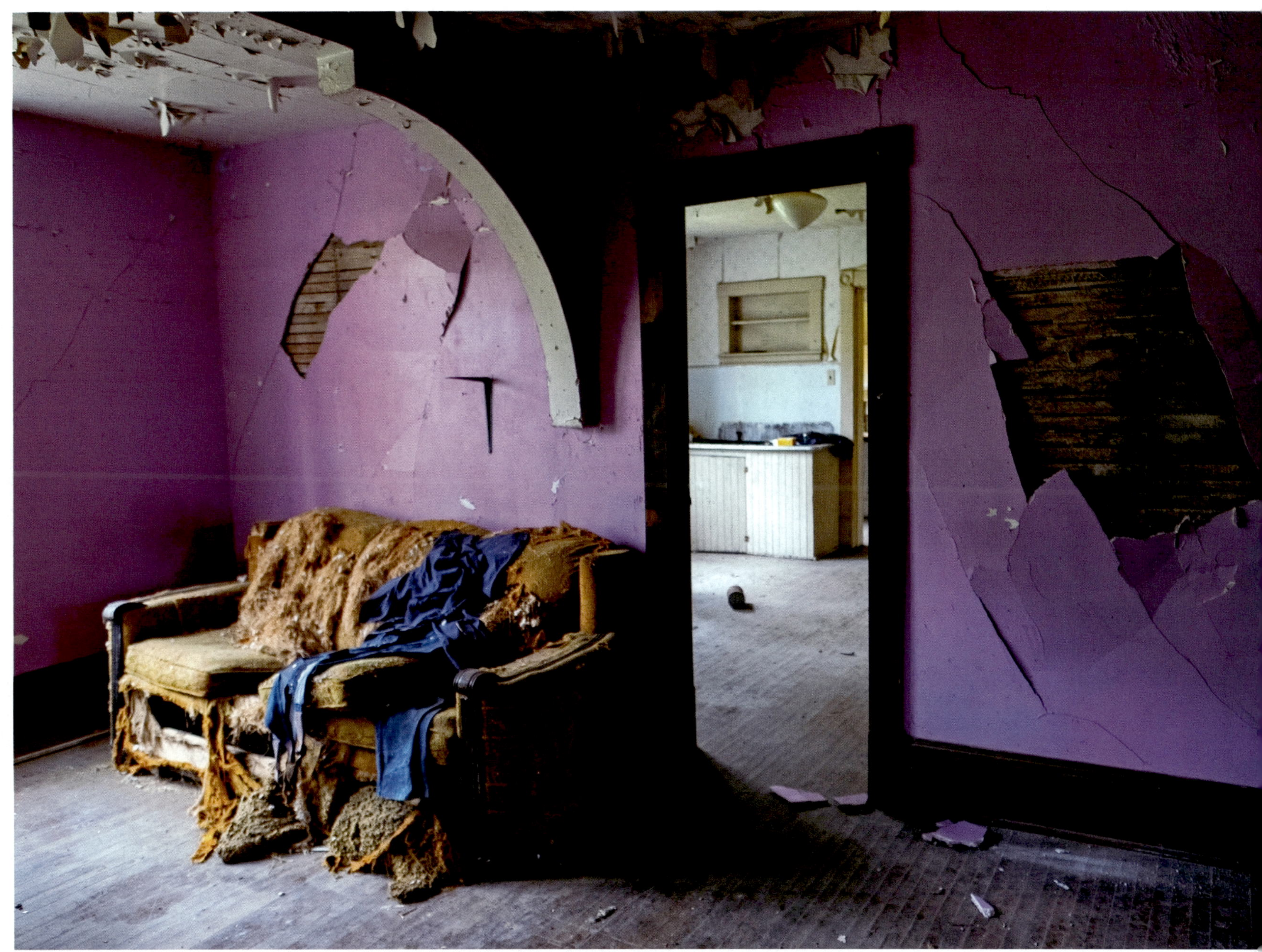

In this same home, the vibrant coloured walls, interesting architecture and original wooden moldings seemed an incongruous match for the decaying sofa tucked away in the corner of what most likely was the living room.

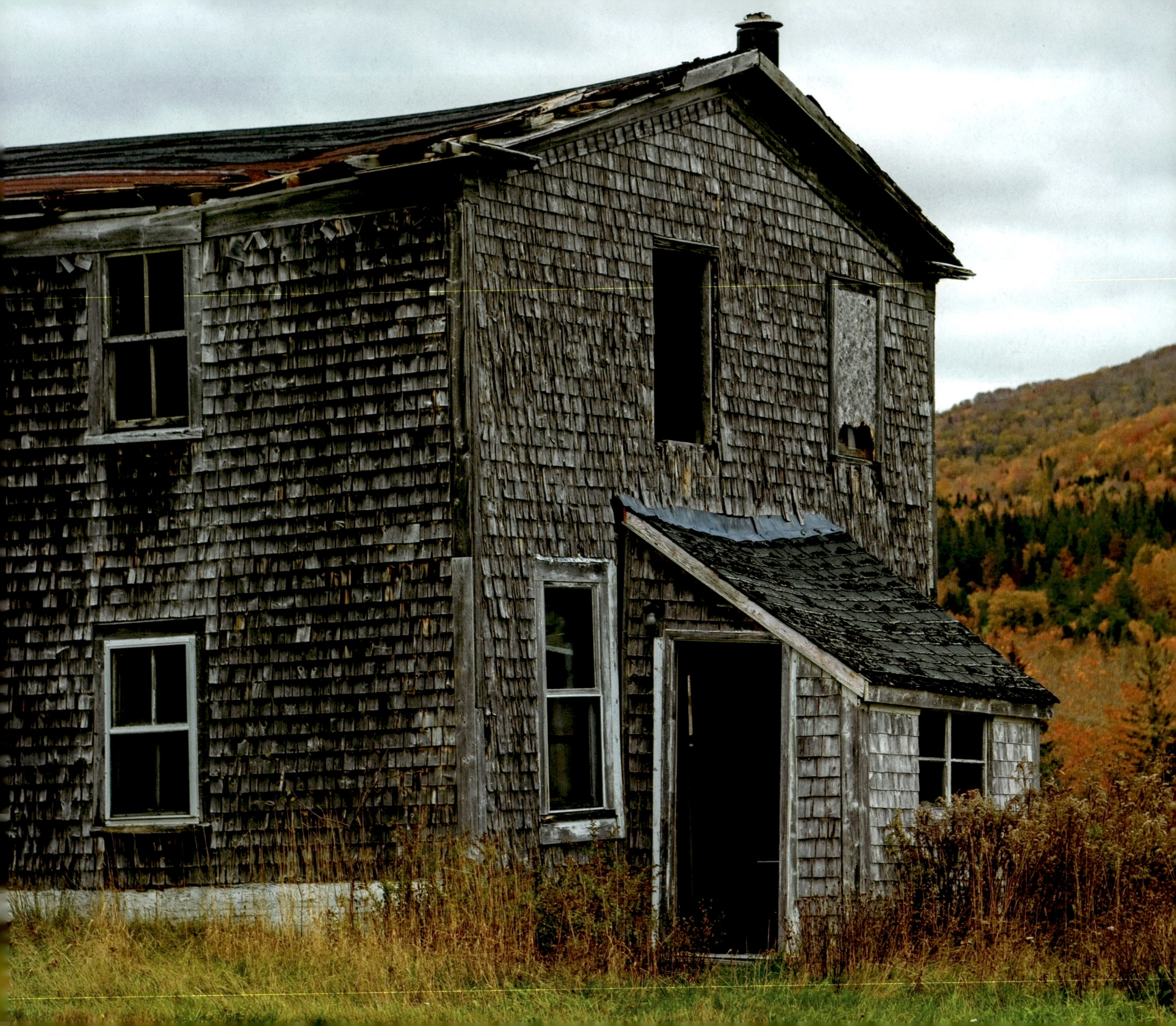

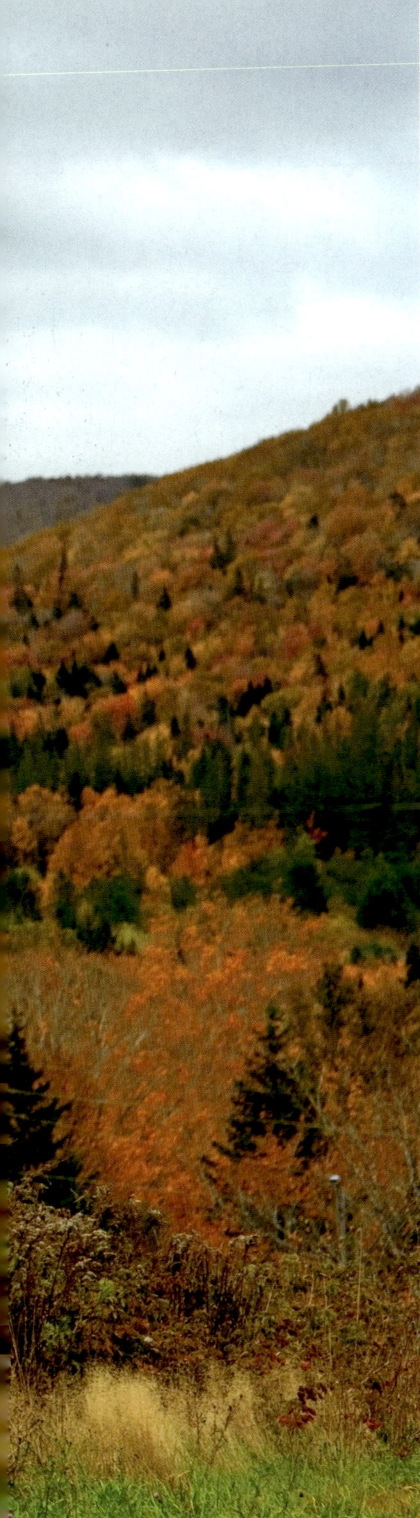

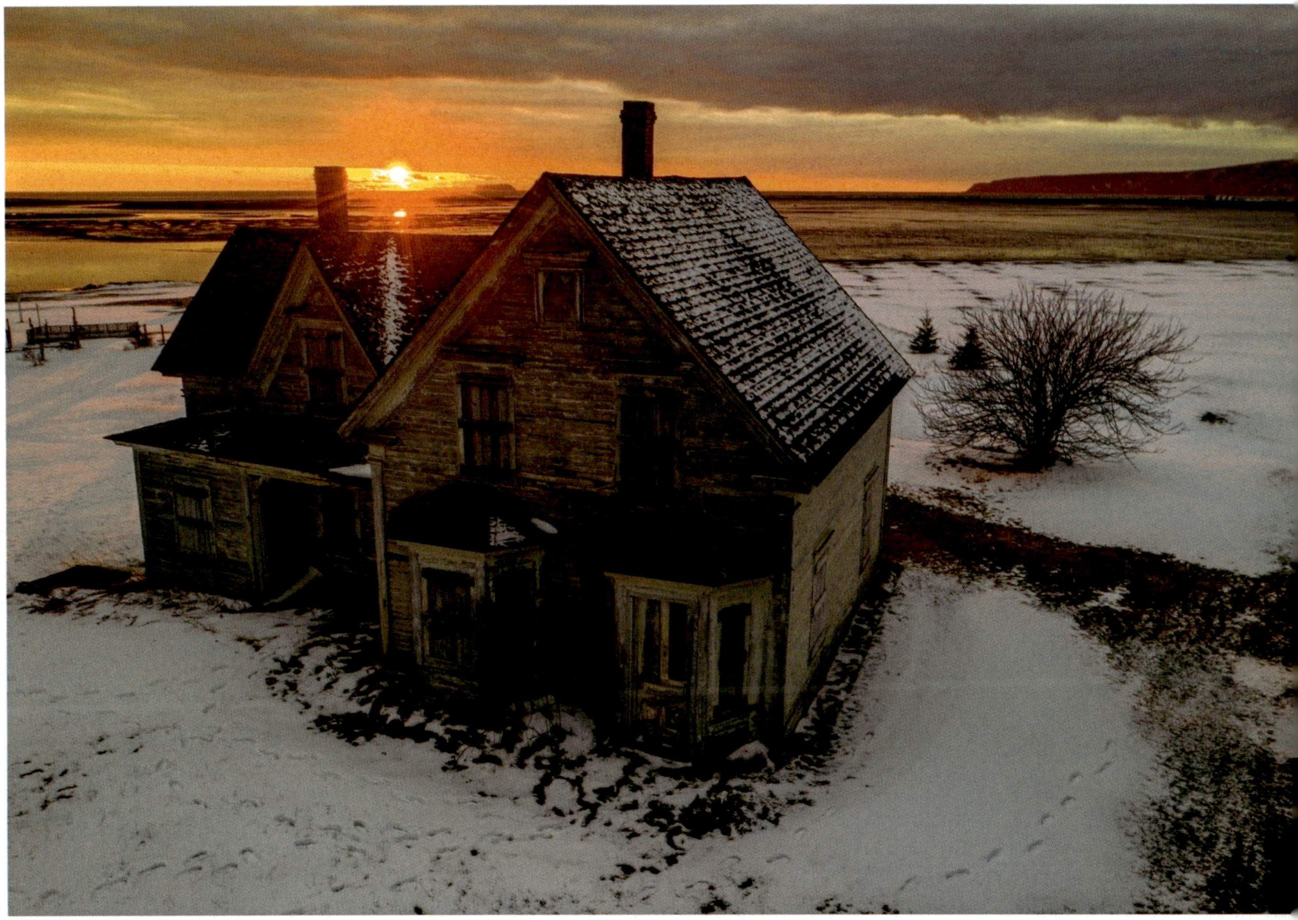

(Opposite) An old farmhouse with the backdrop of fall colours in the highlands of Inverness, Cape Breton Island.

(Above) A drone shot of this abandoned home in Advocate Harbour, Cumberland County, shows off the splendid view the residents would have had from the Bay of Fundy, along with some spectacular sunsets.

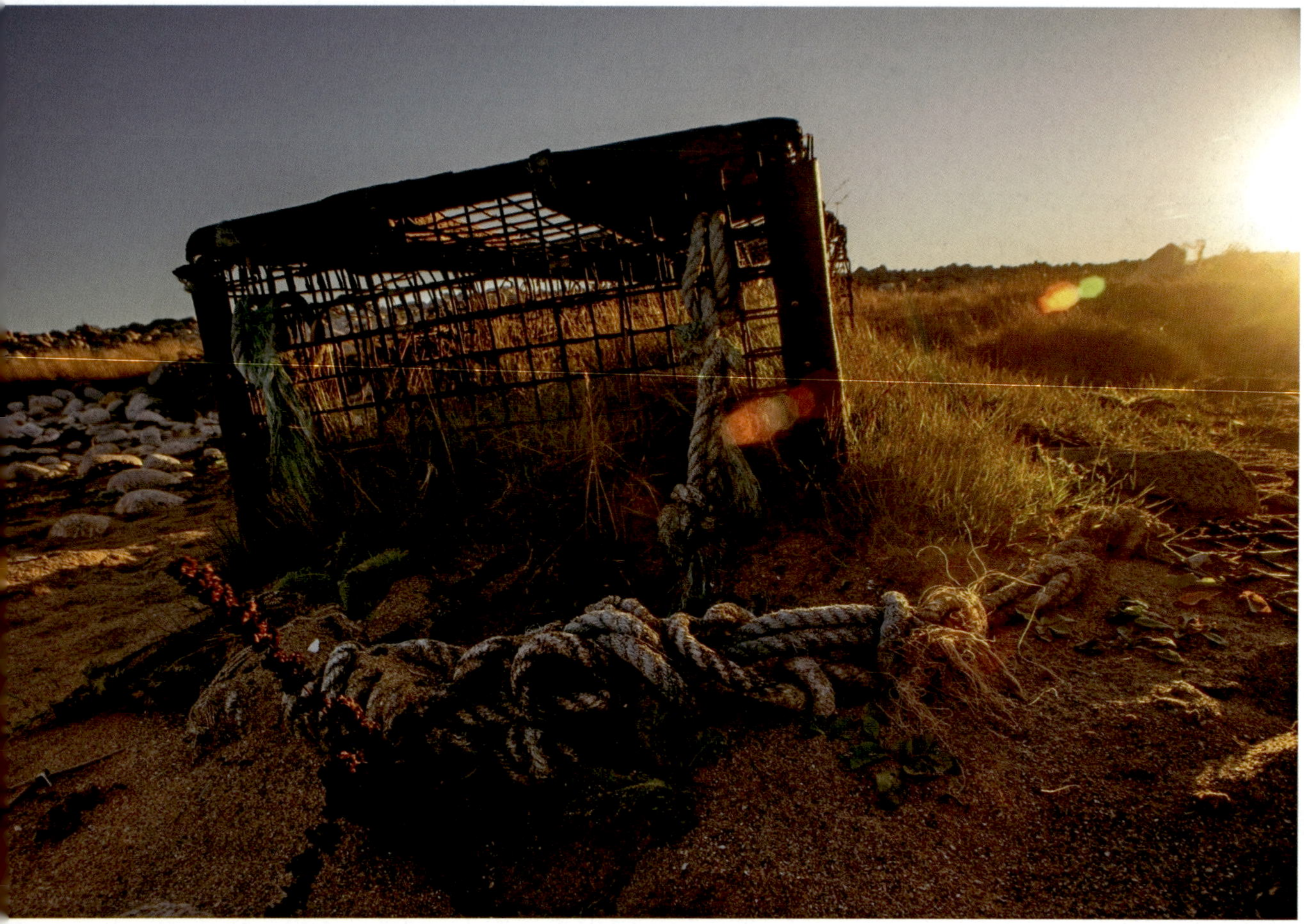

(Opposite) This A-frame house is the only structure left standing on Flat Island, which is off the southwestern tip of Nova Scotia's Yarmouth County. At one time, there were two houses on this tiny island less than a hectare in size, but only this one is left standing. A drone view gives a better perspective of how isolated these homes would have been. Flat Island is located about 37 kilometres south of Yarmouth and about 32 kilometres west of Cape Sable Island.

(Above) One of many lobster traps that washed up on shore around Seal Island, which is the outermost of the Tusket Islands off the southwestern tip of Nova Scotia and about 10 kilometres south of Flat Island.

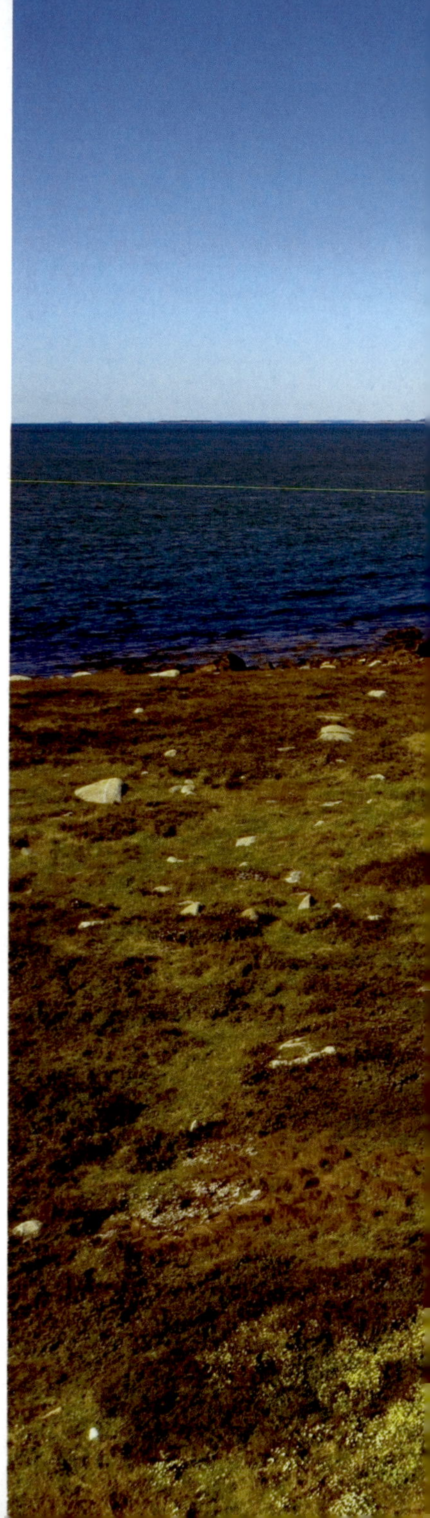

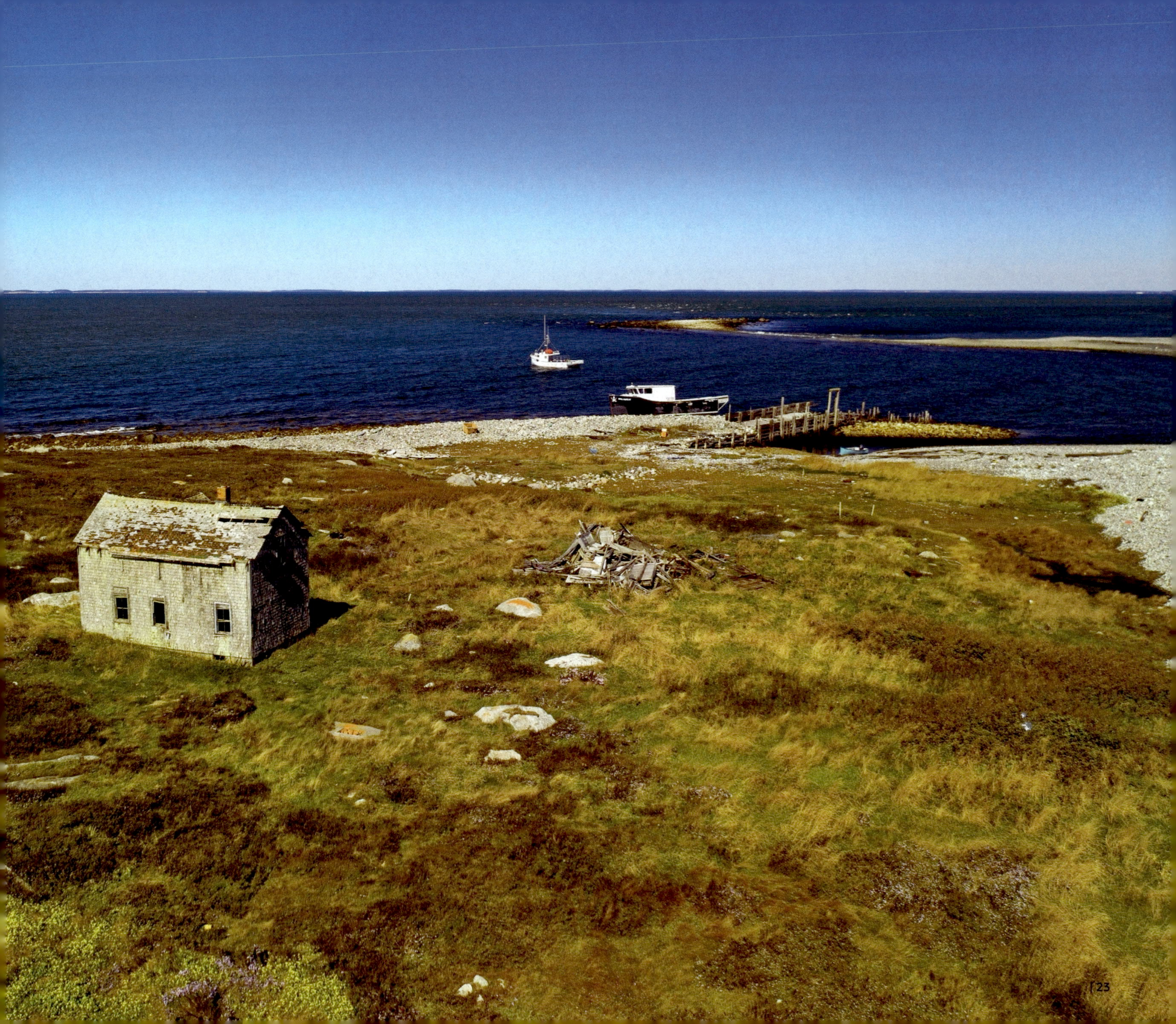

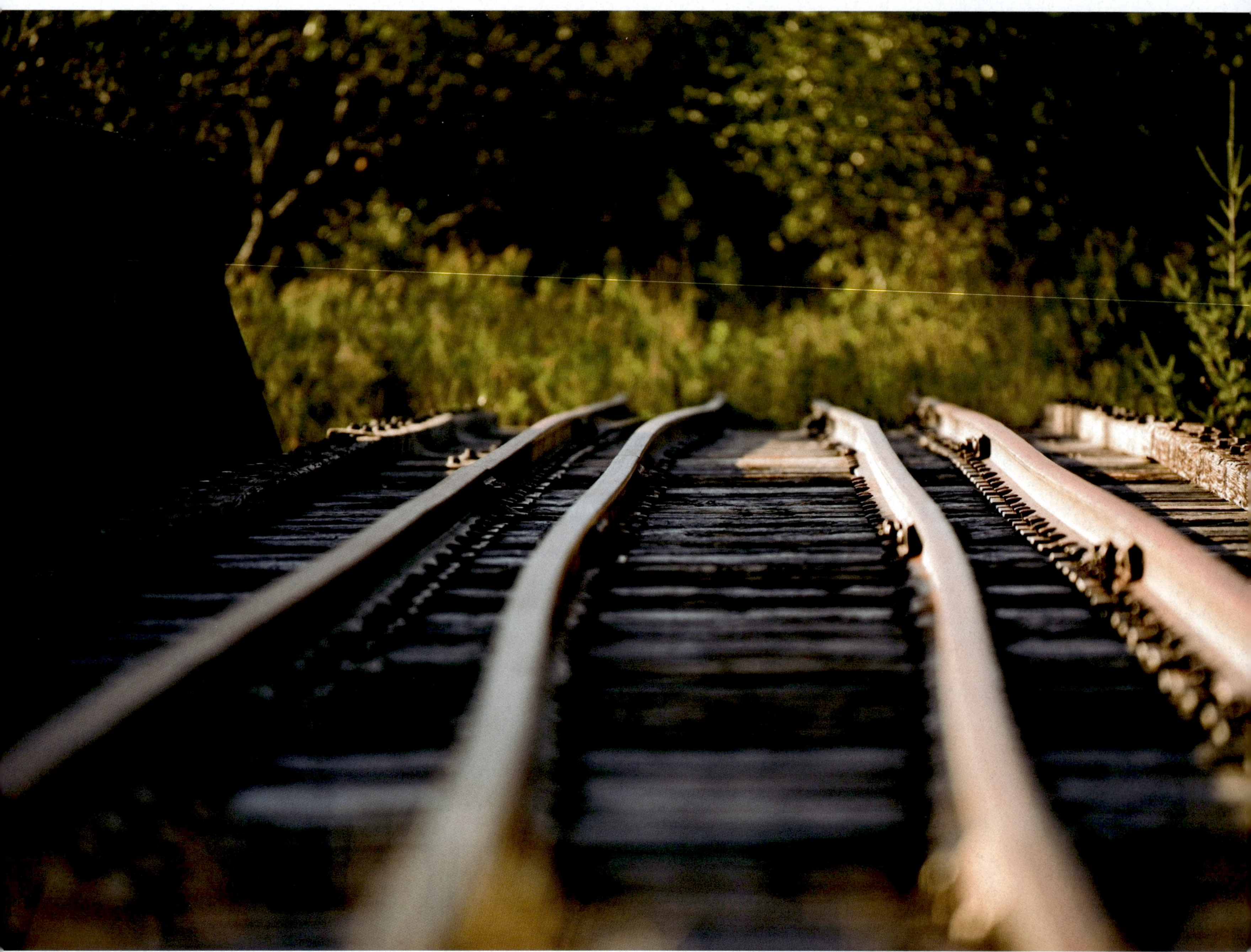

(Opposite and Right) Two views of the old abandoned rail line running from Sackville to the Annapolis Valley. Huge stretches of this derelict line are slowly being overrun by nature while other portions have been incorporated into hiking trail routes.

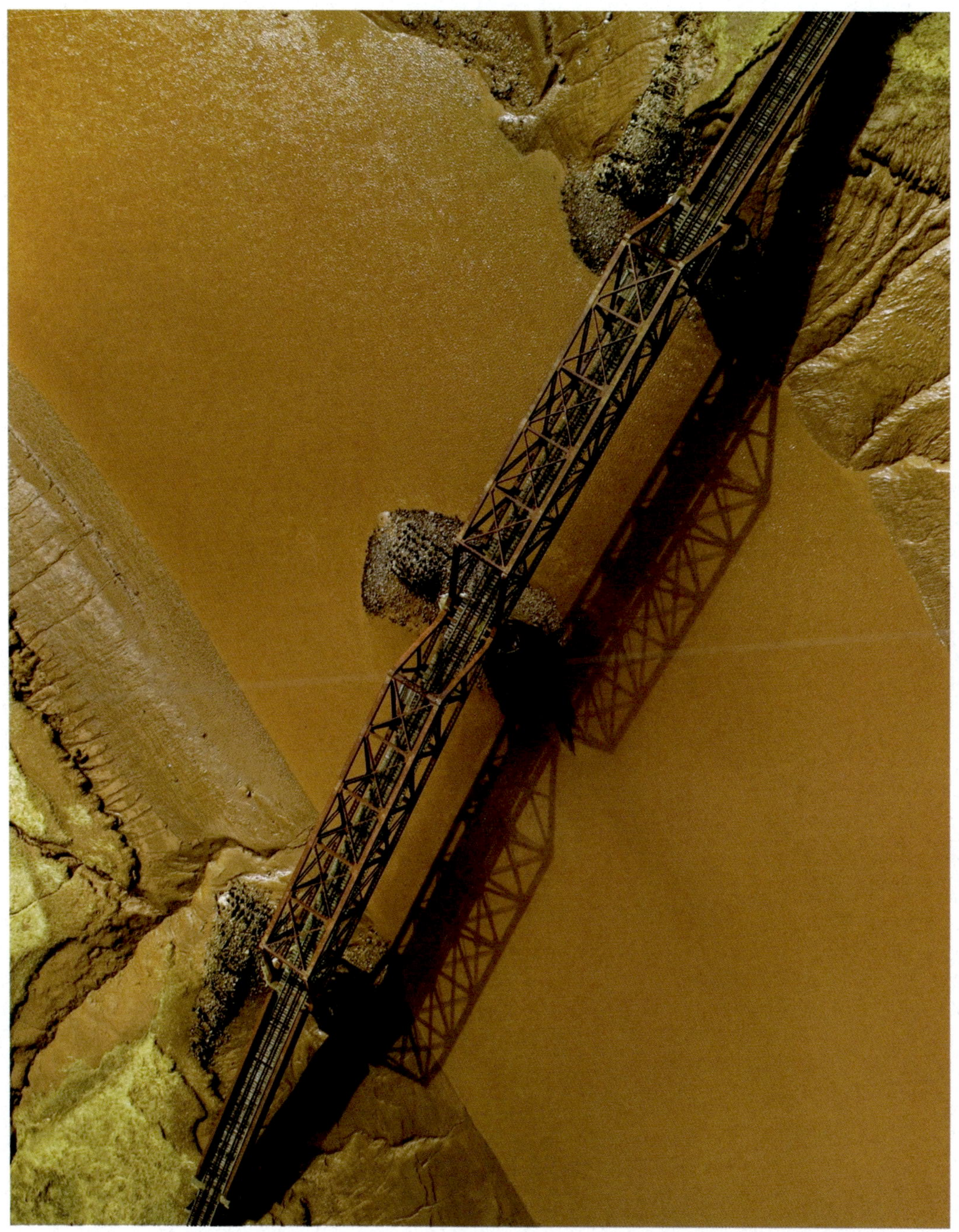

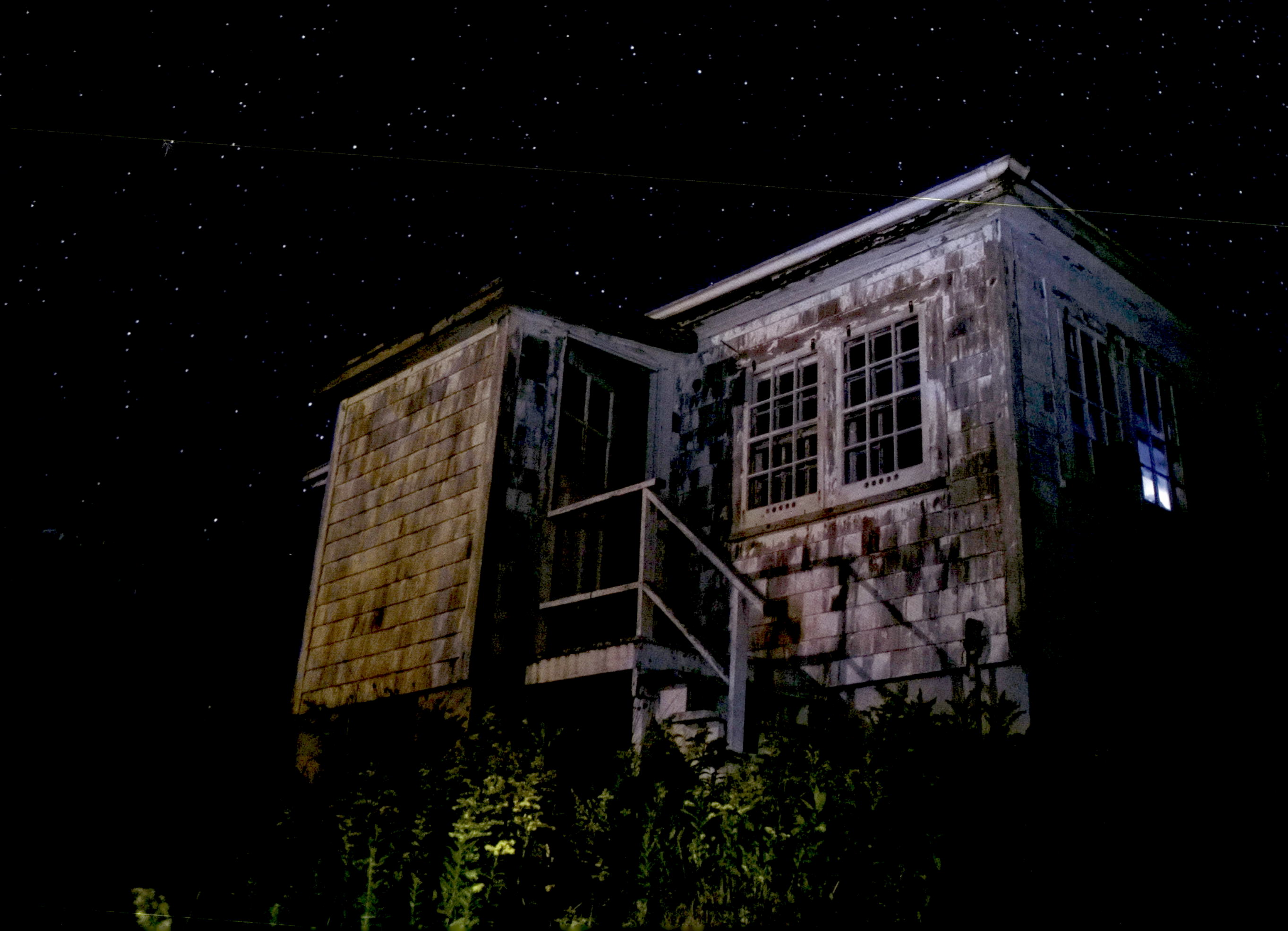

There's a place I'll always cherish, 'neath the blue Atlantic sky
Where the shores down in Cape Breton bid the golden sun to rise
And the fragrance of the apple blossoms sprays the dew-kissed lawns
Back in dear old Nova Scotia, a place where I was born.

Song lyrics, My Nova Scotia Home

Hank Snow

(Opposite) The abandoned coast guard station on remote Seal Island off the southern coast of Nova Scotia. After the local lighthouse was automated, a keeper and staff were no longer needed. The facility is now empty and abandoned.

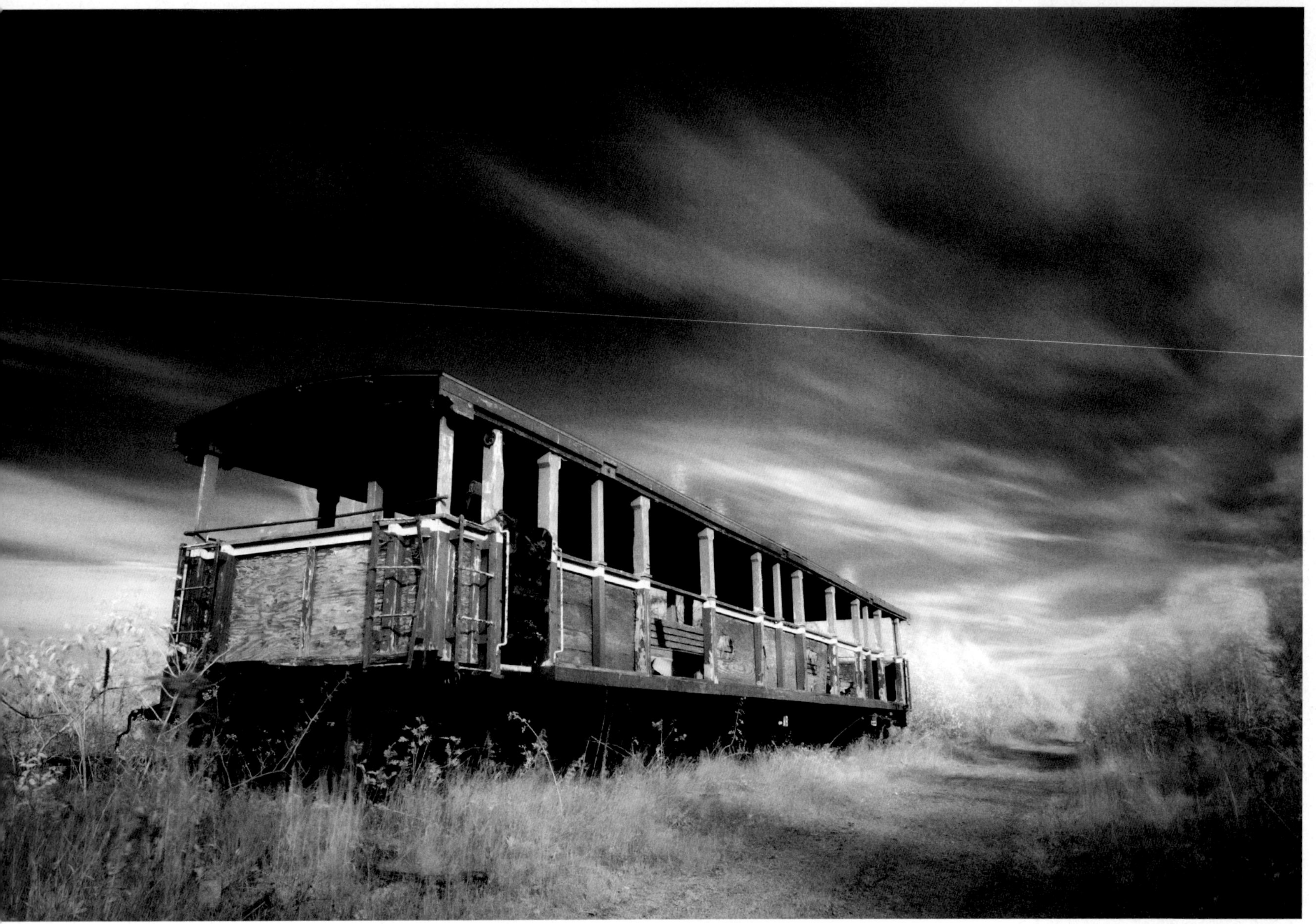

An infrared photo of an old trolley on a spur line in Windsor, Hants County. The Windsor spur was part of a 90-kilometre rail line between Windsor Junction, which is just outside Halifax, and New Minas, Kings County. The rail line was suspended in 2011 when the gypsum quarries shut down due to lack of demand for gypsum in the United States, where most of the exported gypsum was used for plaster or Gyproc in construction.

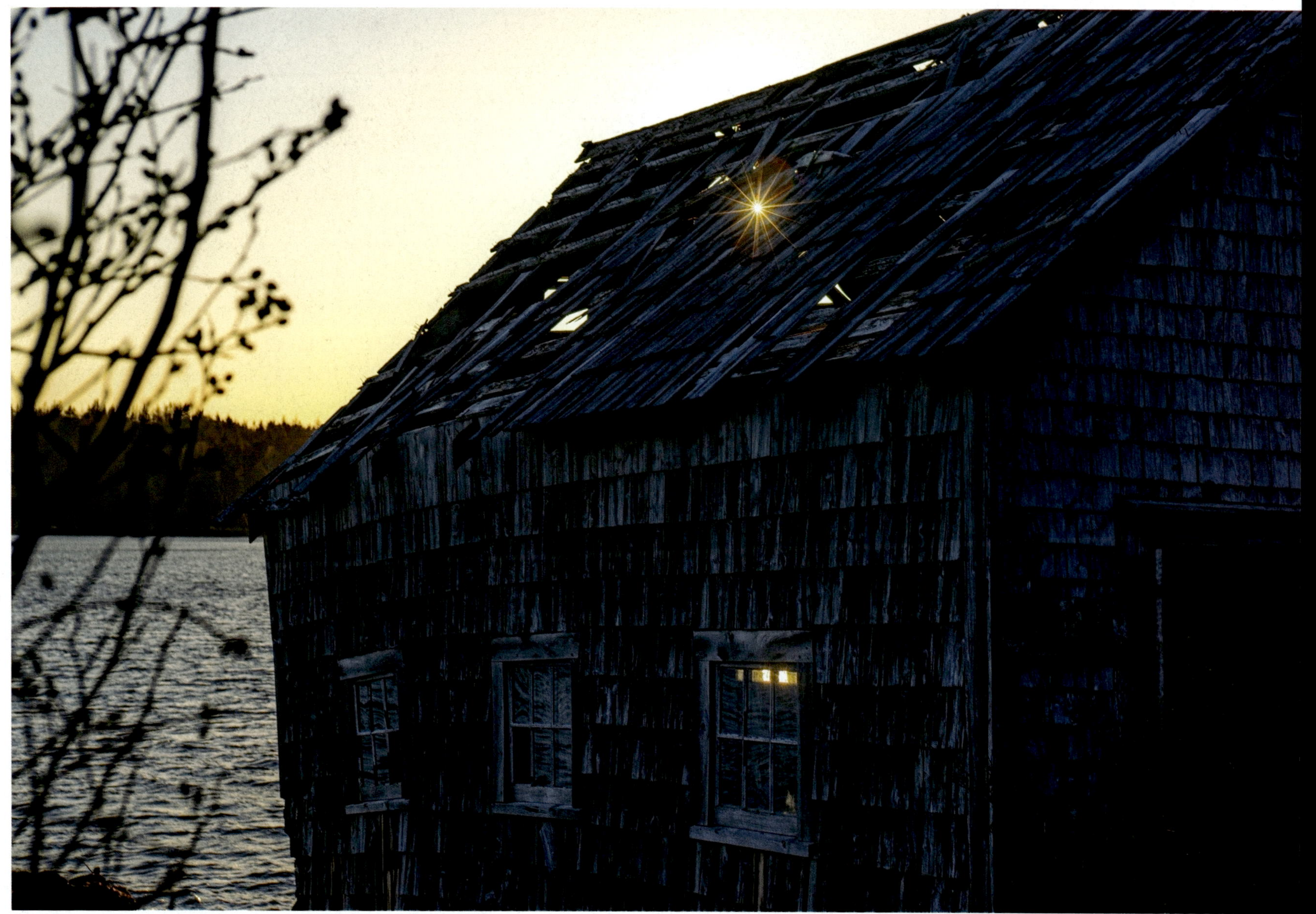

Slates of sunlight shine through gaps in the roof of a derelict fishing shack along the Eastern Shore.

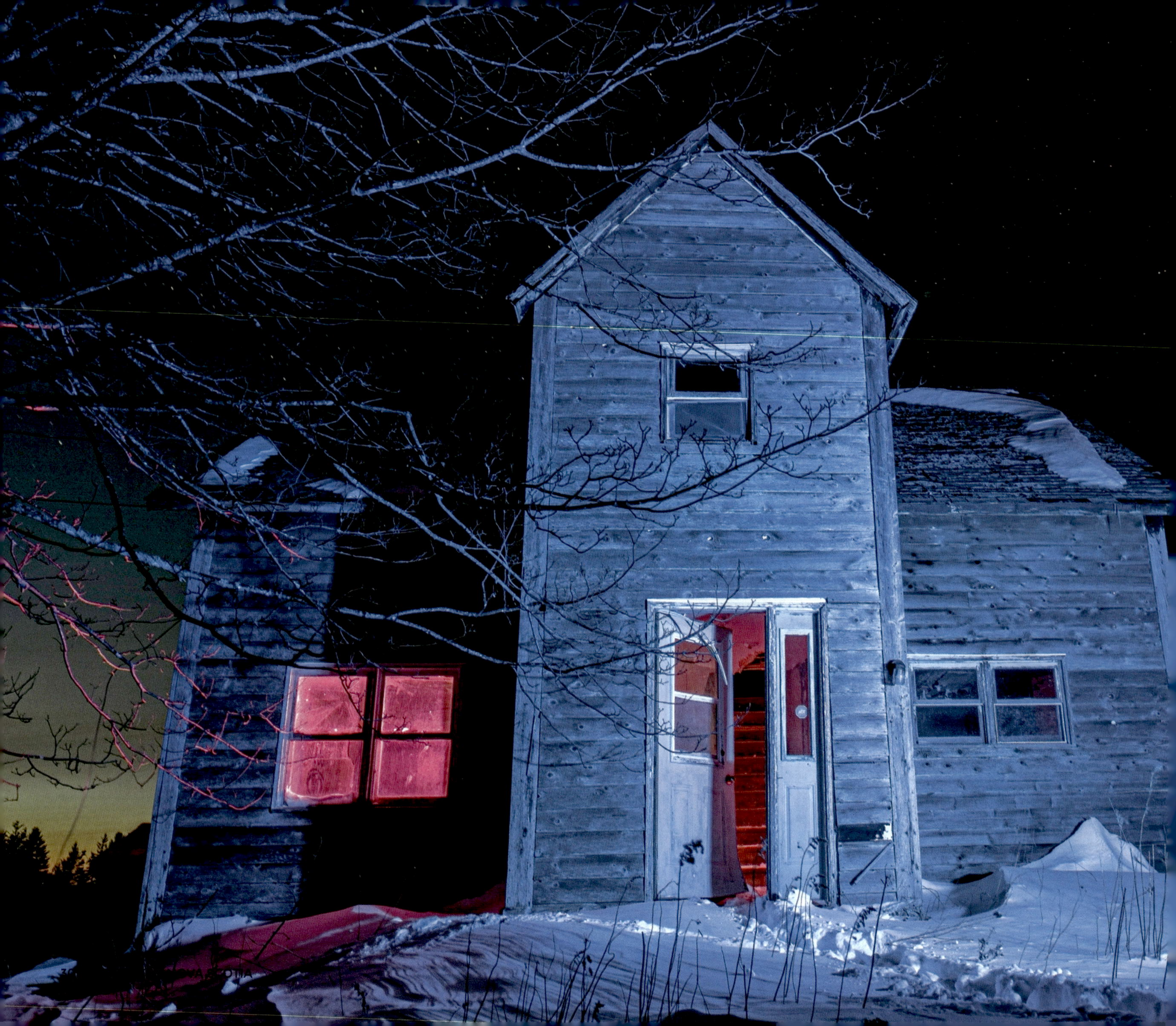

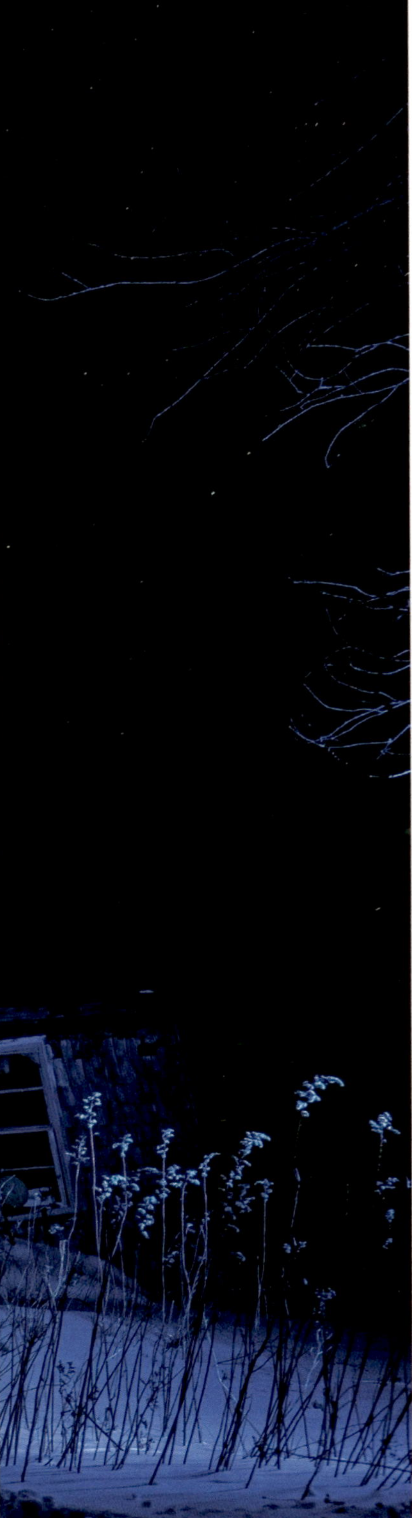

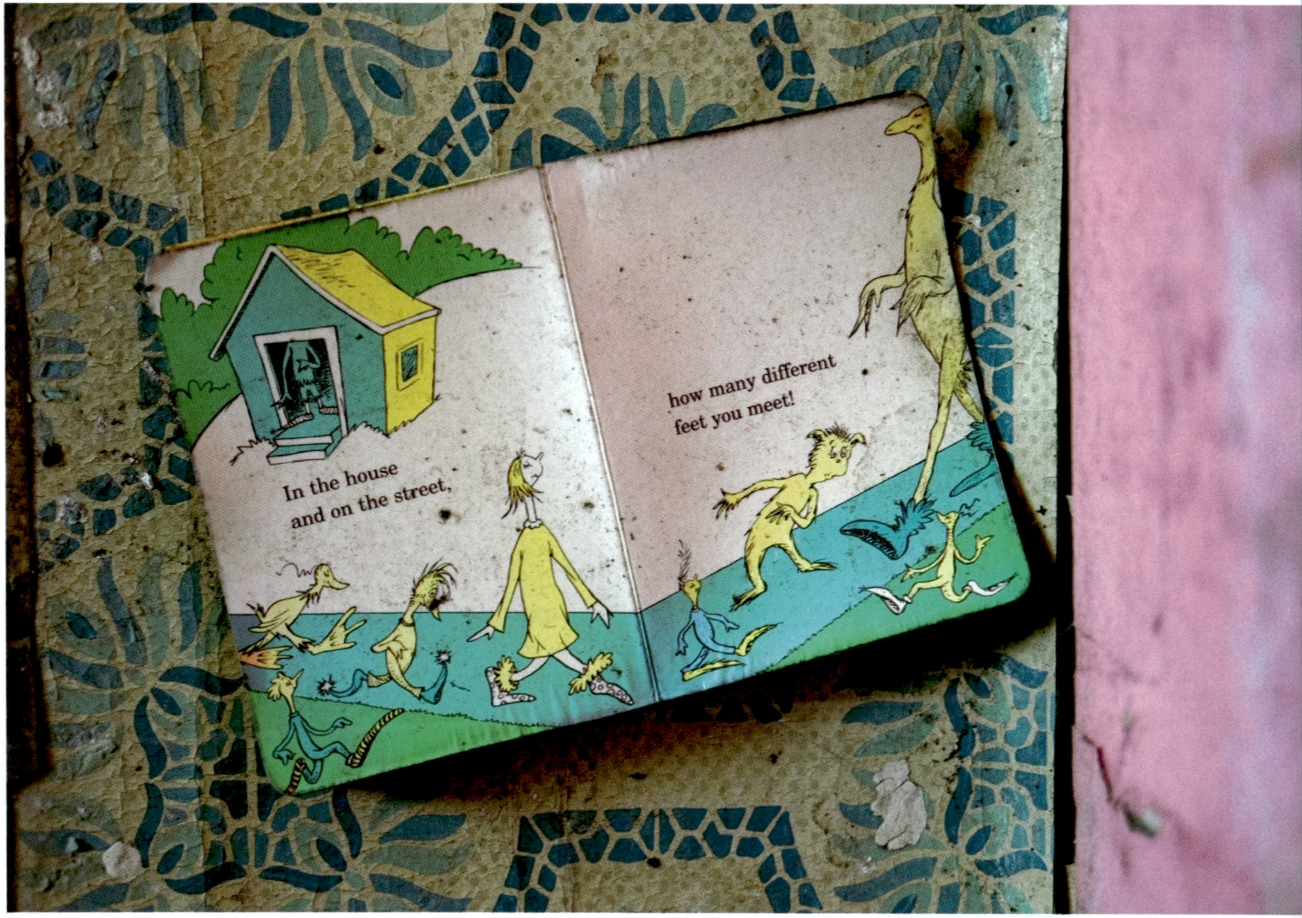

(Opposite) Using coloured gels on our strobe light, we were able to bring some life back into this old house in Paradise, Annapolis County.

(Above) Newspapers and books are often left behind in these old homes, but this children's book left open to a page referencing a house was pure serendipity.

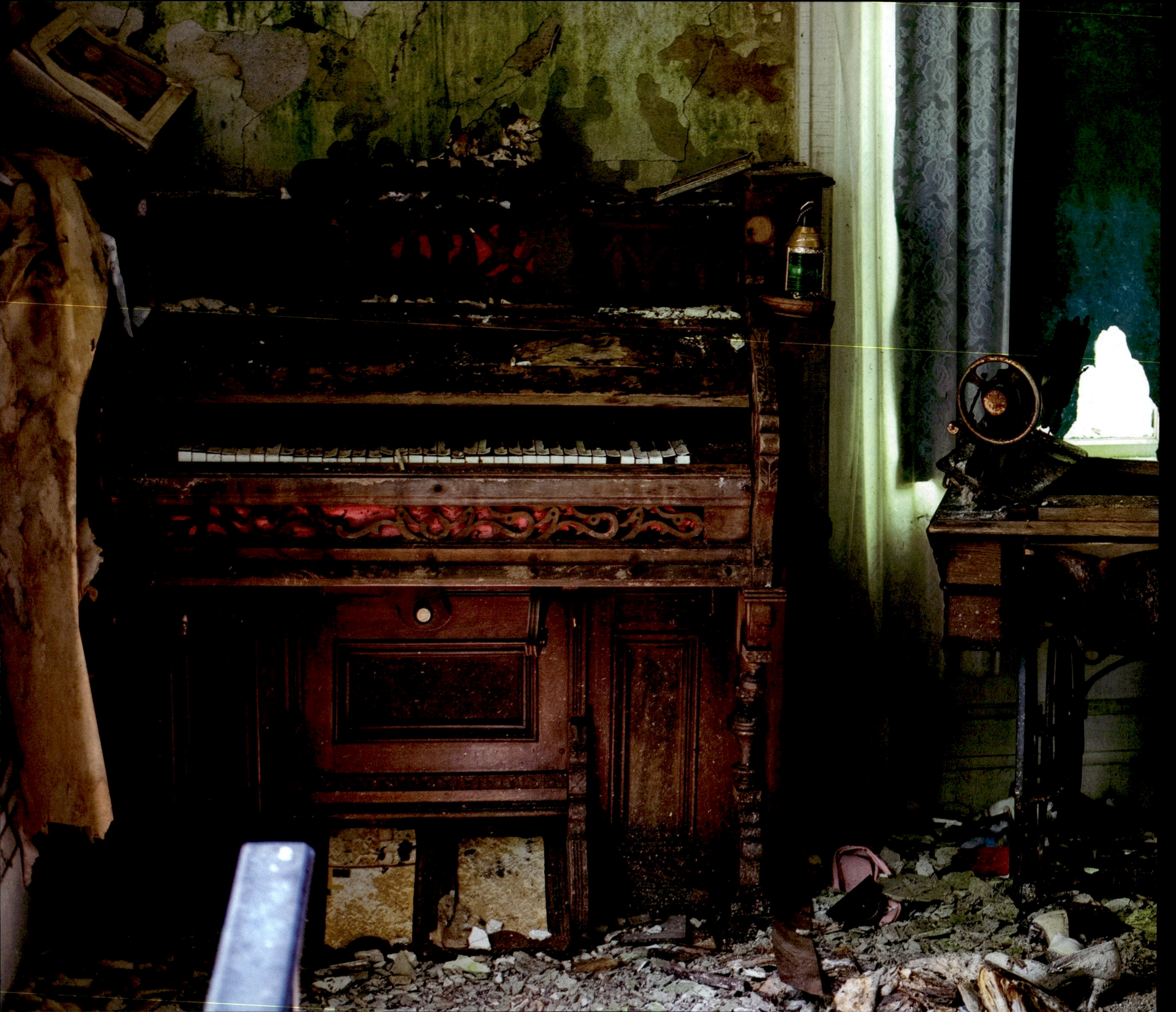

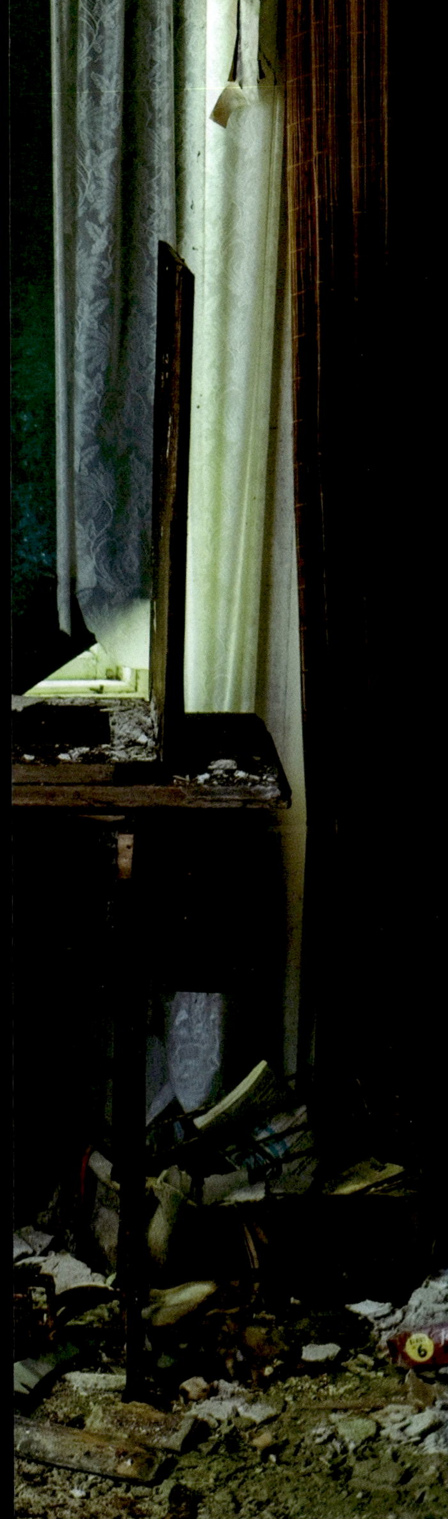

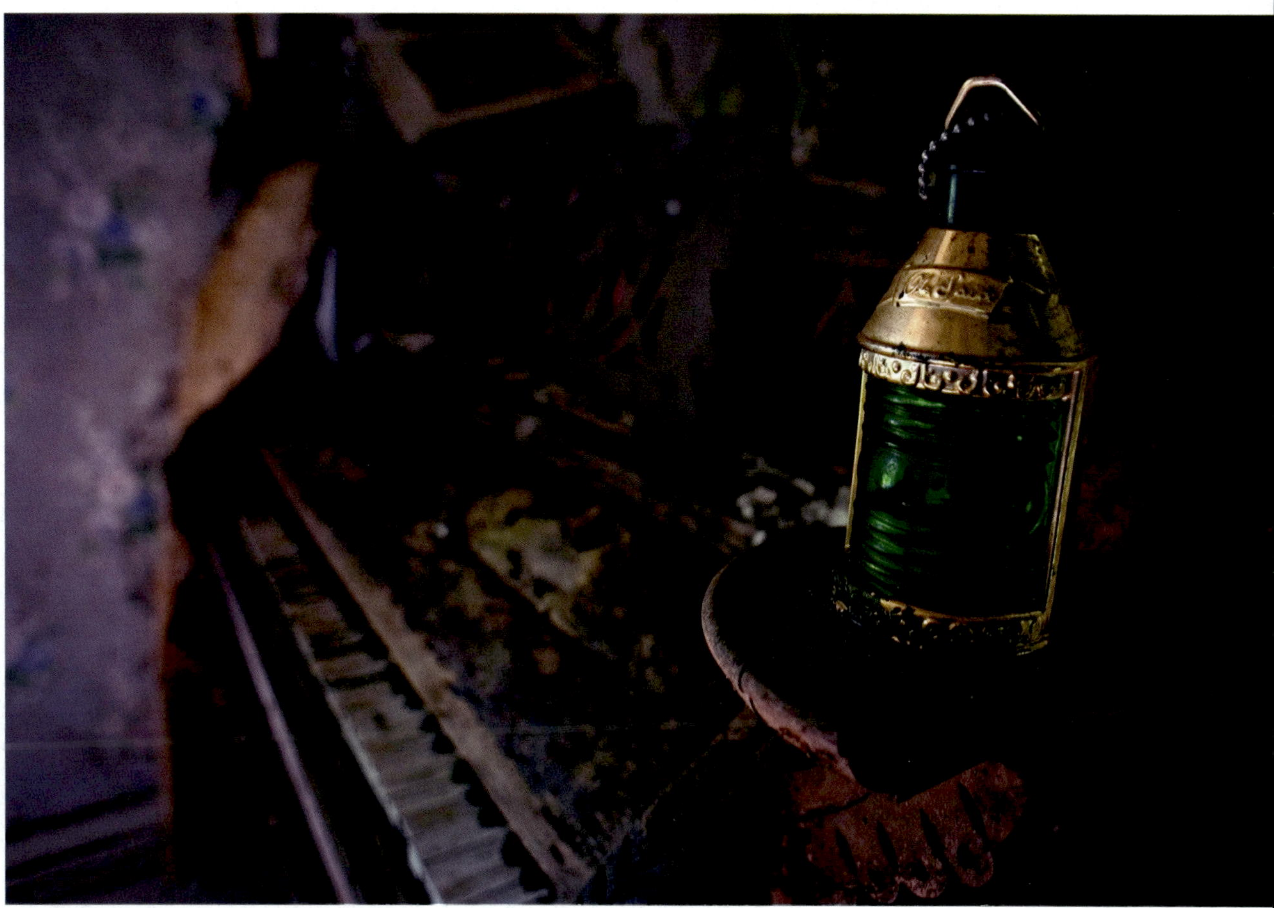

(Opposite and Above) An ornate piano and parts of a sewing machine remain untouched in the bedroom of this home in central Queens County of southern Nova Scotia.

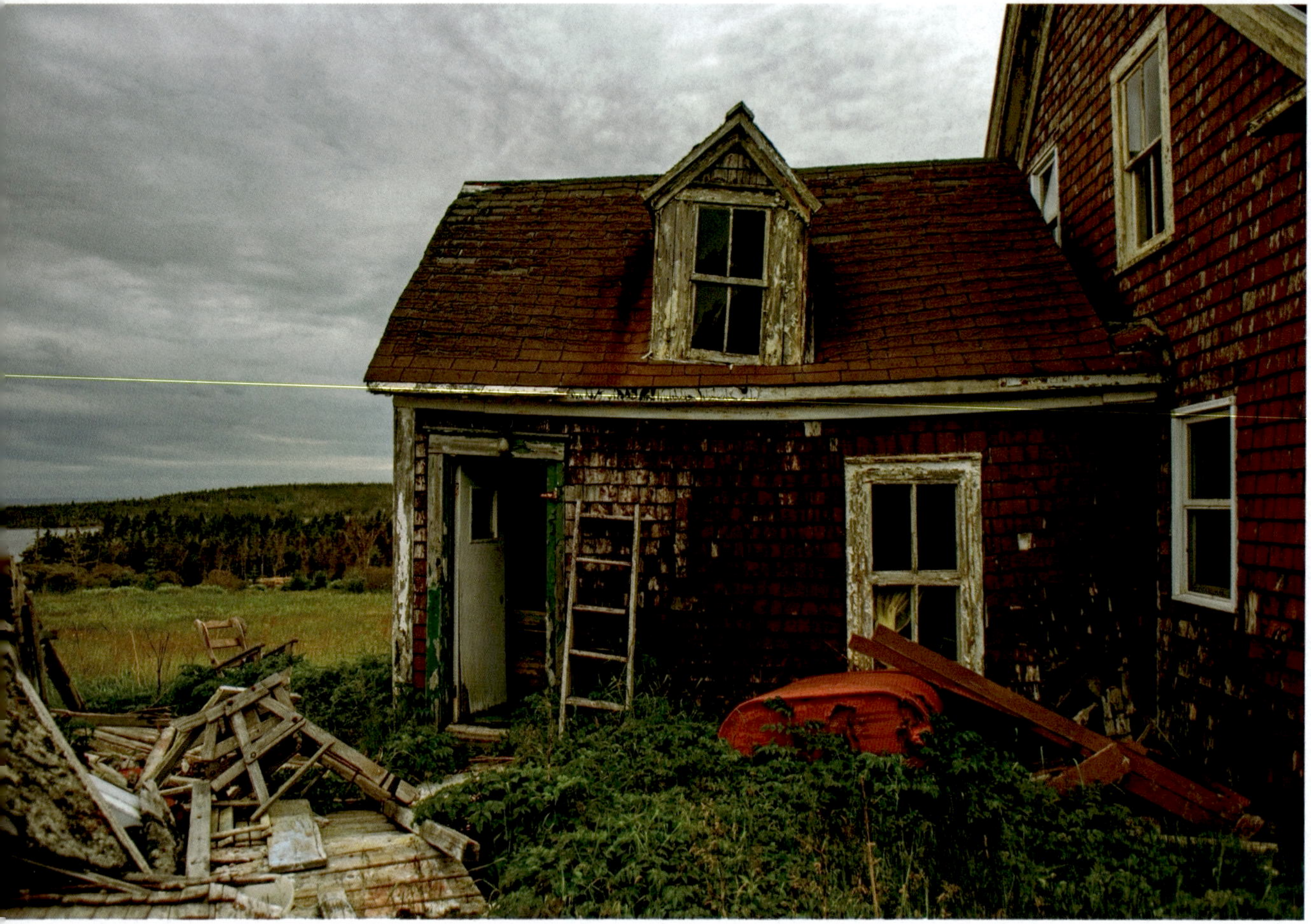

(**Above**) Debris lies scattered around the sagging facade of a home near Lower Whitehead in Guysborough county.

(**Opposite**) The weather-beaten hulk of a vessel named *Schwalbe* lies beached and abandoned on the shores of Lunenburg Bay.

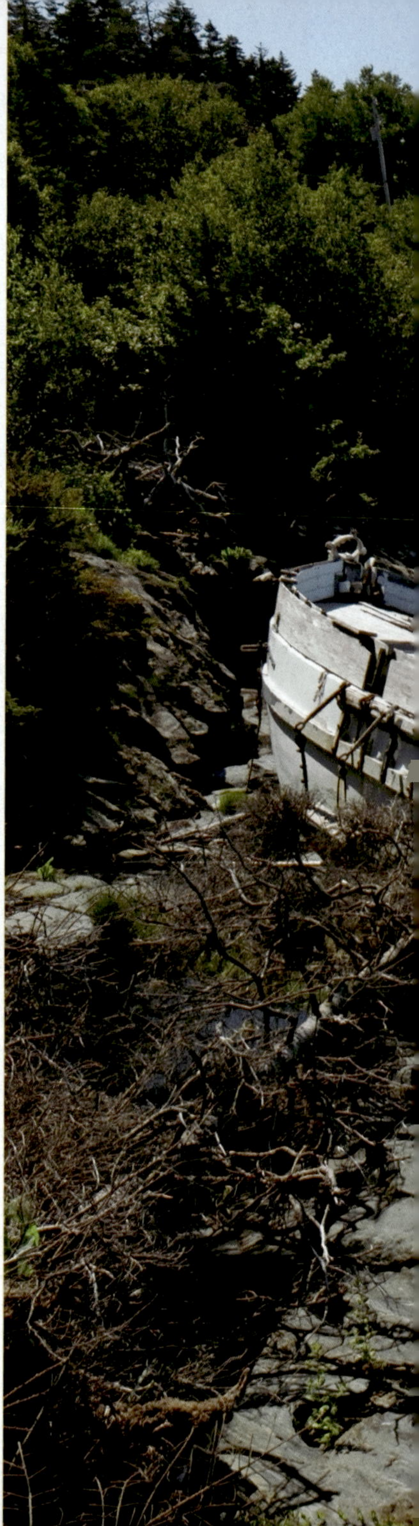

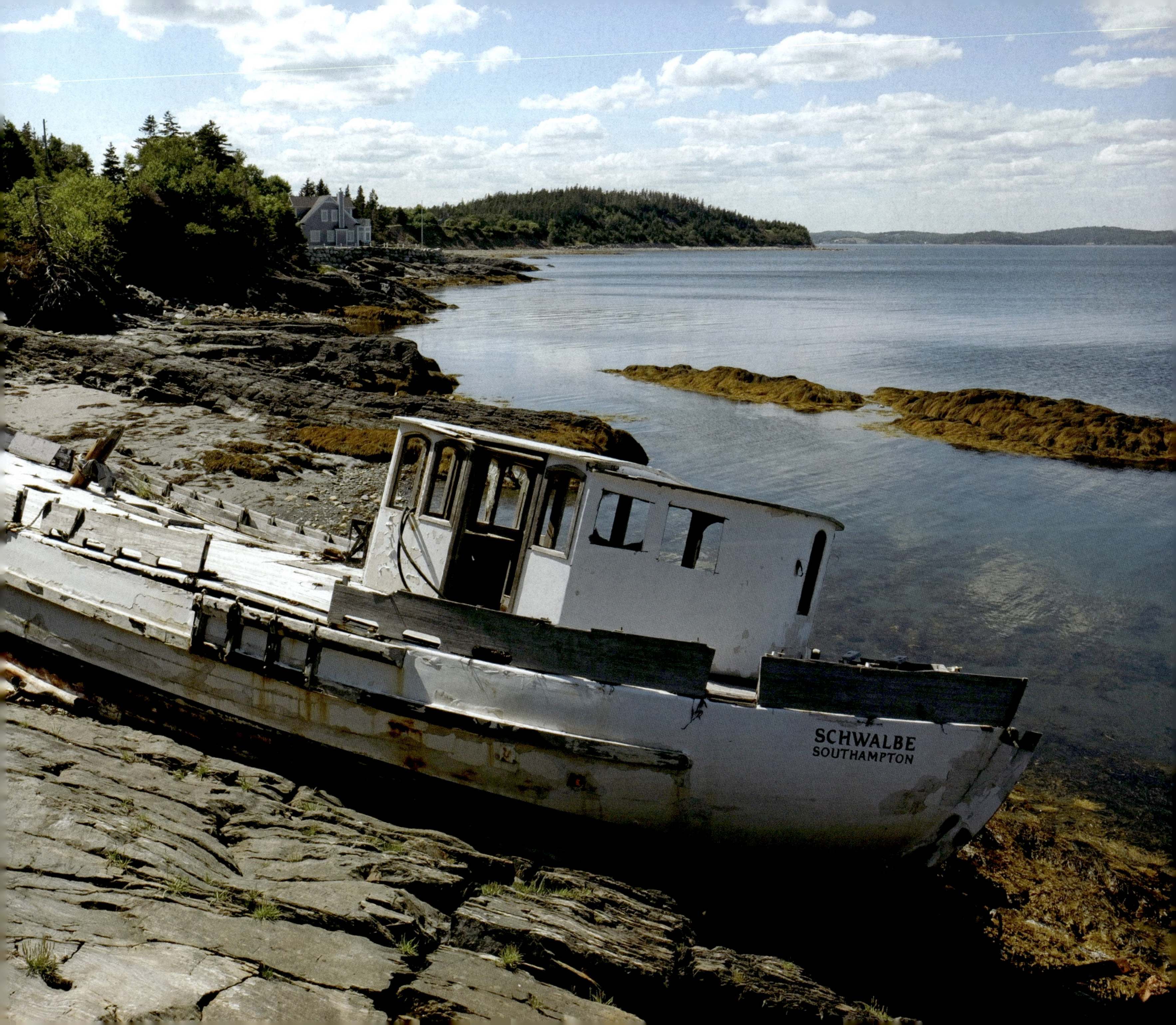
SCHWALBE
SOUTHAMPTON

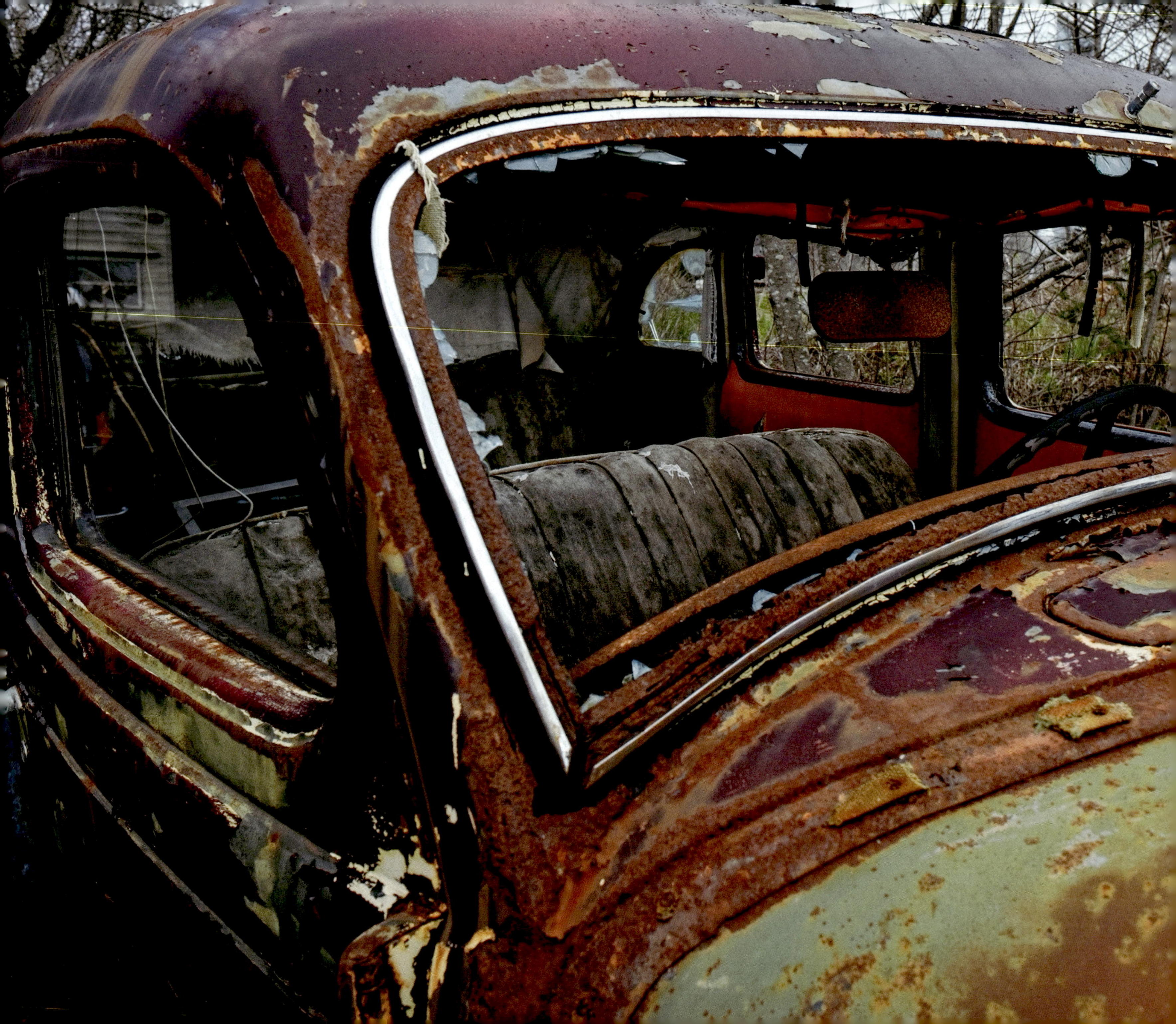

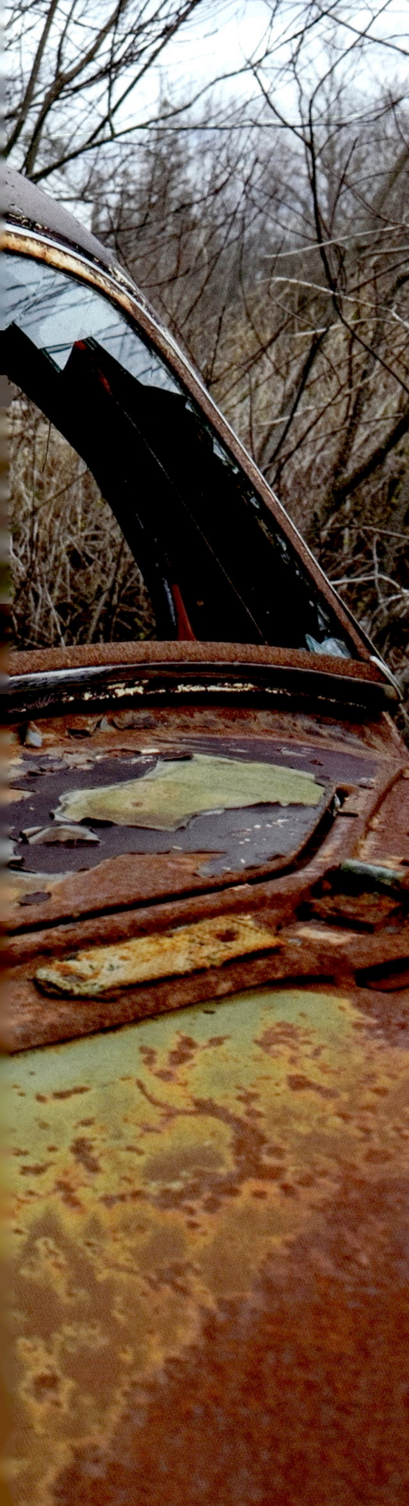

(Opposite and Right) Another old classic car sits rusting in a lot with other vehicles in Middle Musquodoboit.

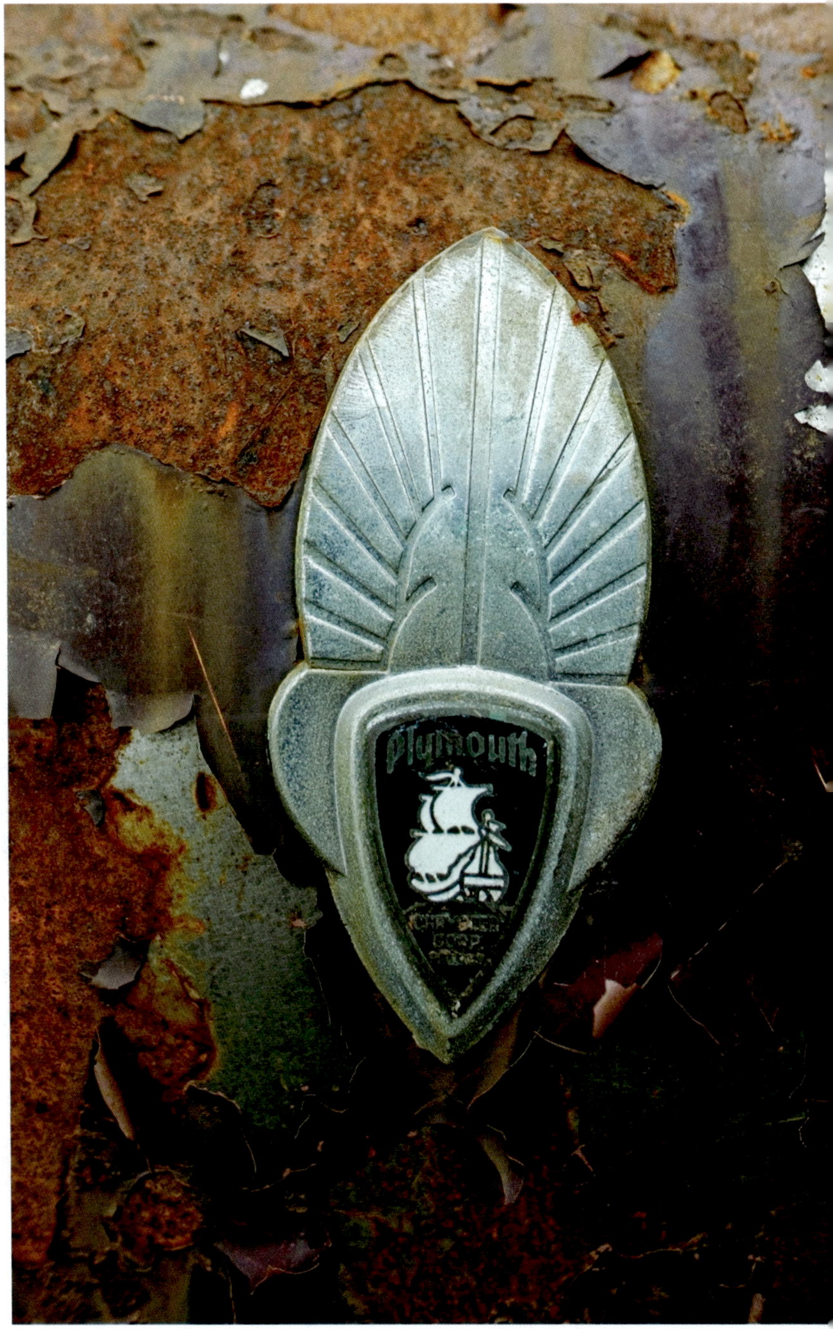

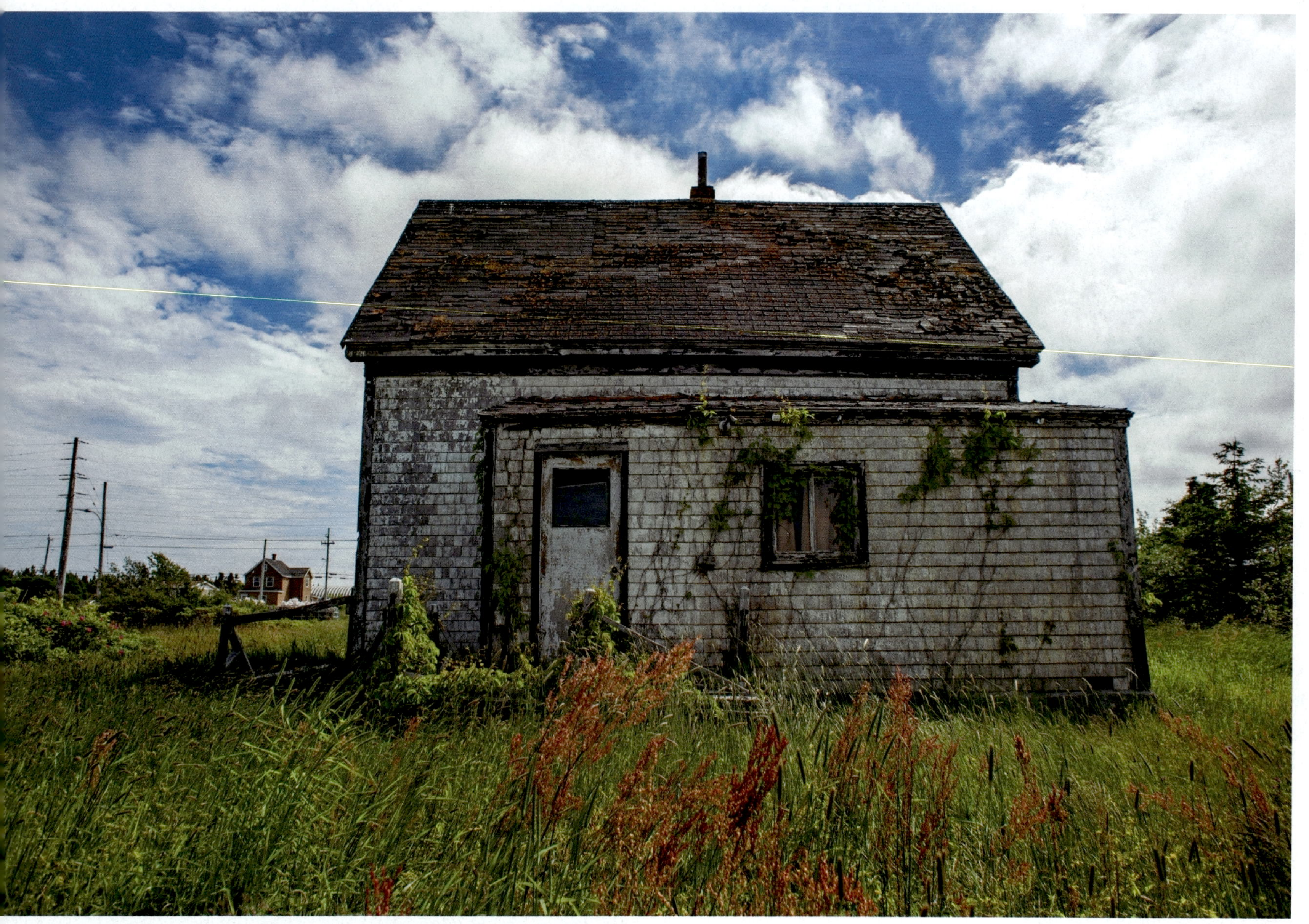

In a small area in downtown Canso, there were three houses left abandoned, all in close proximity to one another. This one was on a small hill surrounded by tall grass.

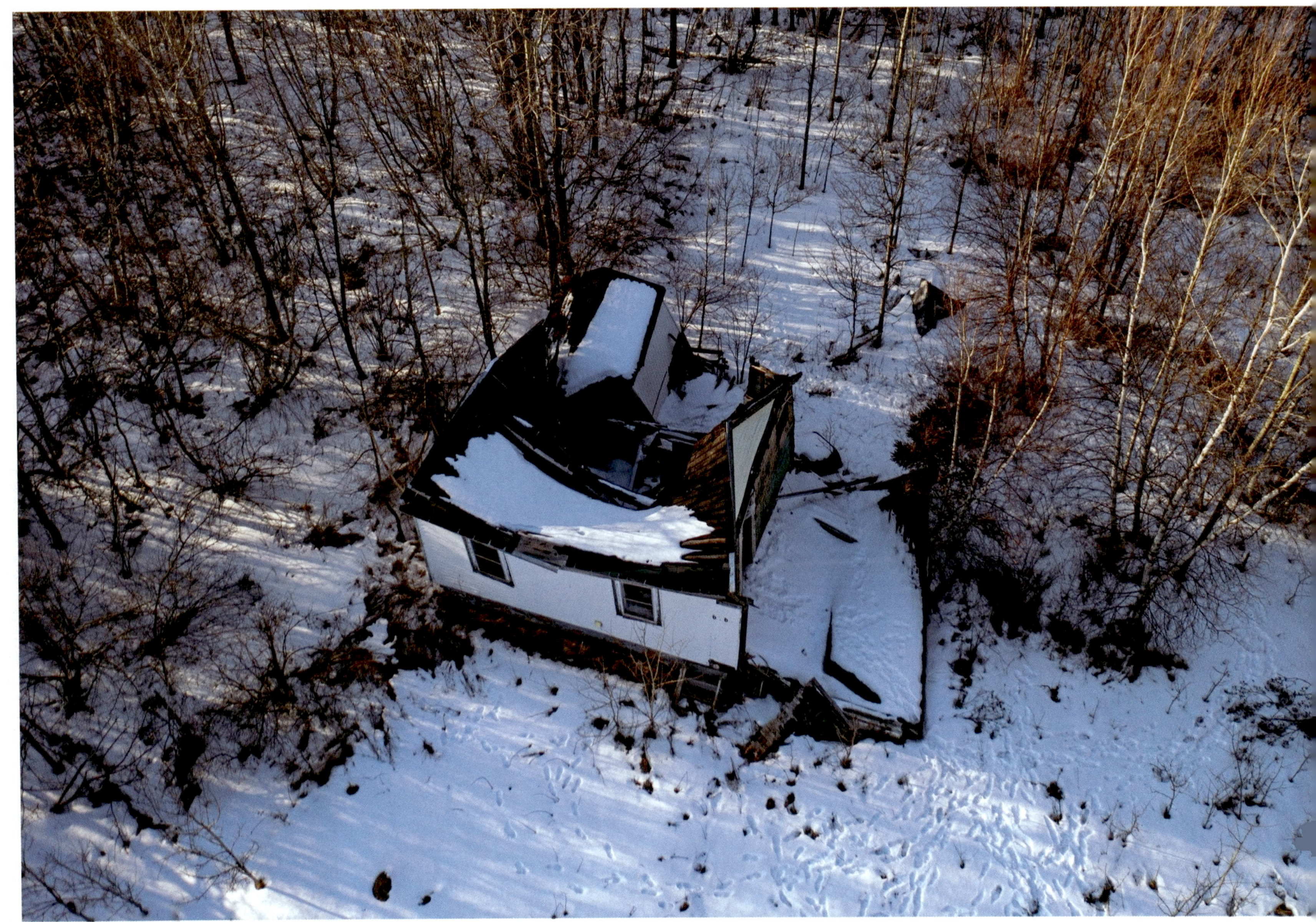

This home in Cumberland County was not far from the road and had been vacant for some time. You can see that the roof is caved in and the structure itself is severely compromised.

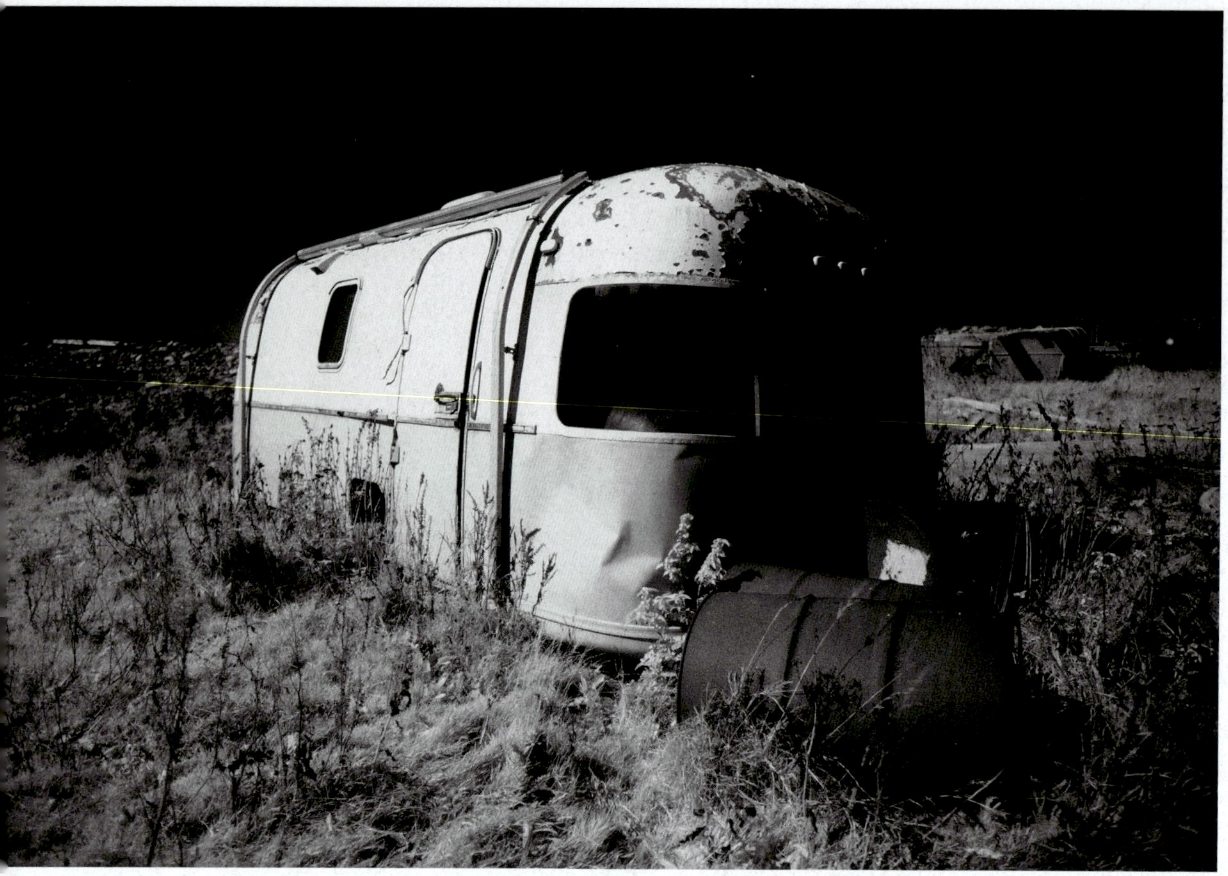

(Above) A recreational vehicle left to the elements on the west side of Seal Island.

(Opposite) With no running water or electricity on Seal Island, owners had to make do with outhouses. This one hasn't had a visitor in quite some time.

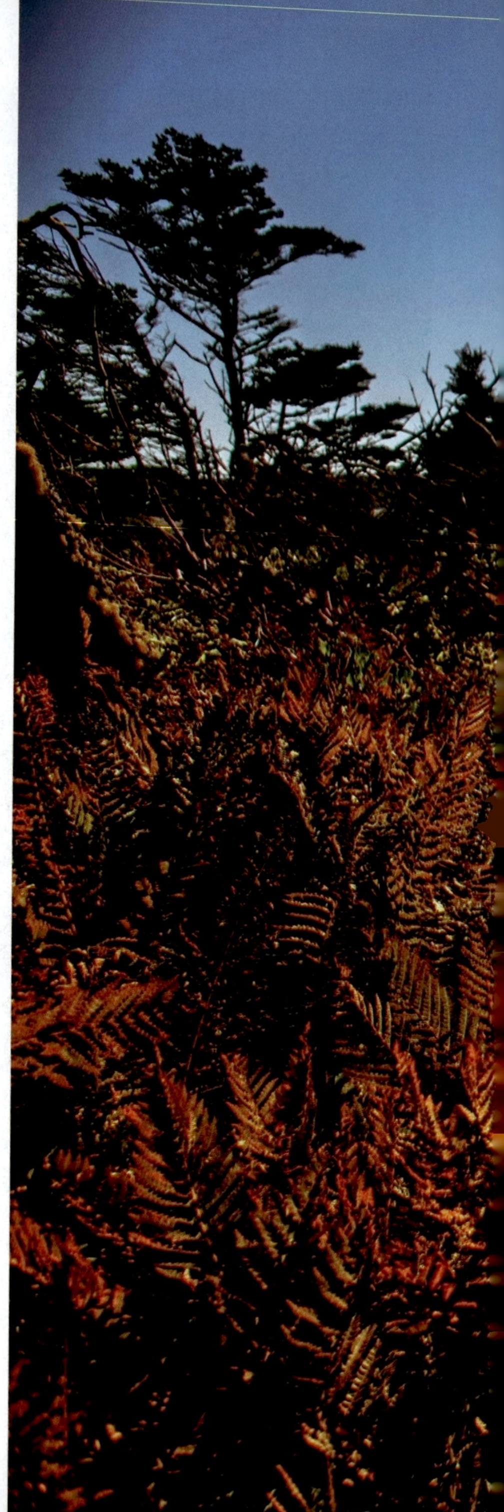

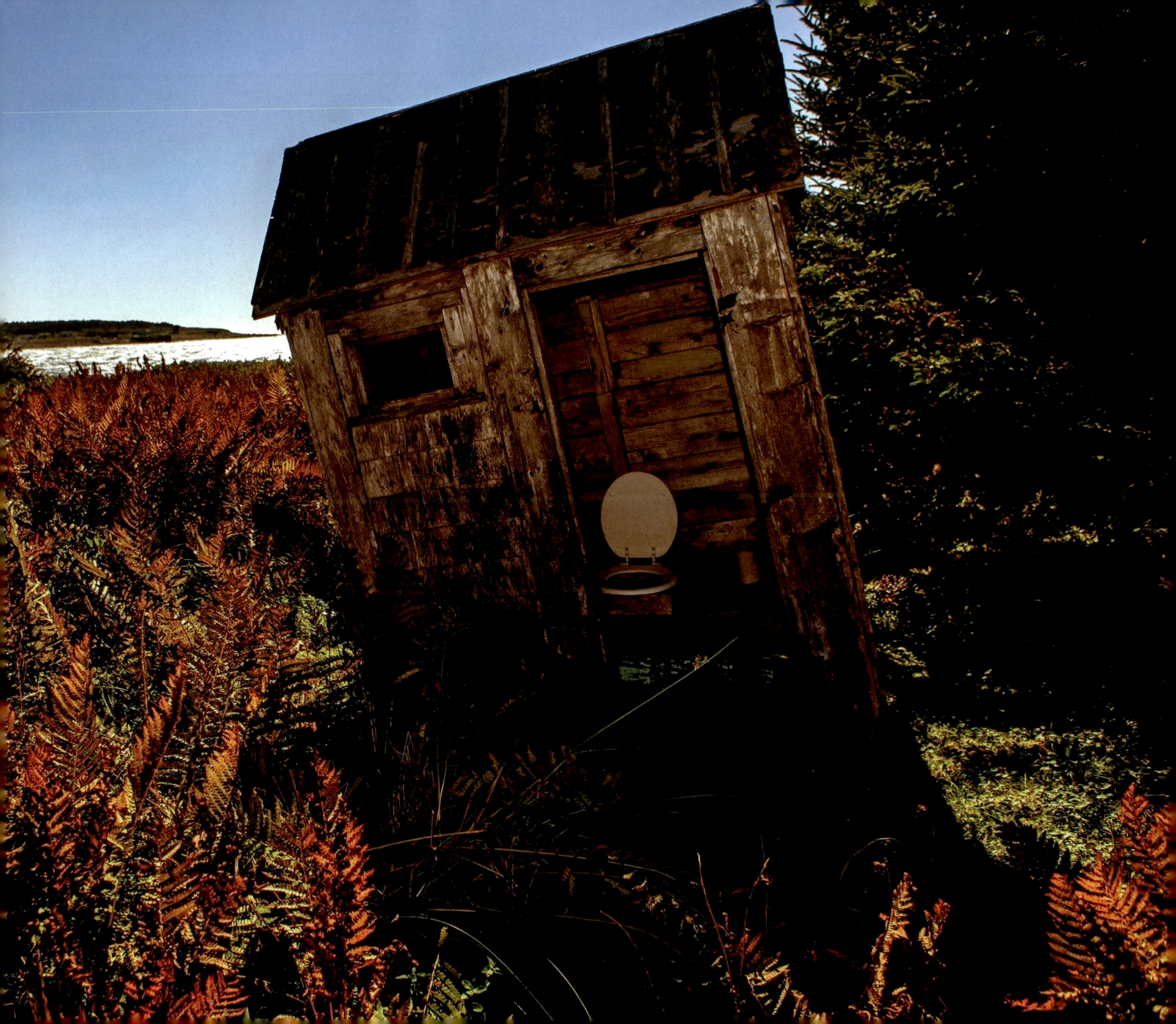

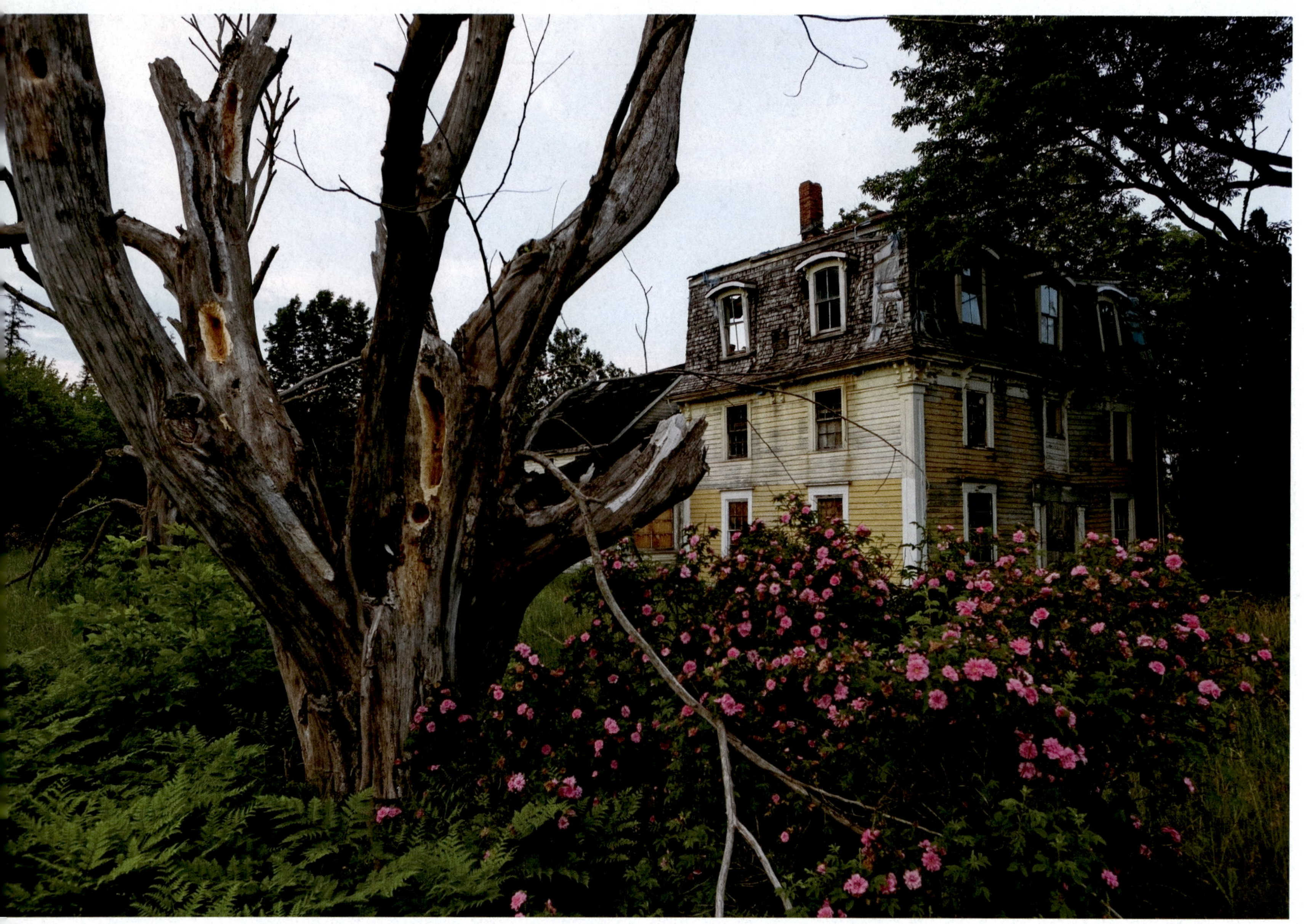

This old Victorian home along the Glooscap Trail near Five Islands Provincial Park on the Bay of Fundy, is hidden in the summer by majestic trees and flowering bushes.

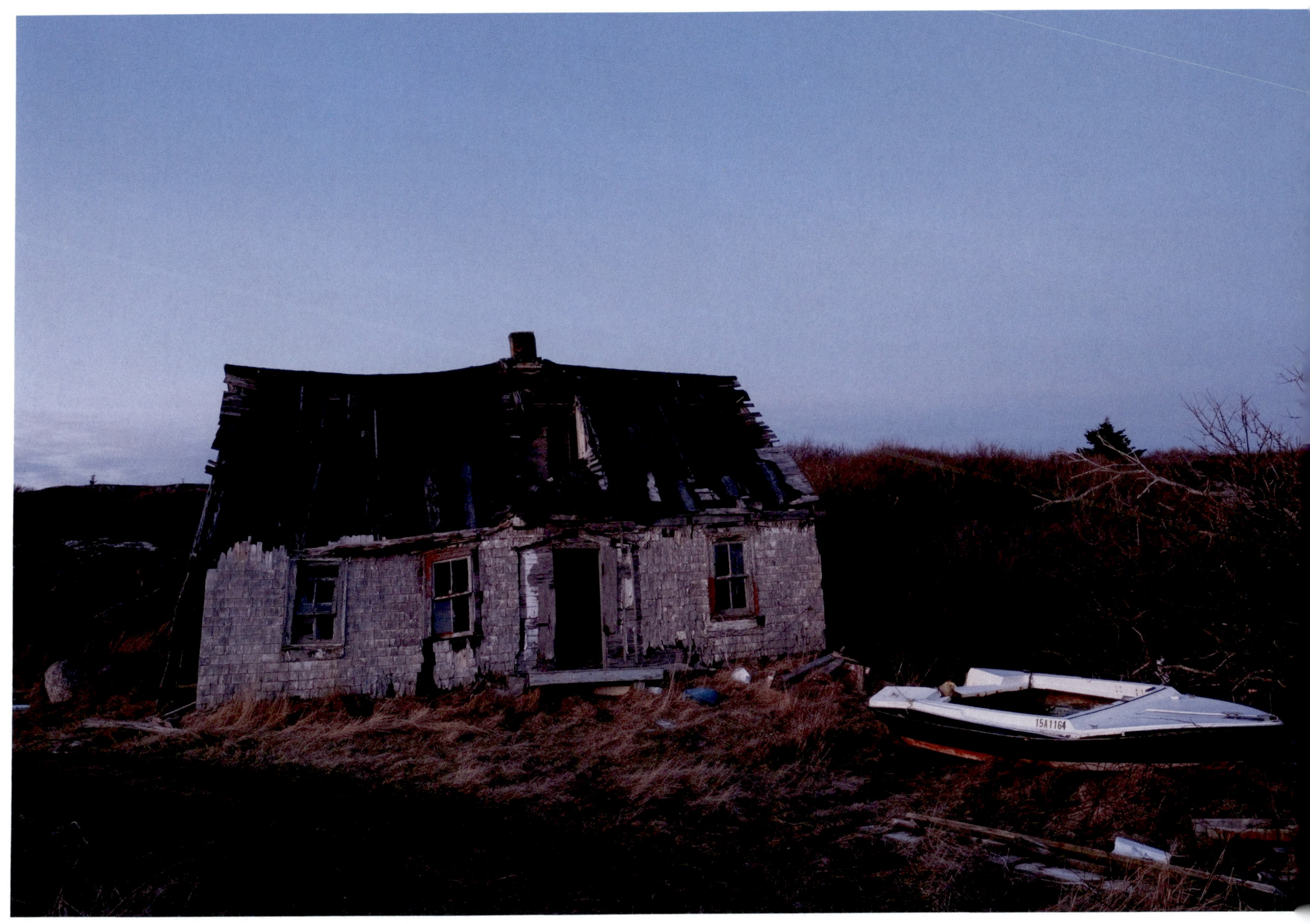

This abandoned home in Lower Prospect near Terence Bay sits among the remnants of its coastal life under a late winter sky.

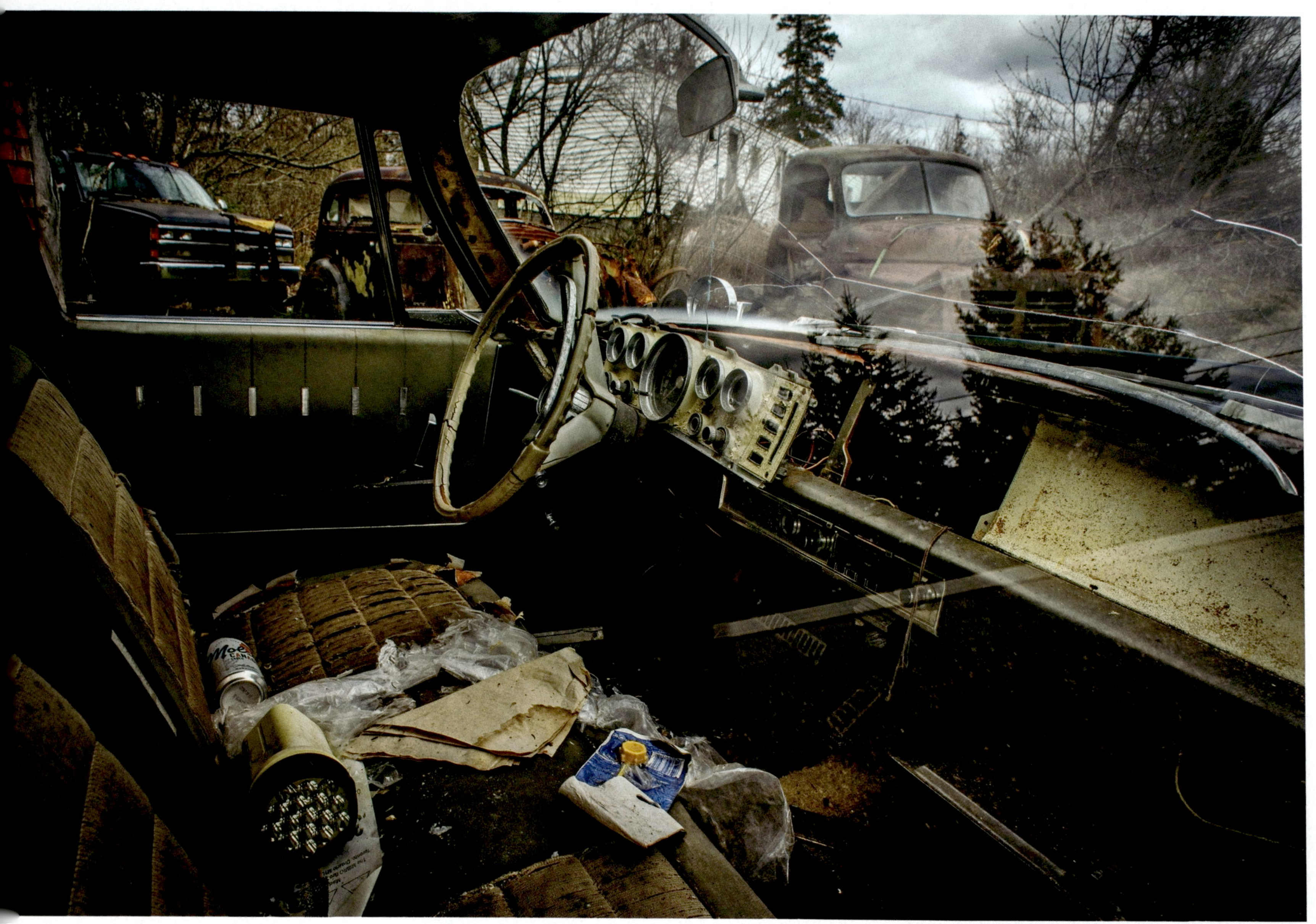

(Above) Inside the vintage abandoned car (featured on page 36) in Middle Musquodoboit.

(Opposite) Only the foundation remains from a house on the Eastern Shore.

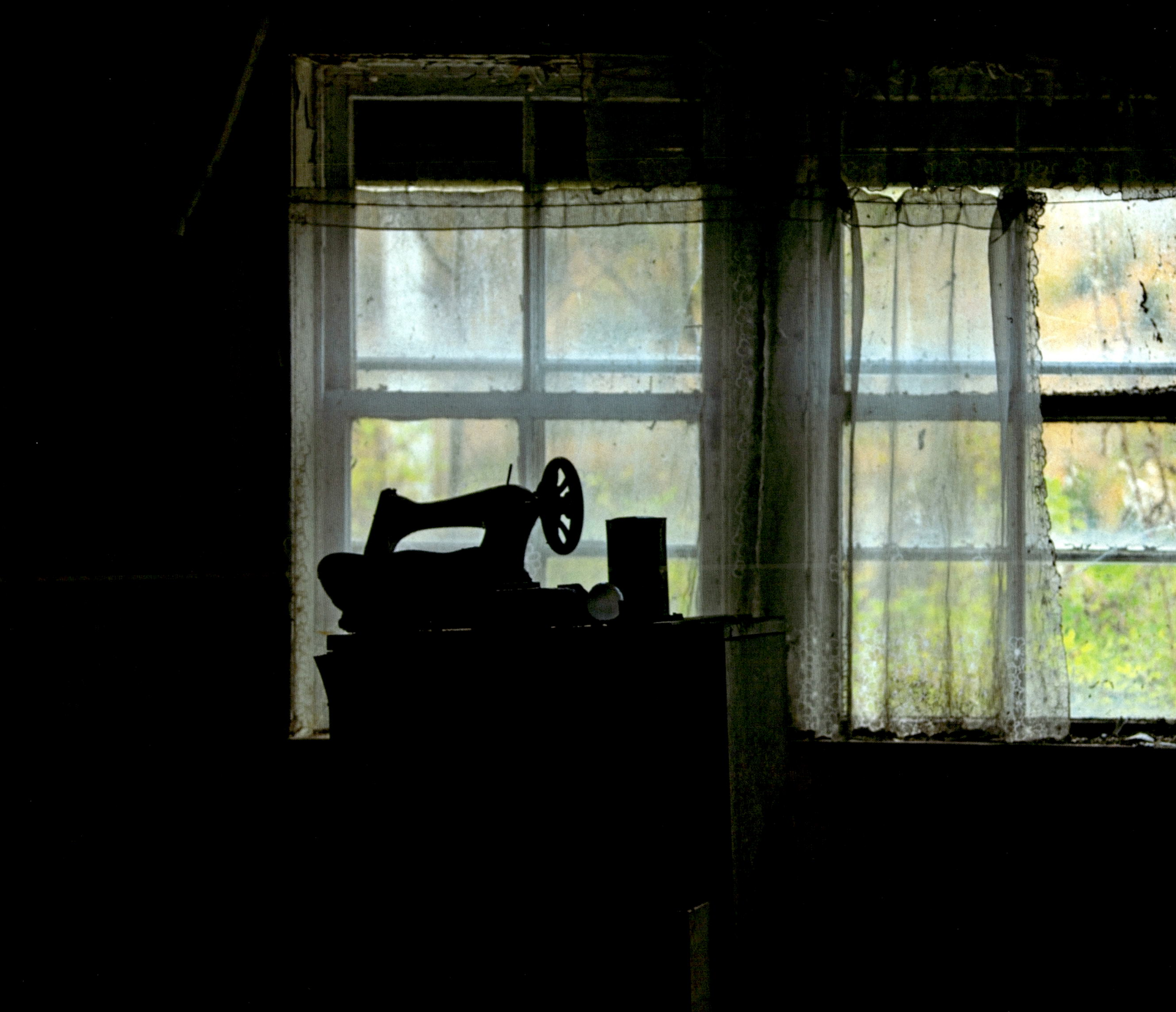

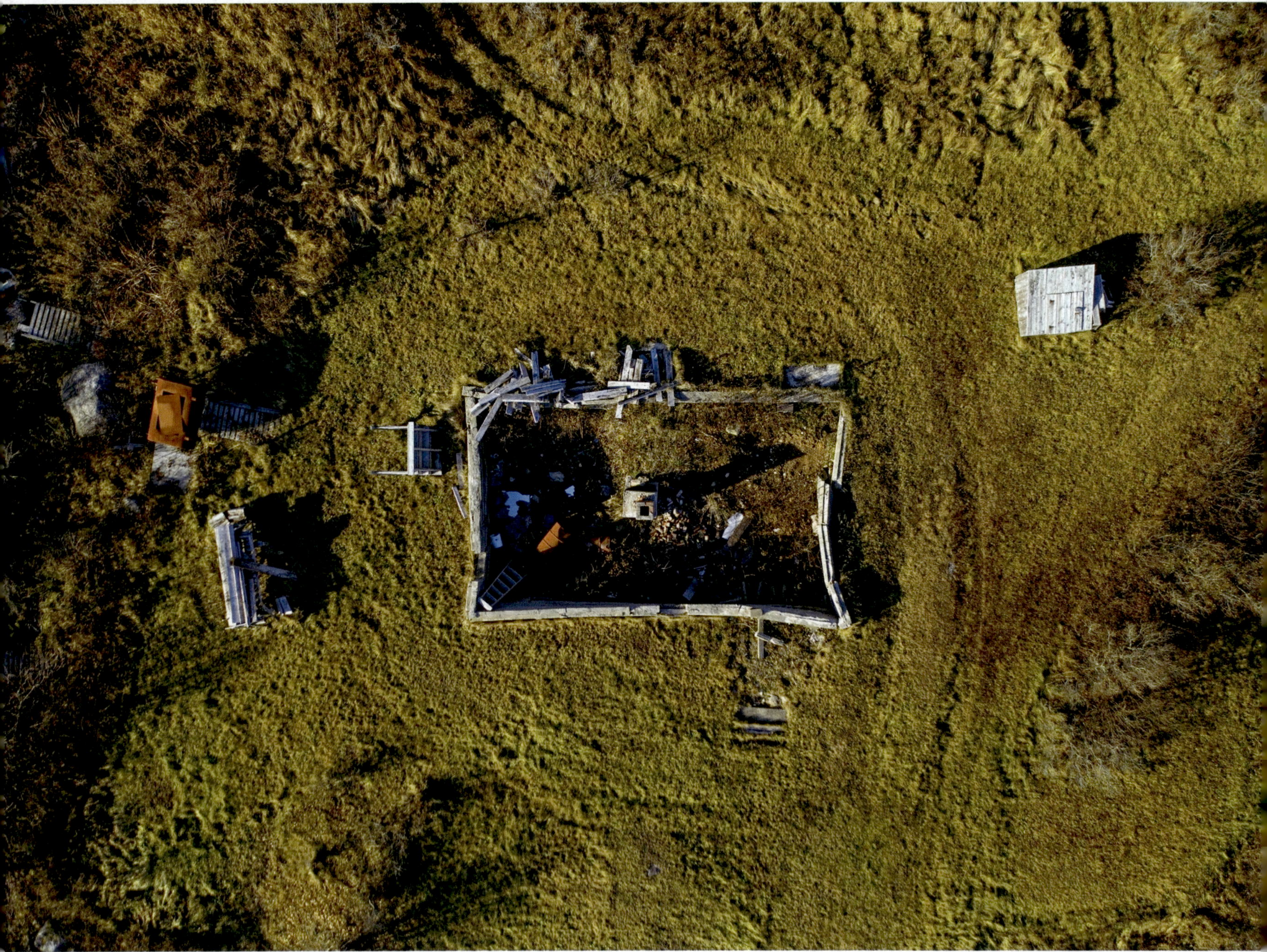

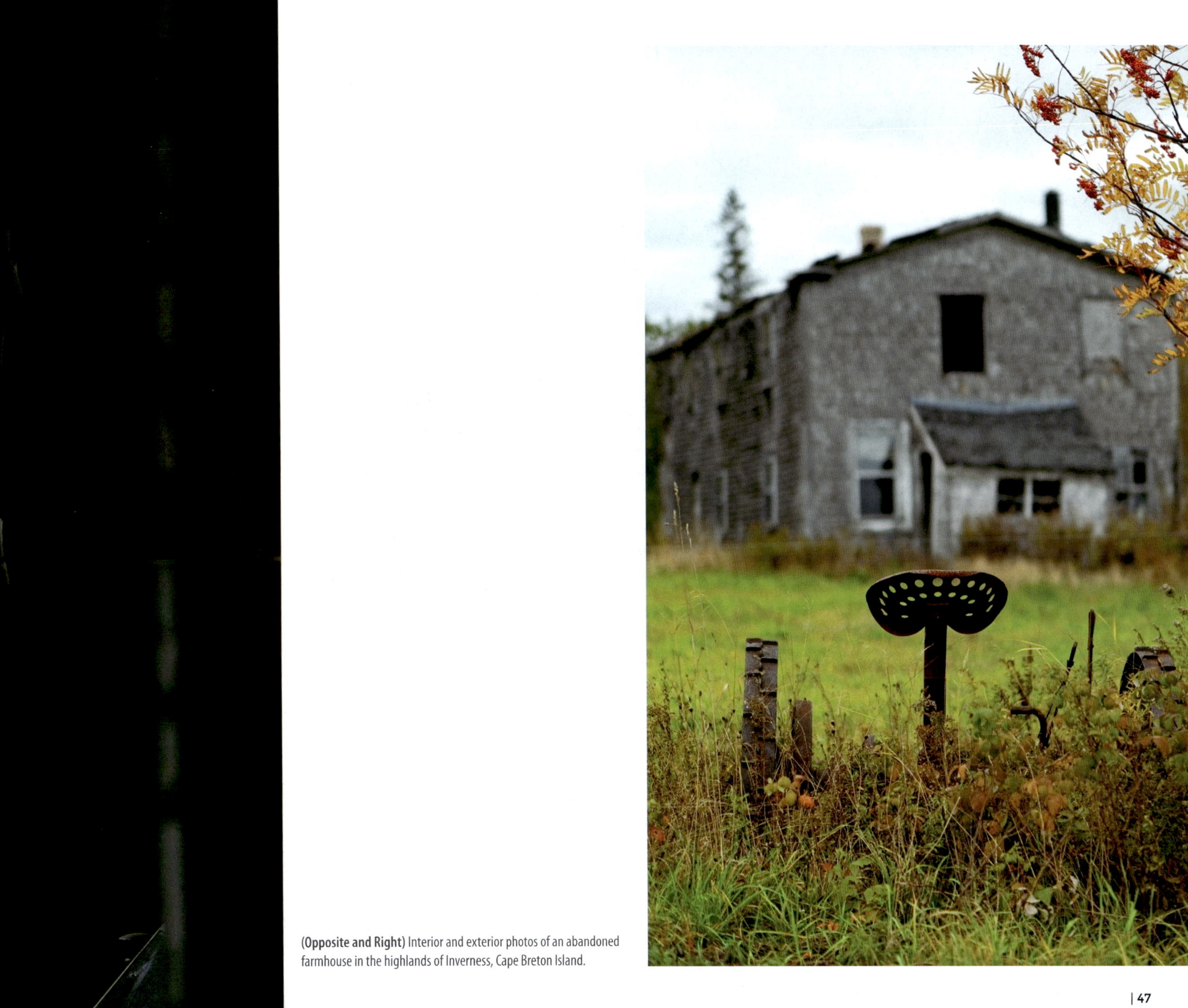

(Opposite and Right) Interior and exterior photos of an abandoned farmhouse in the highlands of Inverness, Cape Breton Island.

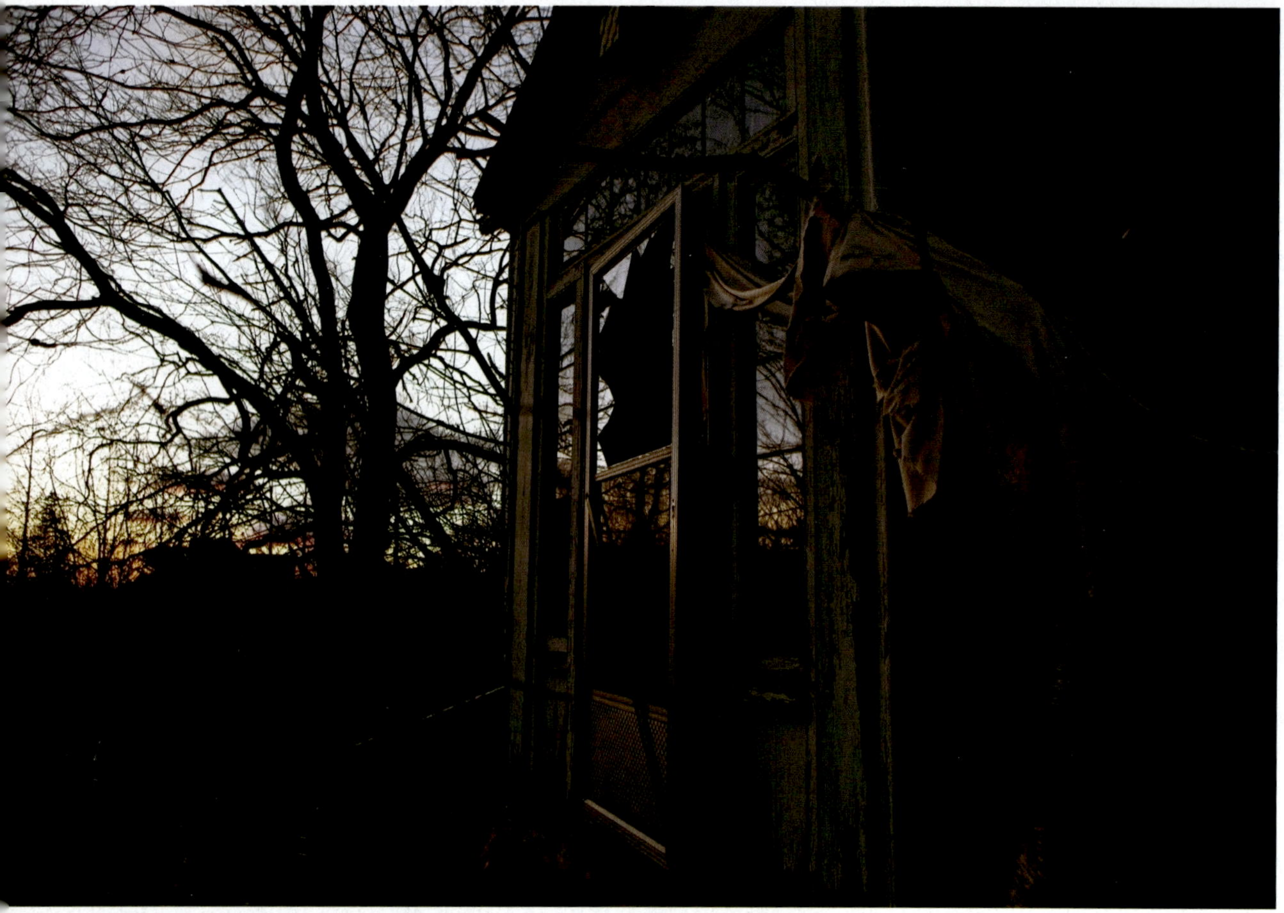

(Above) Hidden by trees and bushes, this broken side door of an abandoned dwelling near Annapolis Royal allowed us access to what would have been a lovely home in its time.

(Opposite) A derelict fishing shack on the waters of the Eastern Shore at the blue hour.

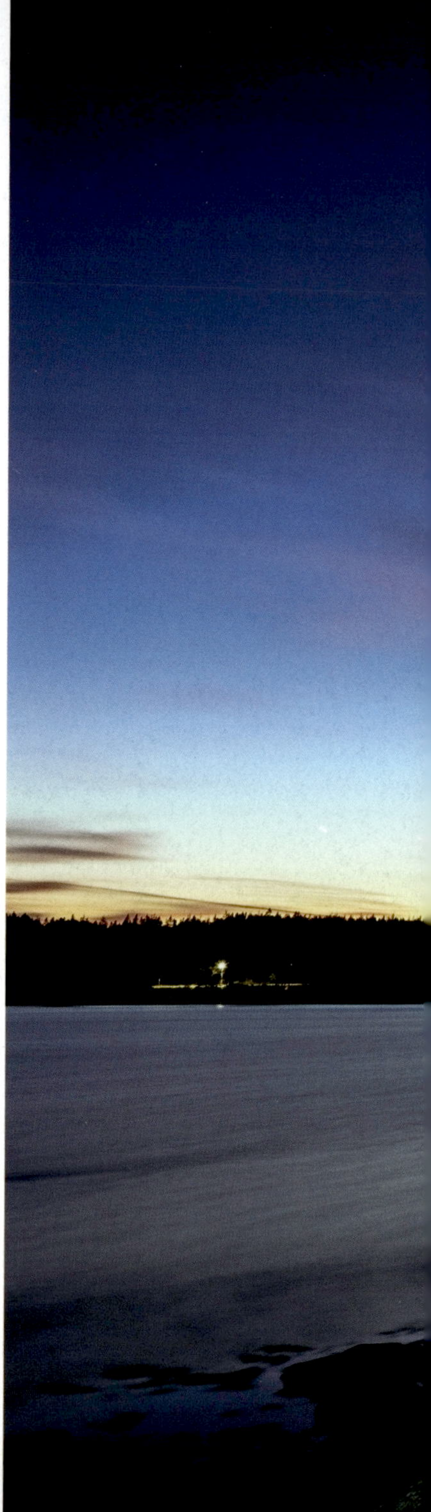

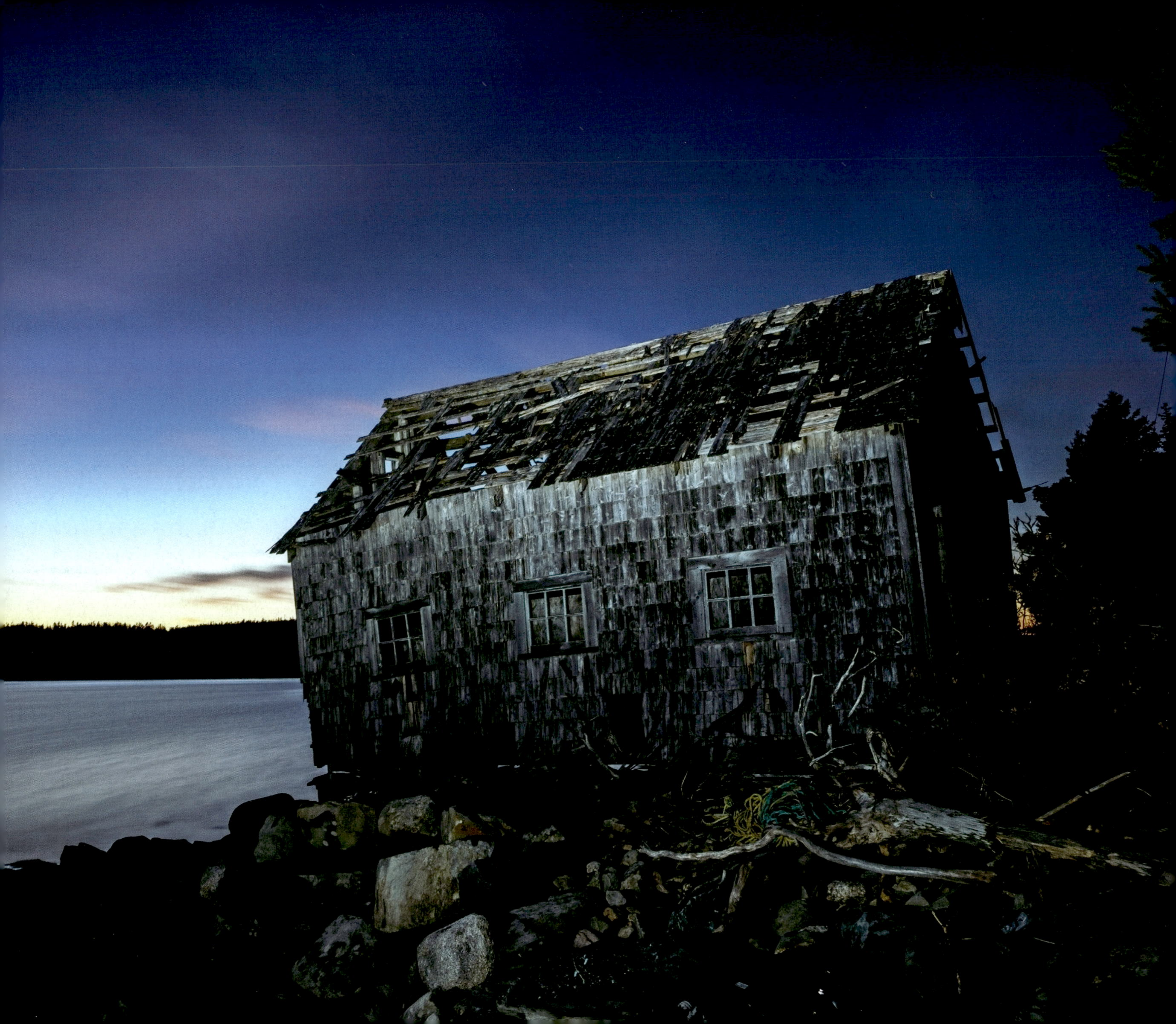

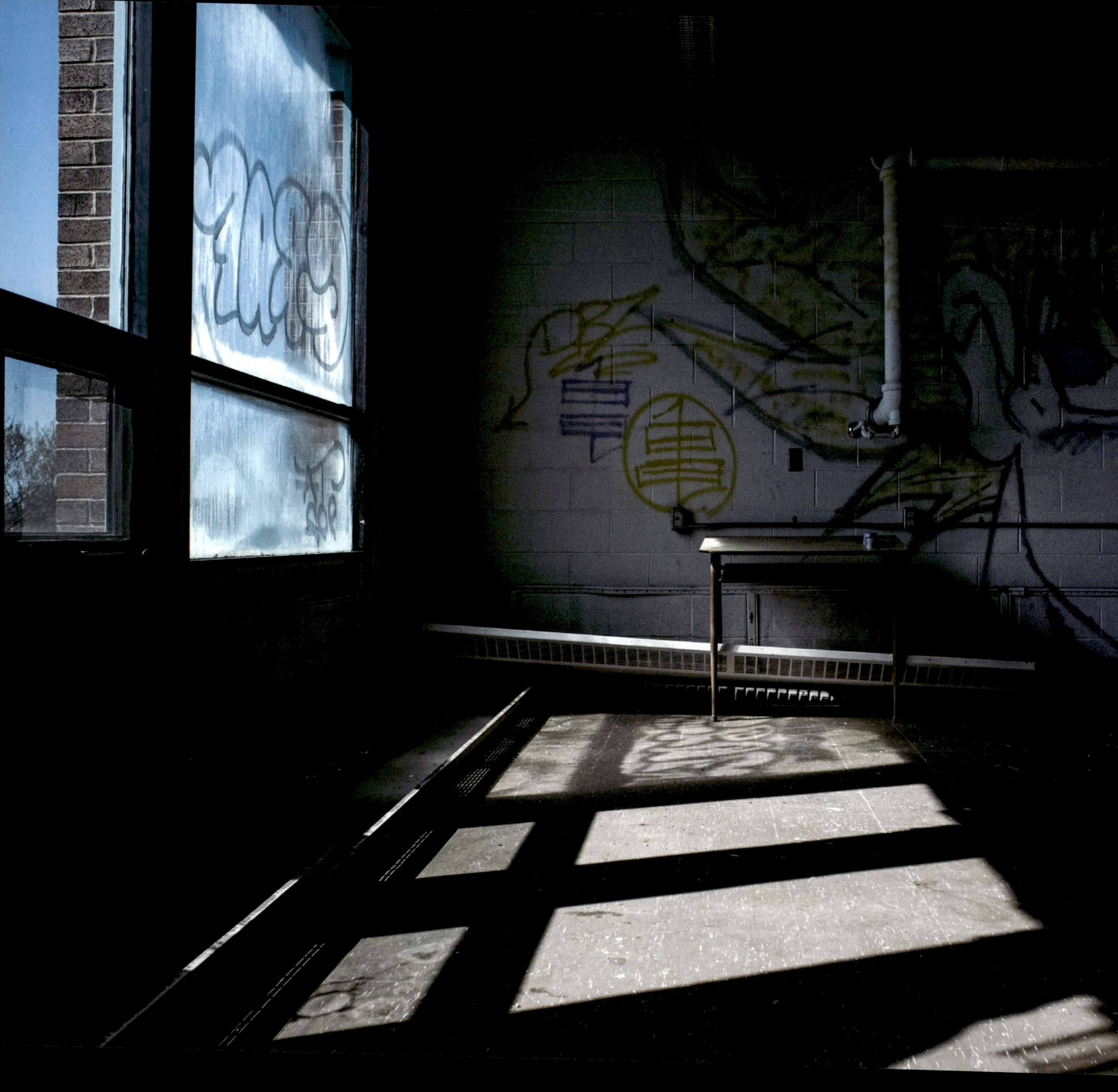

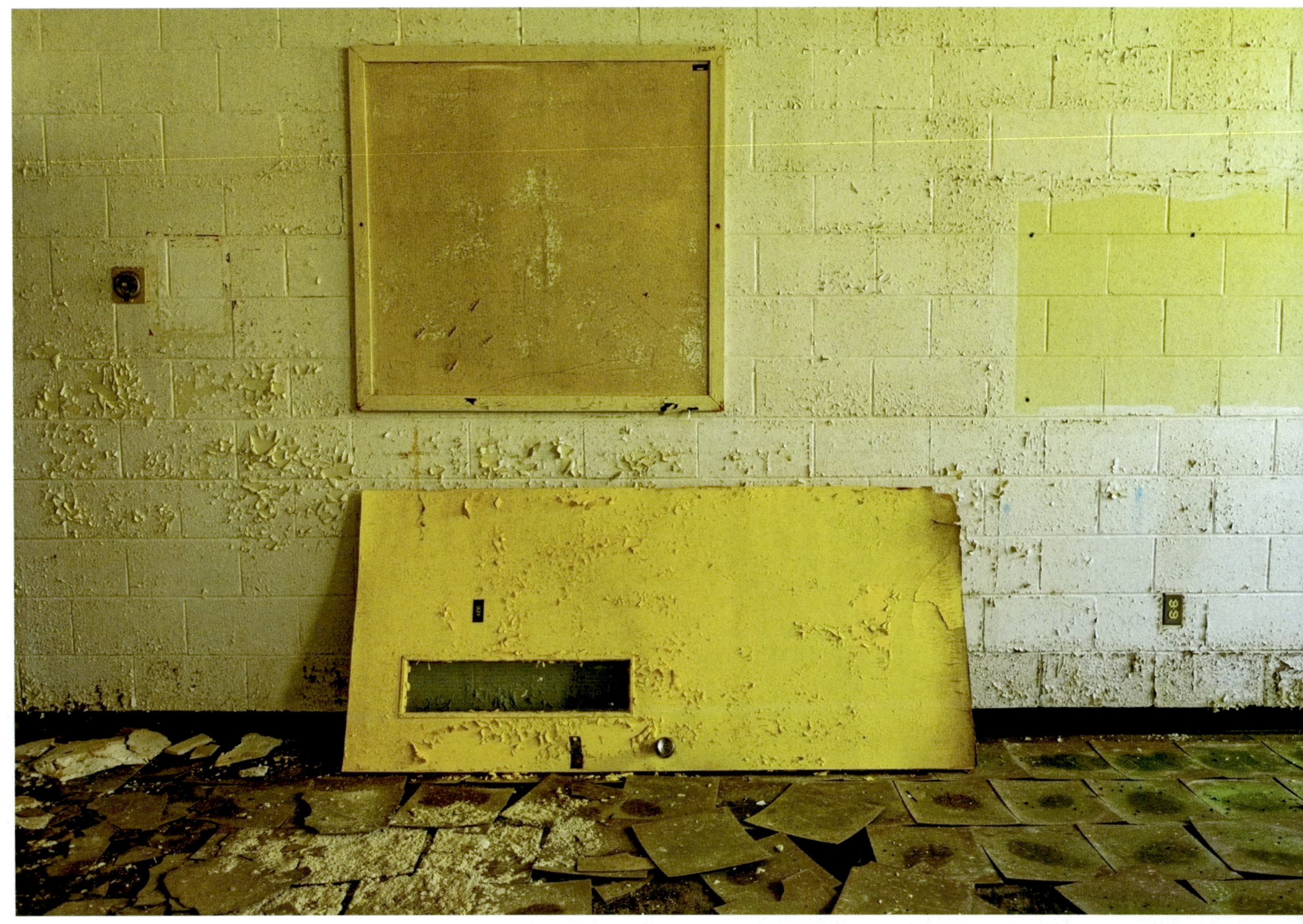

(Opposite and Above) The face of a young man looking out the window of a large room in the former Shelburne Youth Centre in the town of Shelburne. The graffiti seems to encapsulate the troubled history of this detention centre. In 1948, the then-Nova Scotia School for Boys was relocated from Halifax to the Shelburne facility, about 220 kilometres from Halifax. The reform school typically housed about 70 boys until 1985 when residents from the Nova Scotia School for Girls moved into the facility which was then renamed The Shelburne Youth Centre. In the early 1990s, allegations of sexual and physical abuse started to surface. In 1996, the Nova Scotia government began paying out-of-court settlements to former residents in a controversial compensation process.

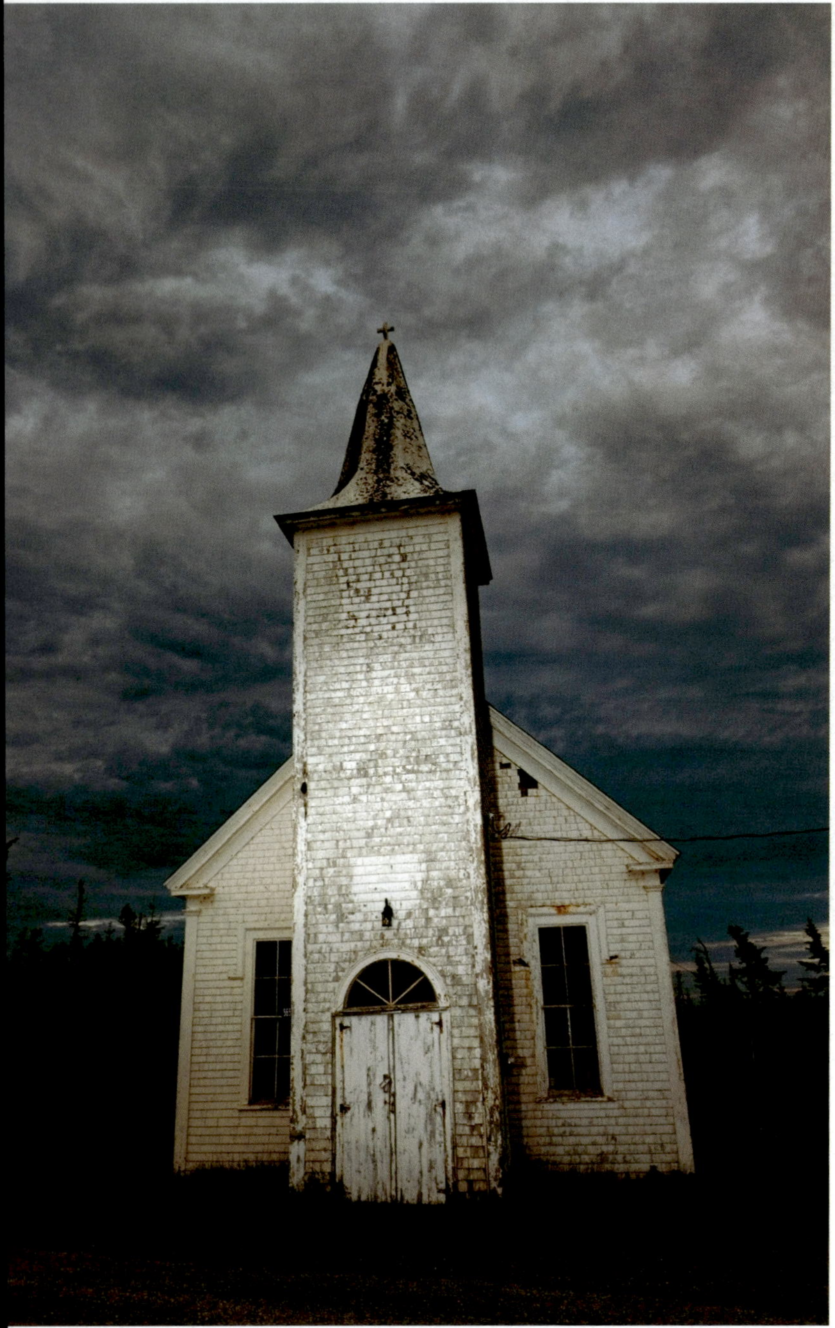

(Left) Grace United Church in Whitehead, Guysborough County, was built in 1880. Similar churches to this one line the winding roads along Guysborough County.

(Opposite) The sun sets behind a farmhouse near the small community of Folly Mountain, Colchester County. The area nearby in East Folly Mountain is believed to have been settled in the 19th century.

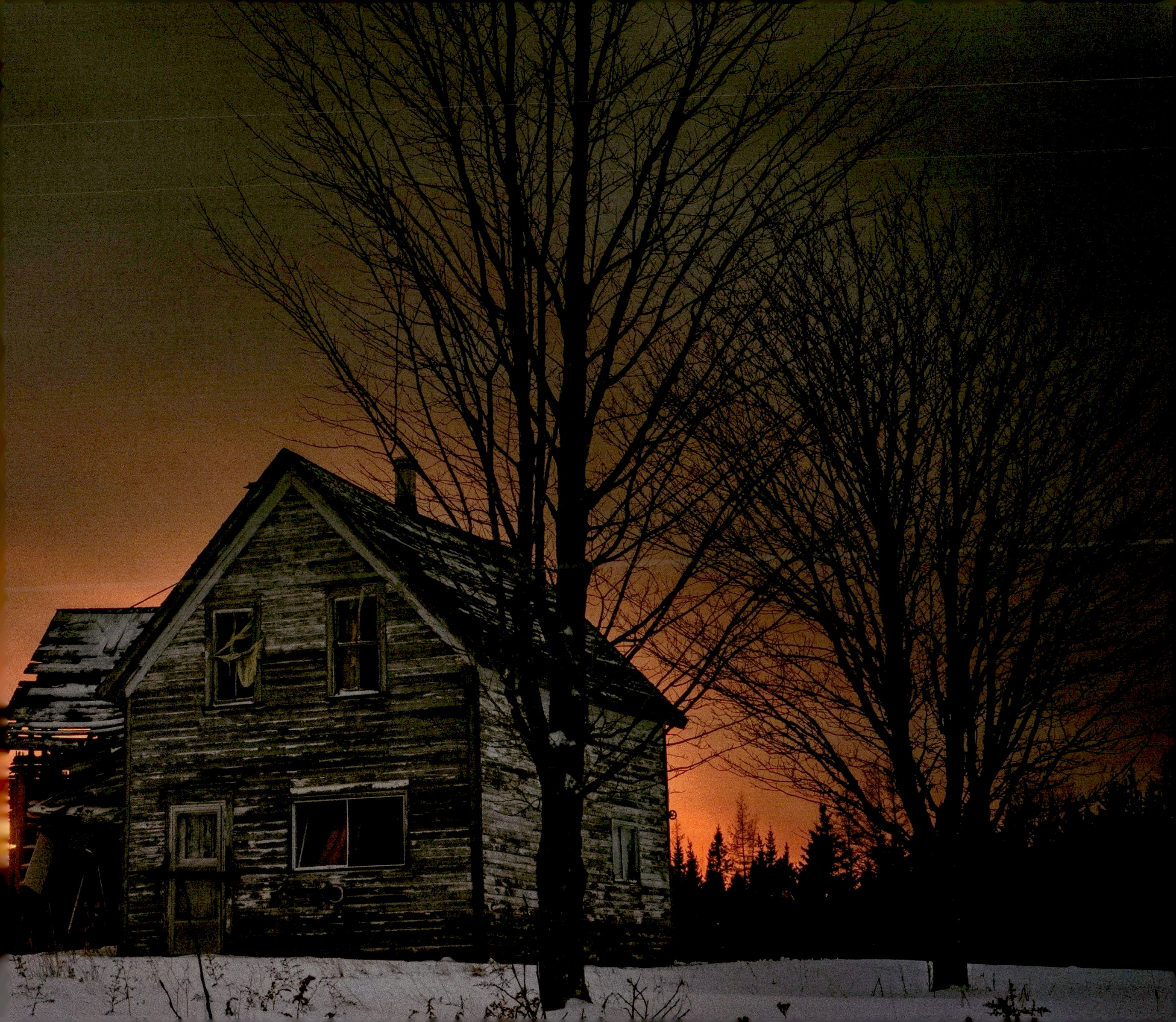

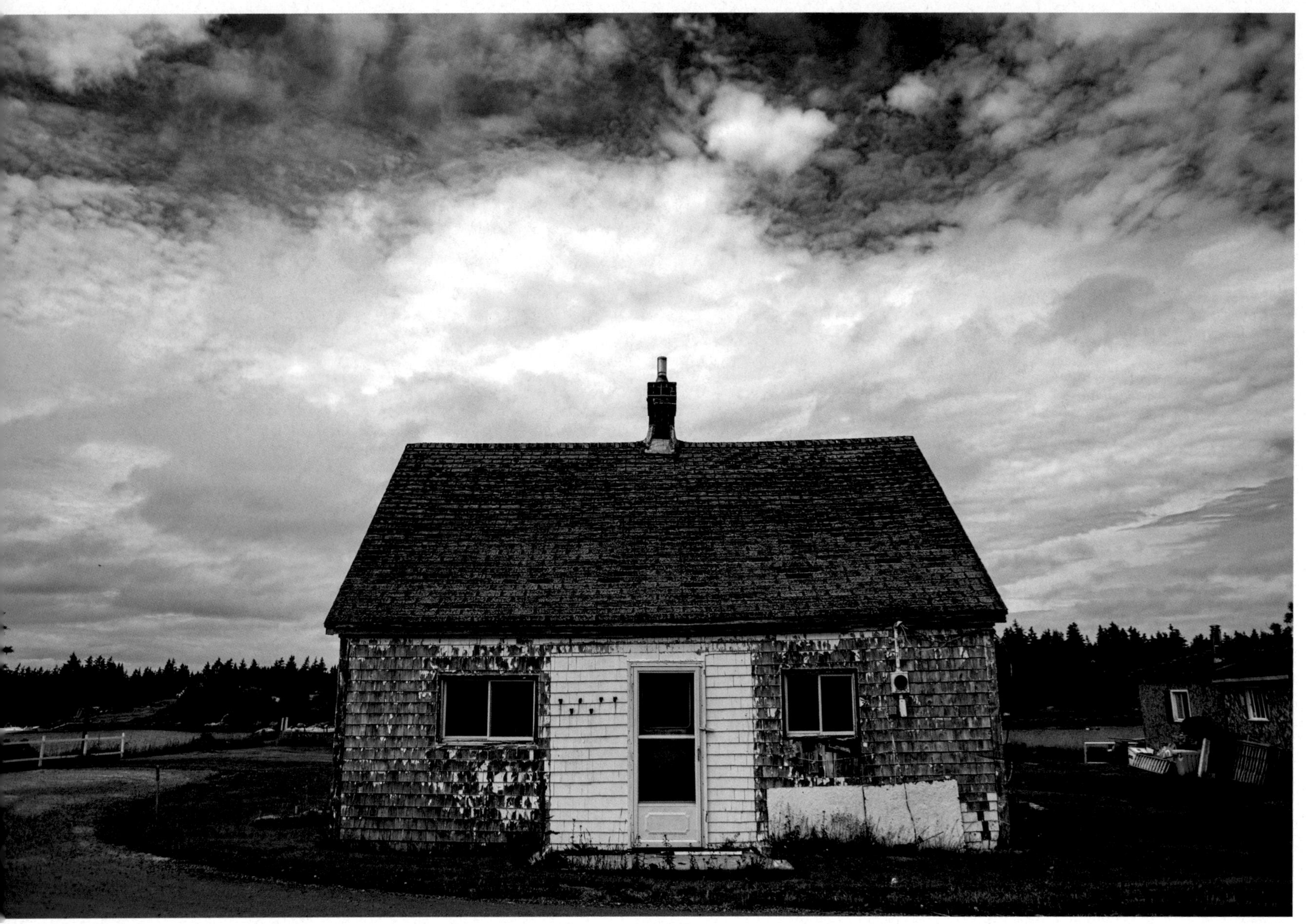

This small, weathered house along the water in the community of Canso, Guysborough County, was kept very neat and tidy. The name Canso is believed to derive from the Mi'kmaq word kamsok, which means "the place beyond the cliffs." It has been a vital fishing port since 1604. Between 1881 and 1894, it was the communications link between North America and Europe. In 1912, the cable building, which was located just outside the town of Canso, received the first distress call from the ill-fated Titanic which sank in the early morning hours of April 15, 600 kilometres south of Newfoundland. More than 1,500 passengers lost their lives.

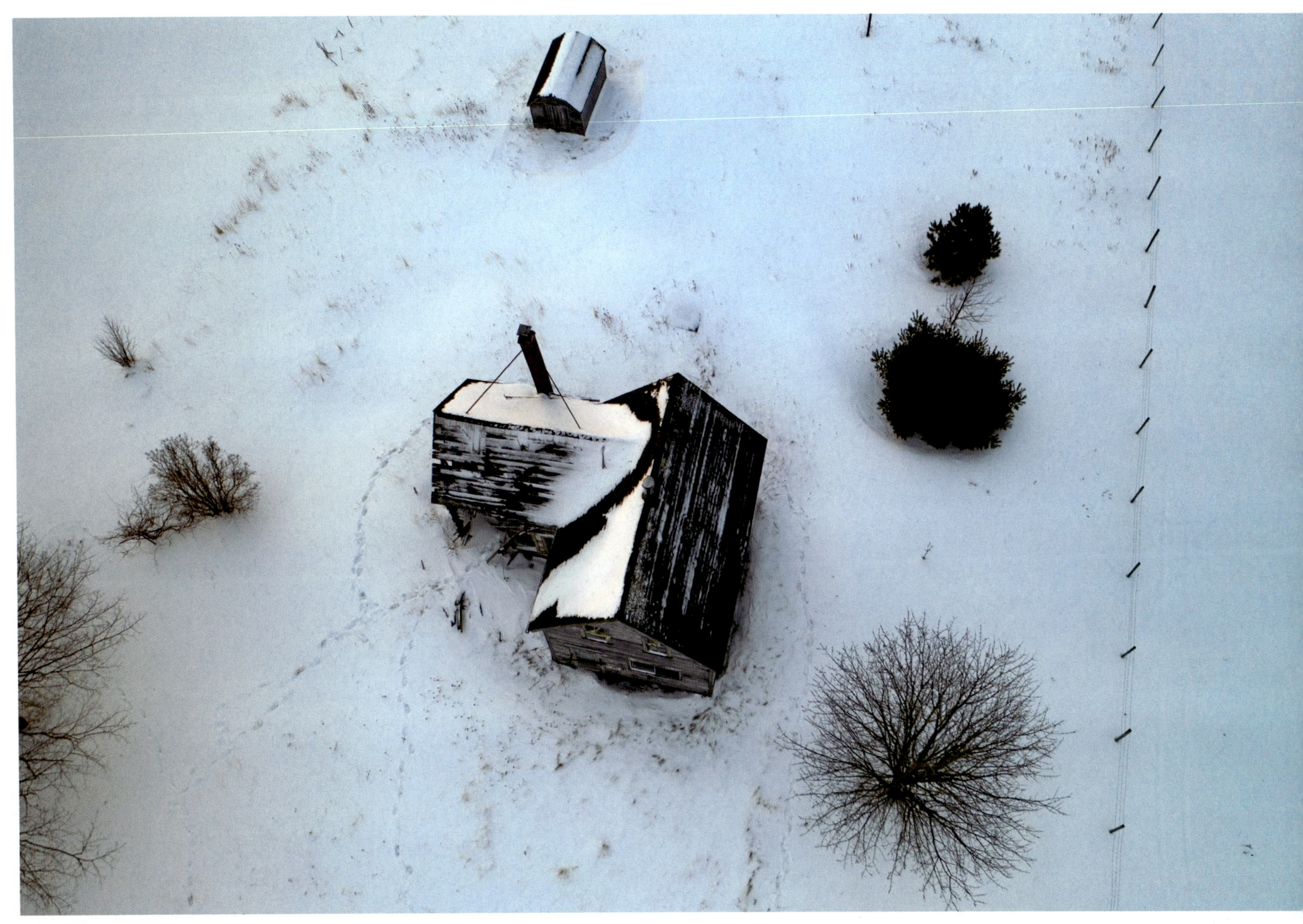

A view from above, this home in Folly Mountain, Colchester County, is starting to crumble but its beauty remains with a blanket of fresh snow to cover its imperfections.

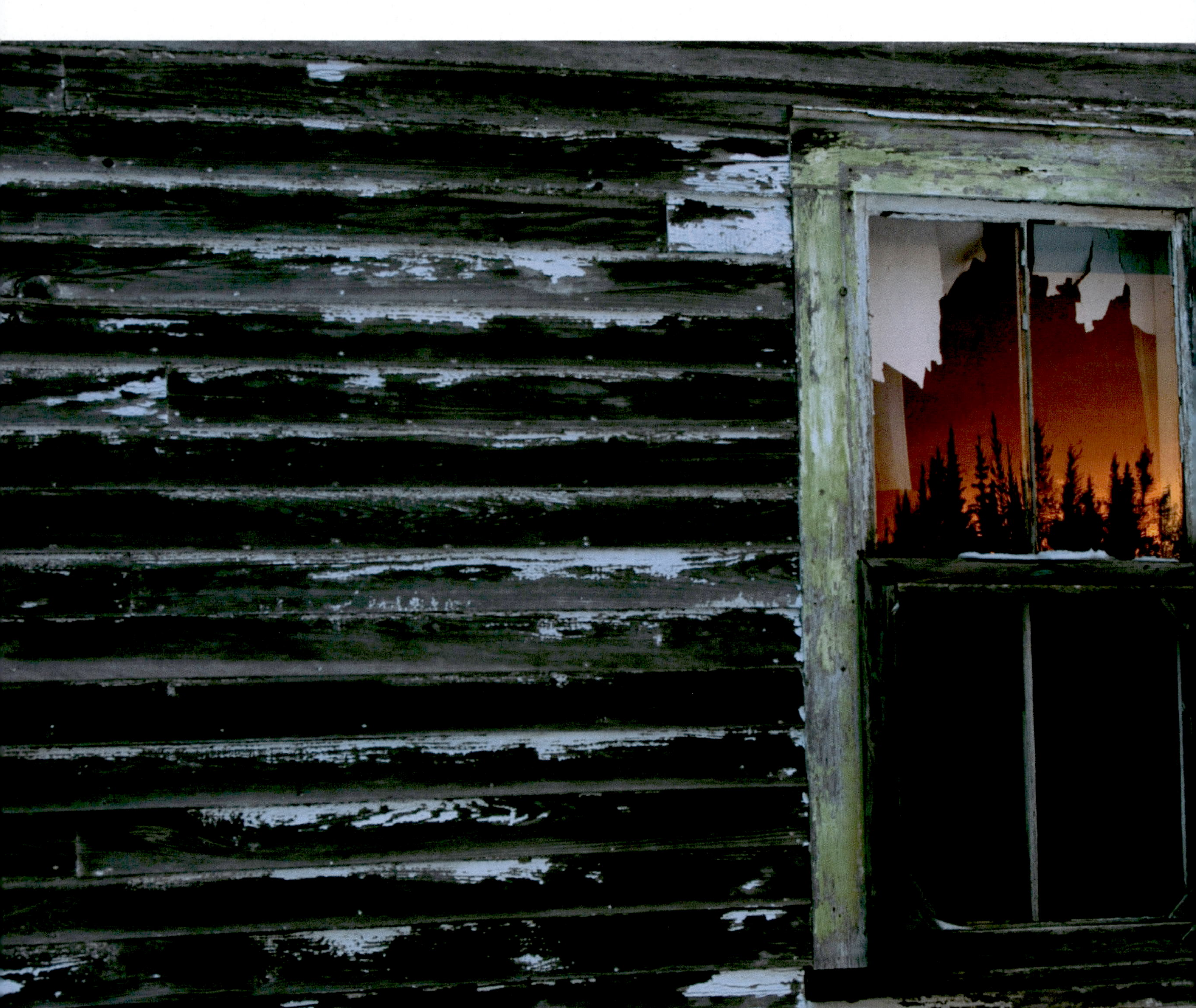

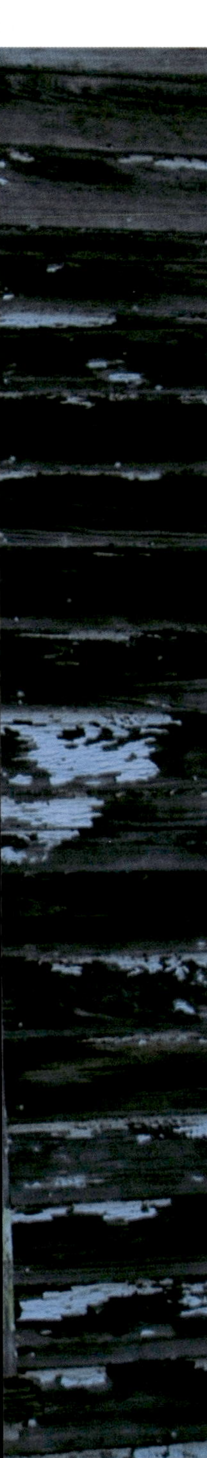

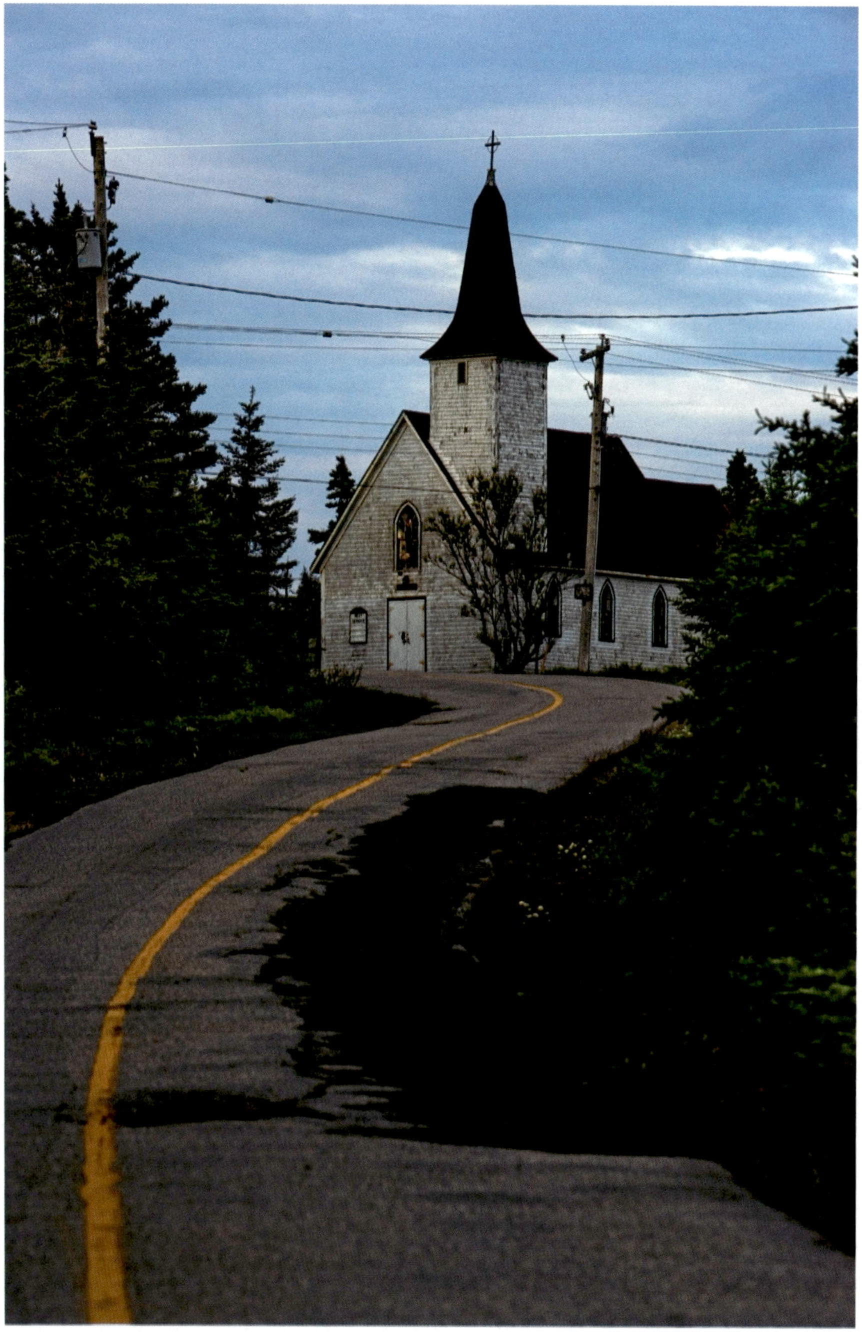

(Opposite) Around the back of the Folly Mountain home, a sunset is reflected in the window.

(Right) Churches like this one can be seen all along the coastal routes in Guysborough County; this one was near the community of Whitehead.

She grows on you slowly the first time you meet
There's just so much beauty the heart can believe
And you want to stay longer and she's ever so pleased
You're one of the many who don't want to leave
So walk through her green fields, Go down to the sea
The fortune in your eyes is more like a dream
She's called Nova Scotia and she so makes you feel
You discovered a treasure no other has seen

— Song lyrics, *She's Called Nova Scotia*
Rita MacNeil

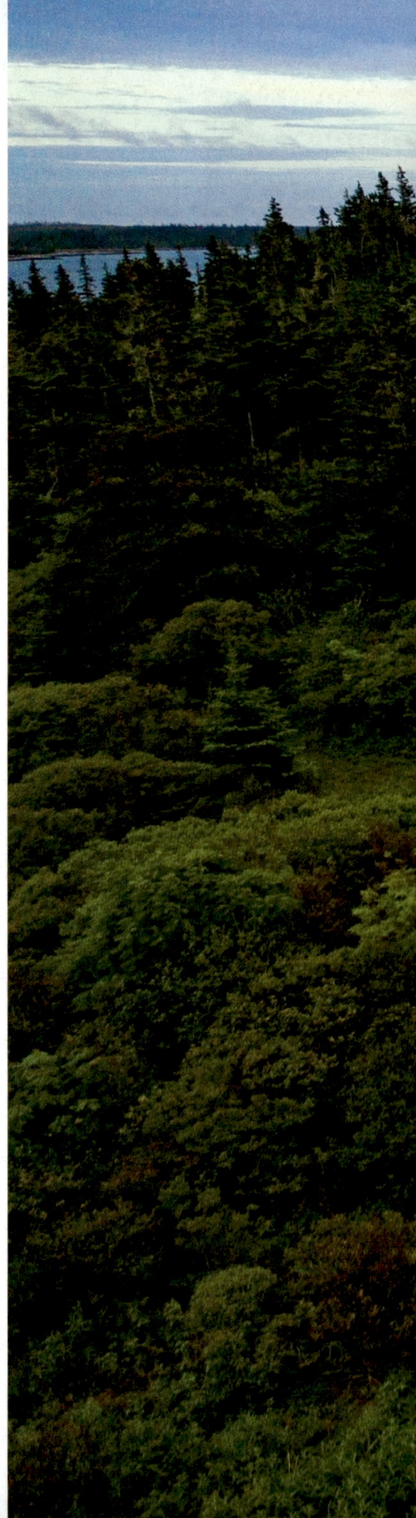

(Opposite) This home in the Whitehead area of Guysborough County was one of several in the same area. There was no obvious point of access so we flew the drone for a closer look, offering us an angle which showed how the ravages of nature overtook this structure. This small coastal fishing village was founded by the French in 1655 and was a popular spot for pirates because of its coves, nearby islands and passageways.

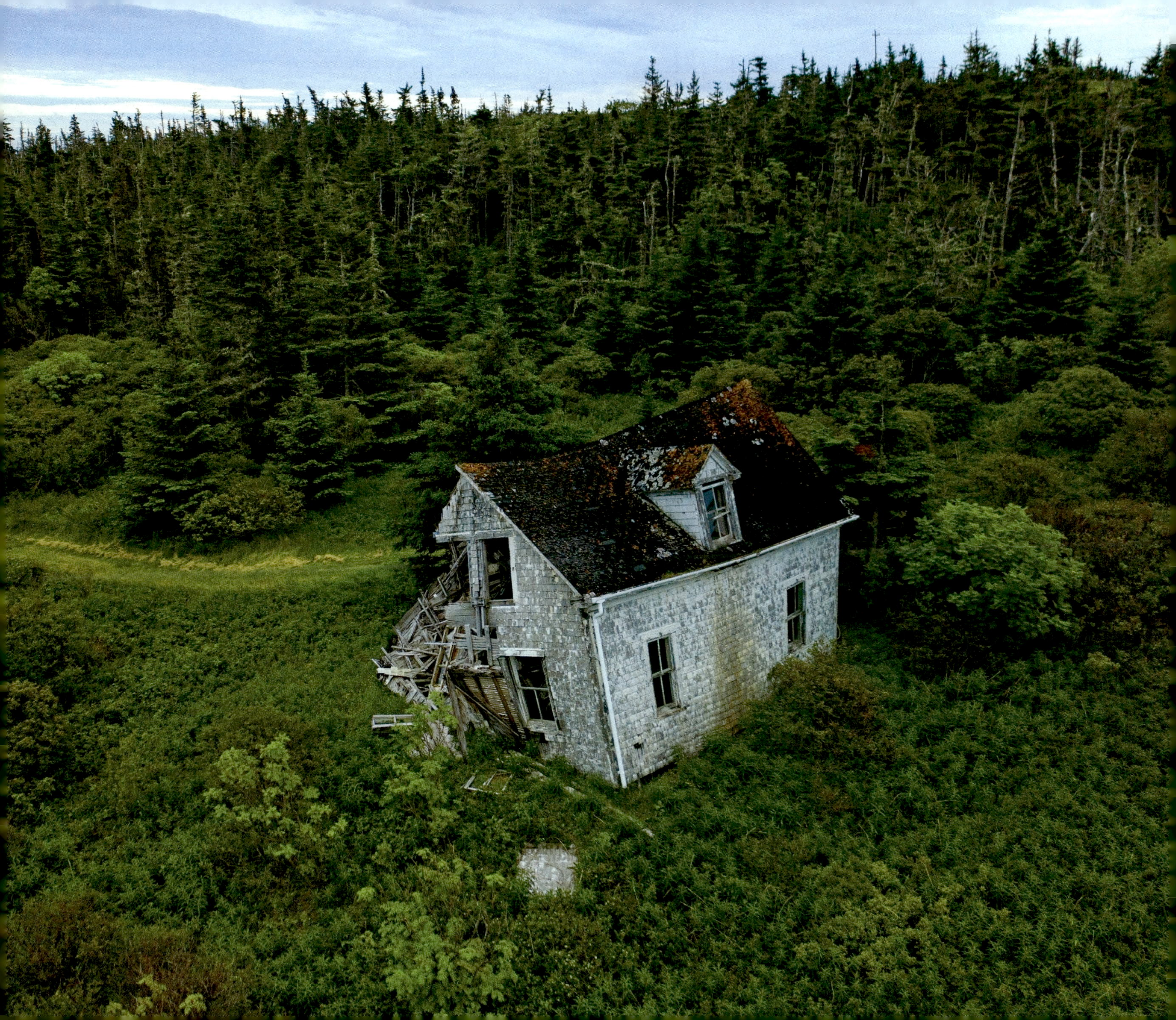

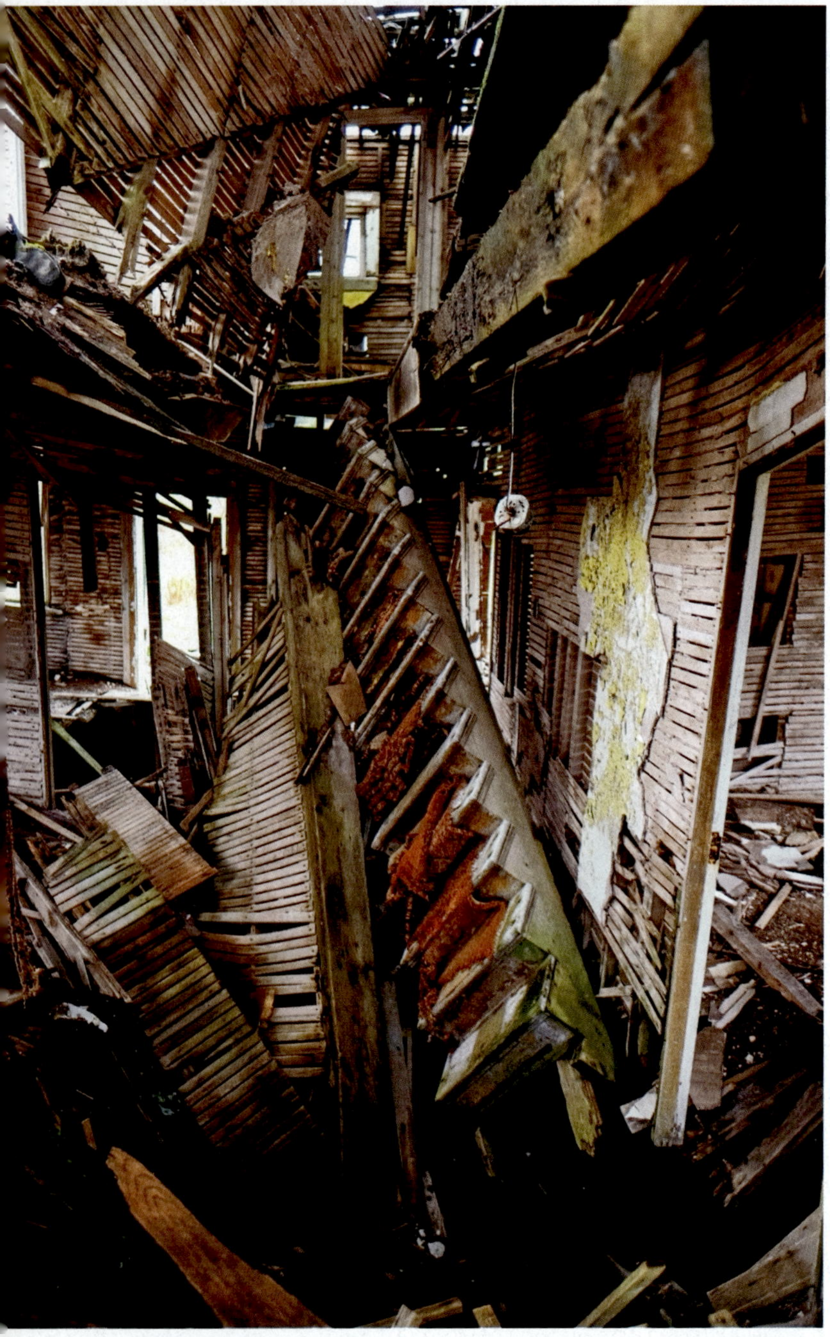

(Left) The twisted staircase is the only remaining discernible feature in this Earltown home.

(Opposite) The beauty of autumn leaves doesn't mask the decline of this iconic Earltown home. This house has a bit of a cult following and was featured in a CBC Land and Sea episode about abandoned structures.

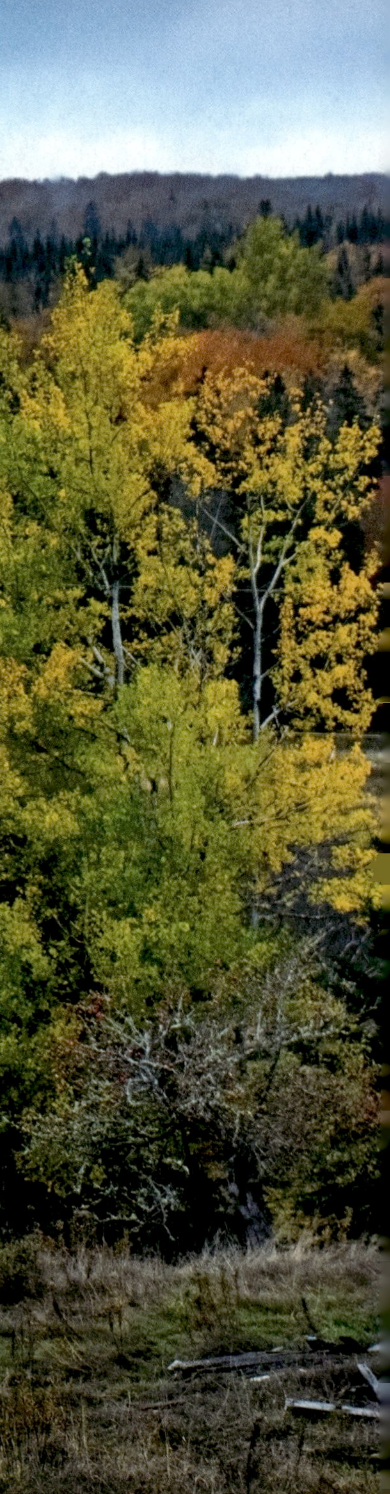

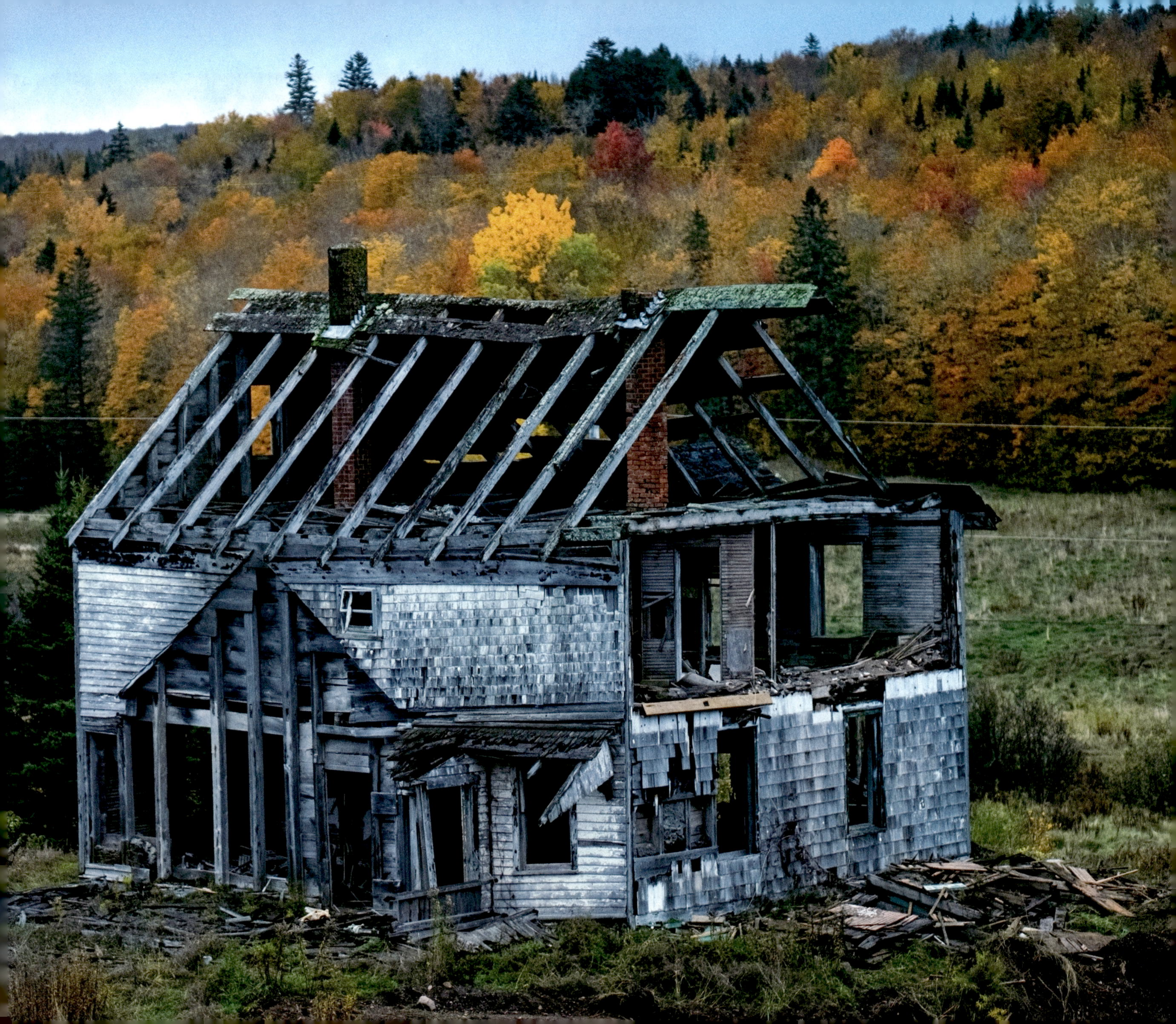

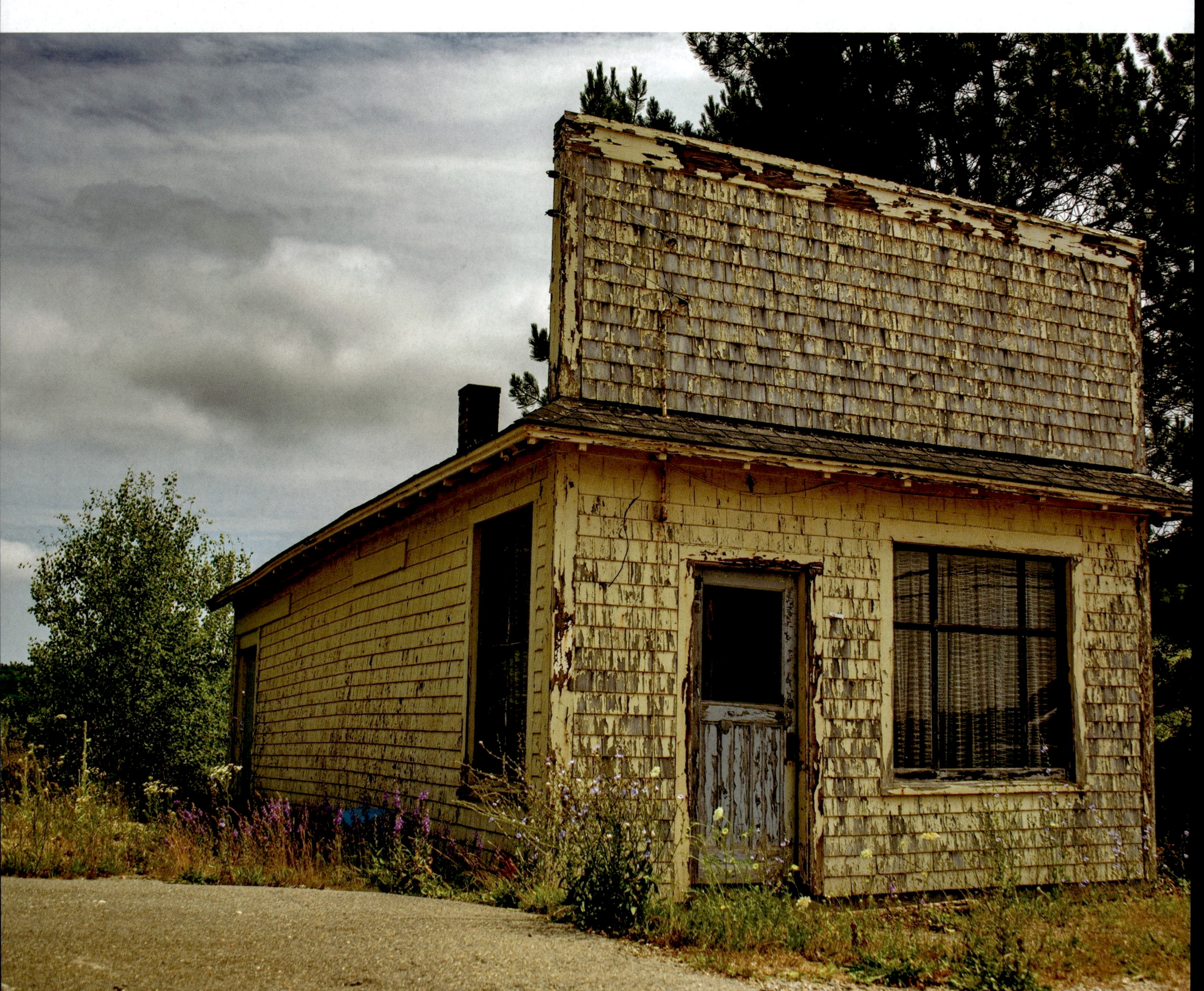

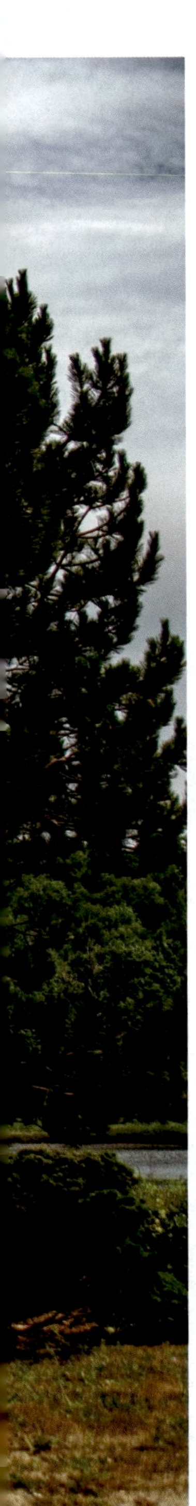

(Opposite) Along the scenic Evangeline Trail route near the Bay of Fundy we came upon this small structure. We don't know for sure, but the architecture suggests this would have been a small store at some point it its history.

(Right) This old farmhouse in Economy, Colchester County, was photographed on a bitterly cold night in February 2020. The ornate cornices decorating the roof line and windows offer a glimpse of the home's previous beauty.

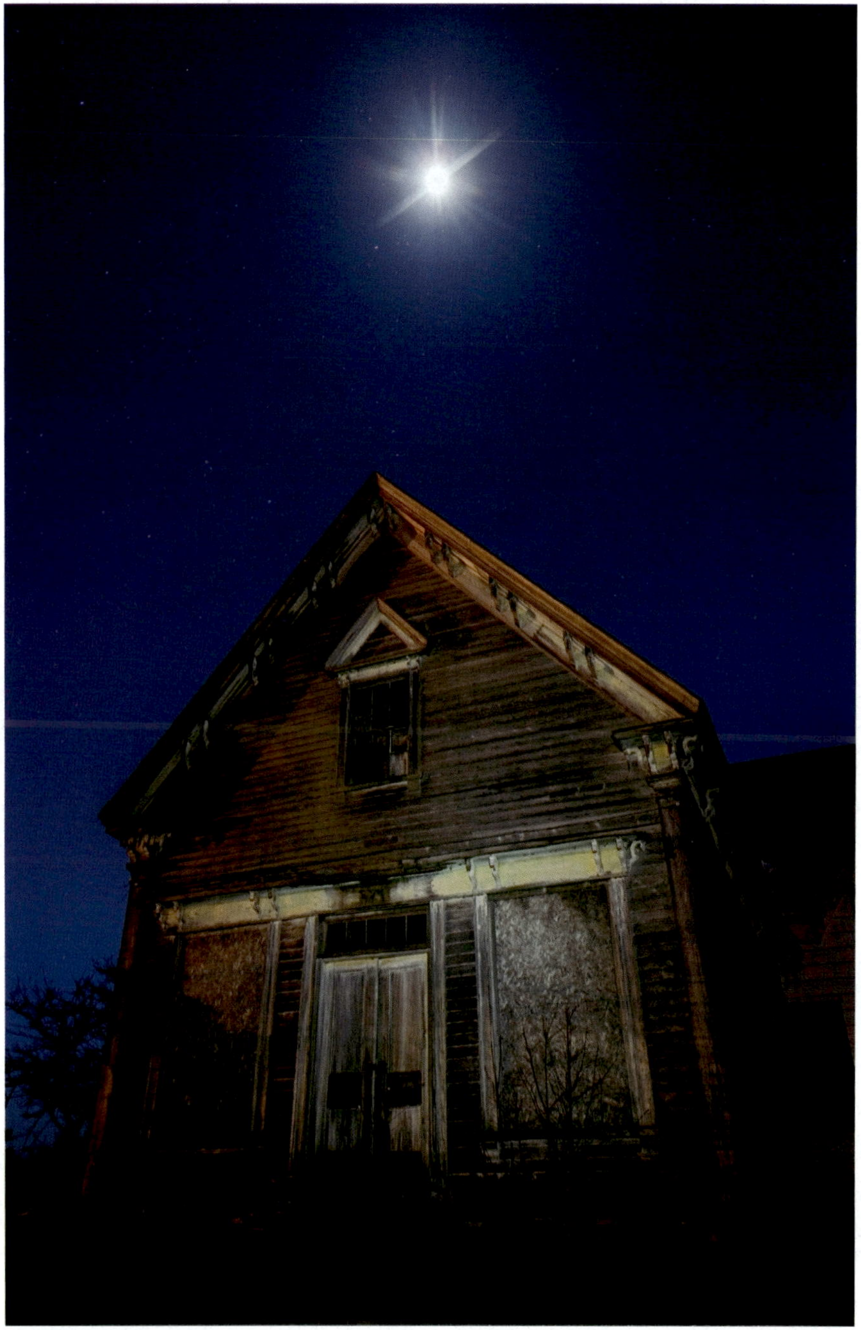

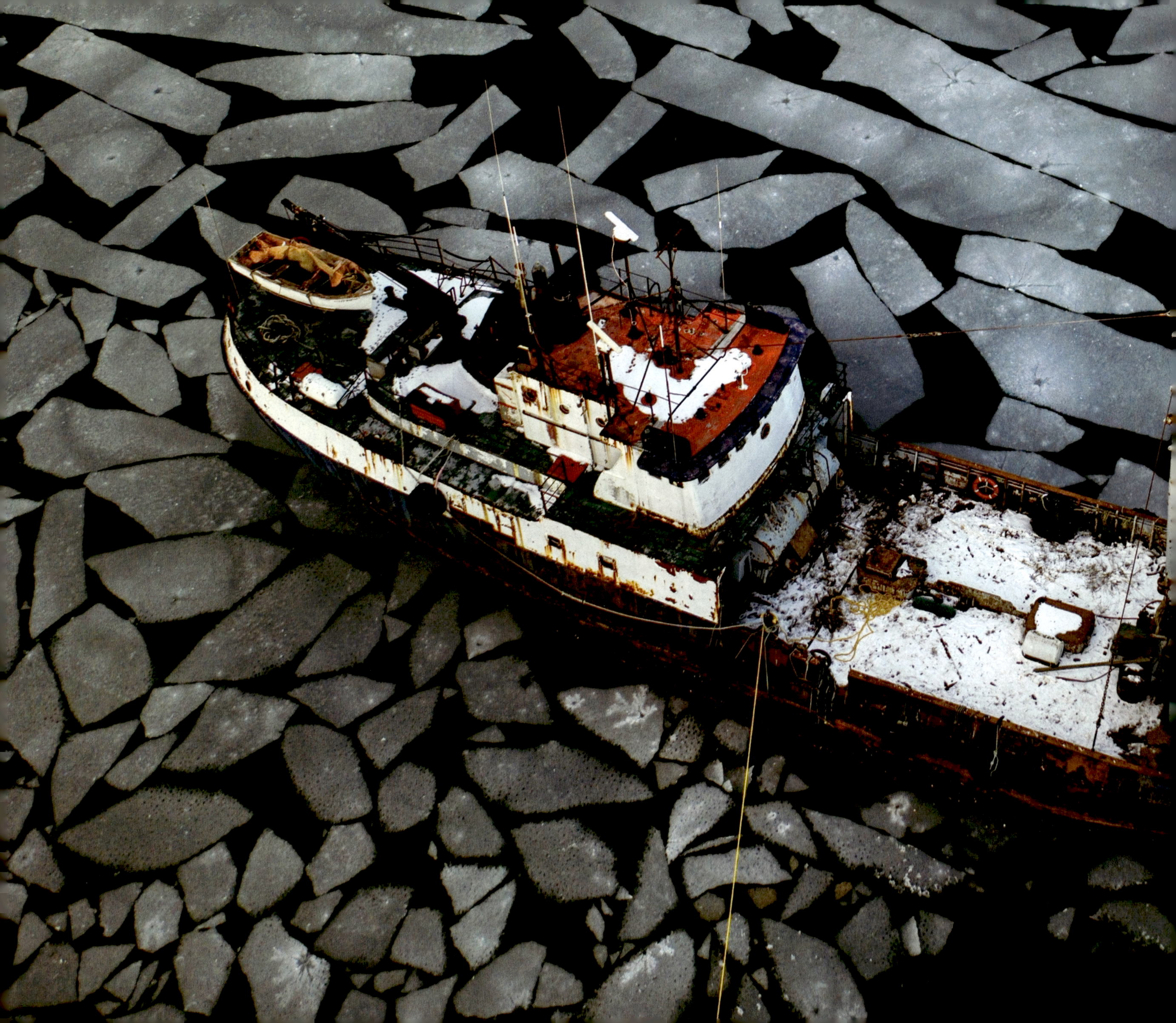

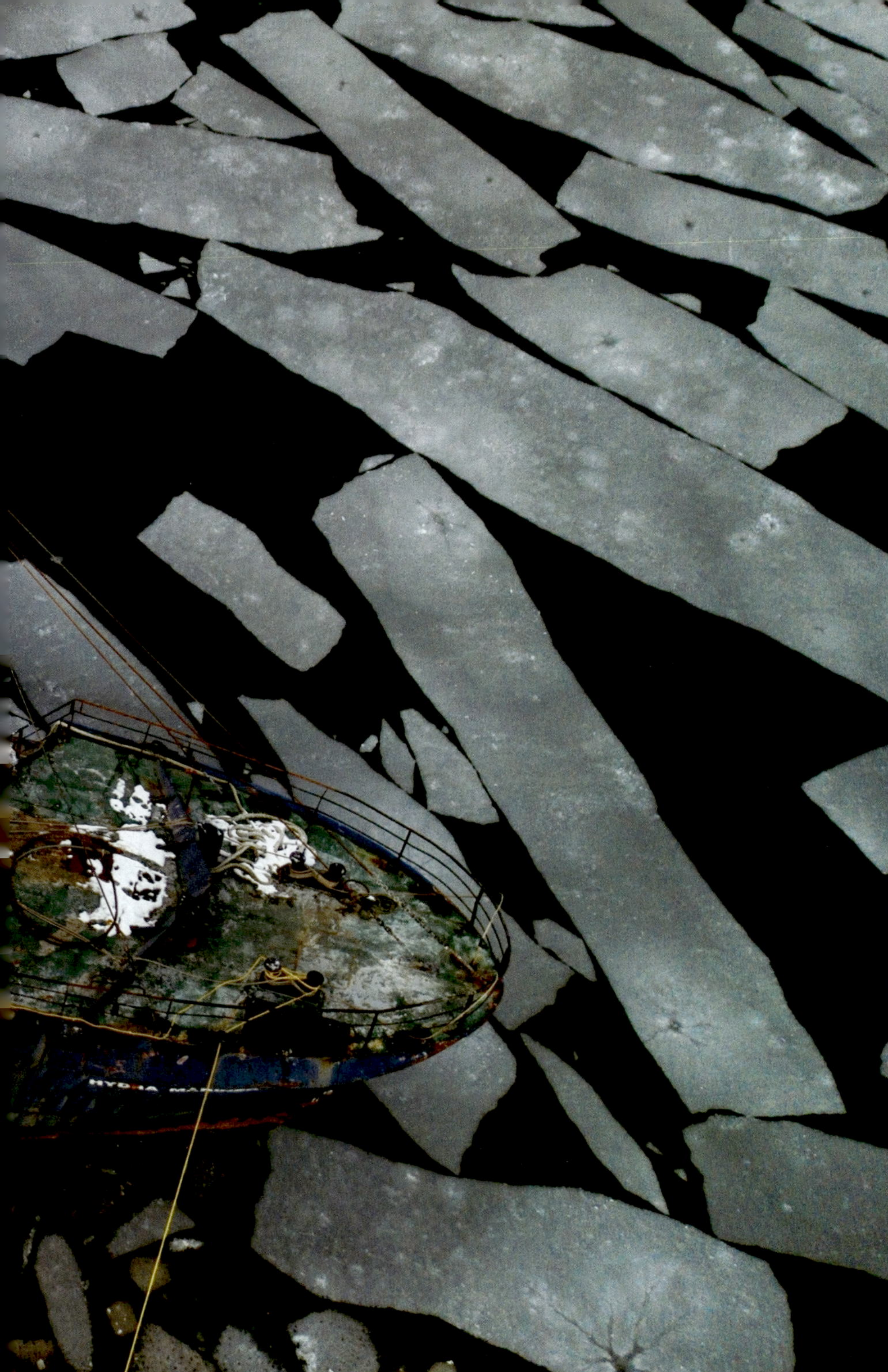

(Opposite) The *Hydra Mariner* sits on the shores of Navy Island, Wrights Cove, Dartmouth, after slipping its moorings in a storm. The vessel has been abandoned by its owner for some time and has become a focus of environmental concern to the Canadian Coast Guard.

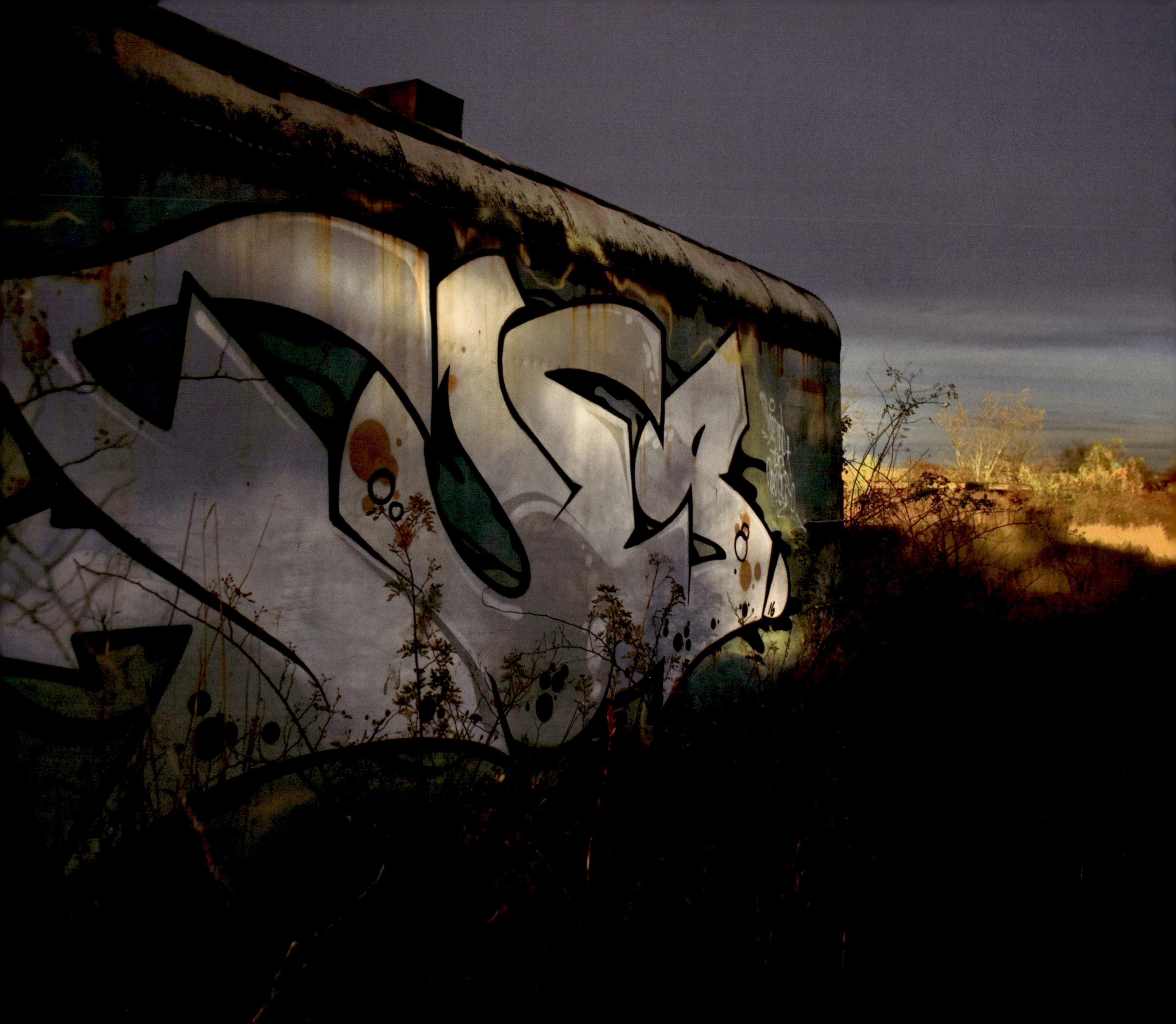

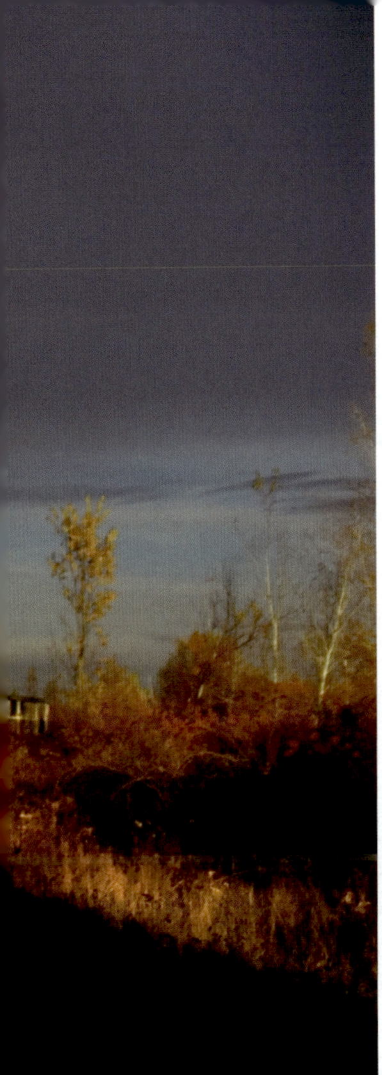

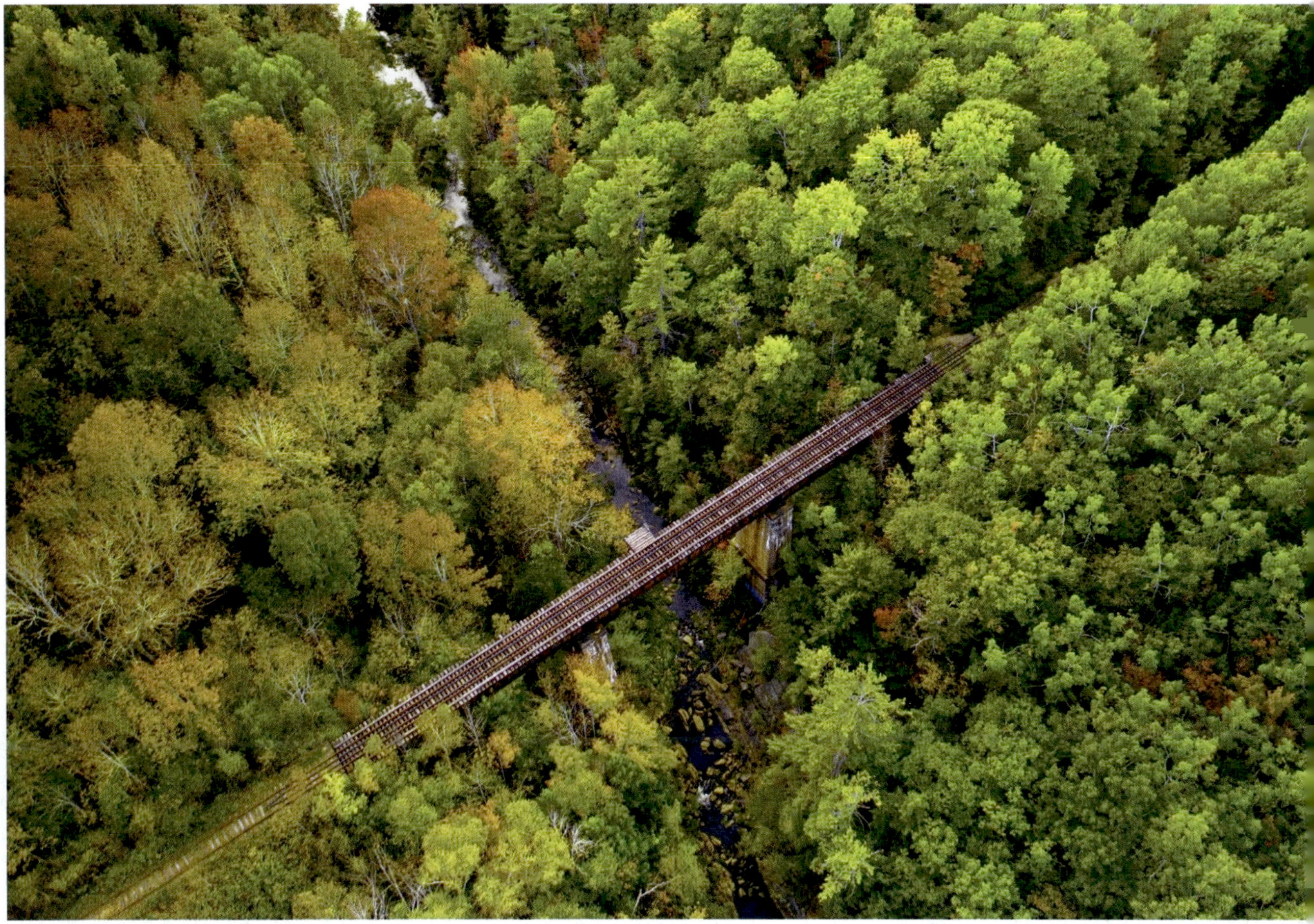

(Opposite) The sun peeks through some cloud in Windsor, Hants County, near an old rail car left on the tracks at the Windsor Spur. The car has become a canvas for graffiti artists who have given it some added colour.

(Above) A drone shot of an overgrown CN rail bridge near Ellershouse in the Municipal District of West Hants. The rail line runs between Windsor, Hants County, and Windsor Junction near Halifax but has not been in service for more than a decade.

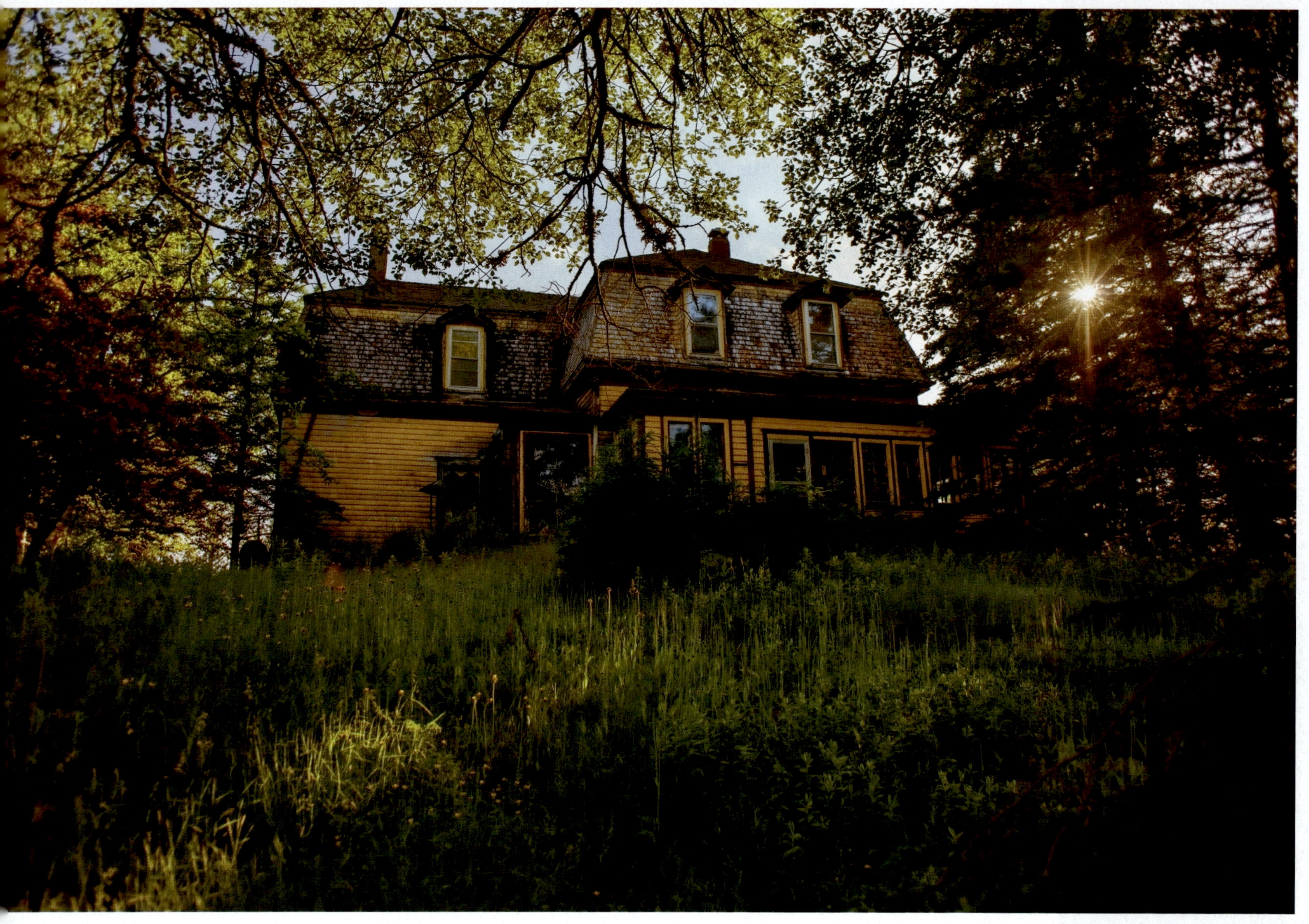

This Empire-style house caught our eye as we drove through a small village in Guysborough County. This stately home overlooked the water and would have been beautiful in its day with its stained-glass windows, and what appear to be handcrafted wooden mouldings embellishing the doorways and windows.

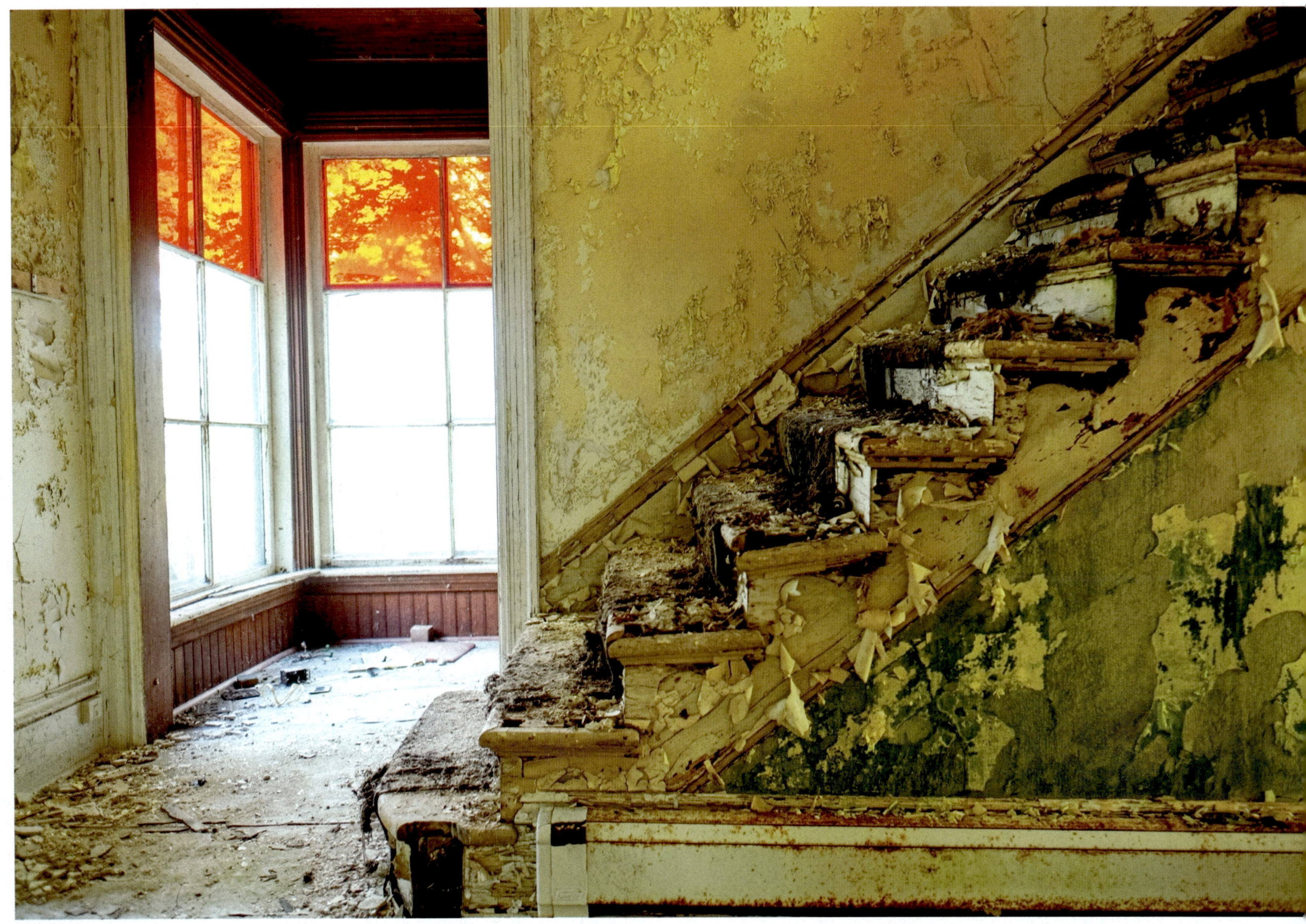

This photo shows the red stained-glass window and the staircase in the foyer of the home on the opposite page.

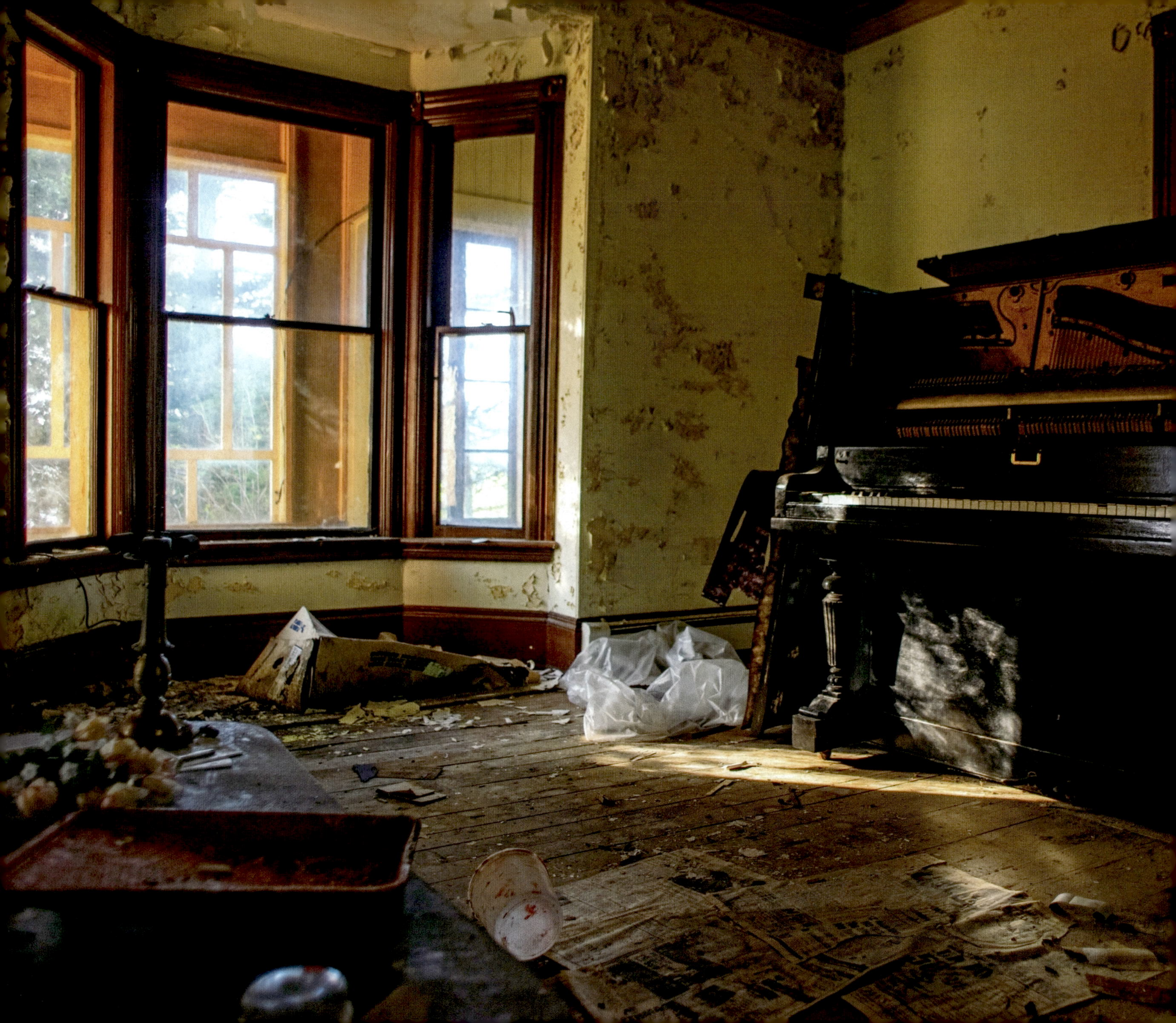

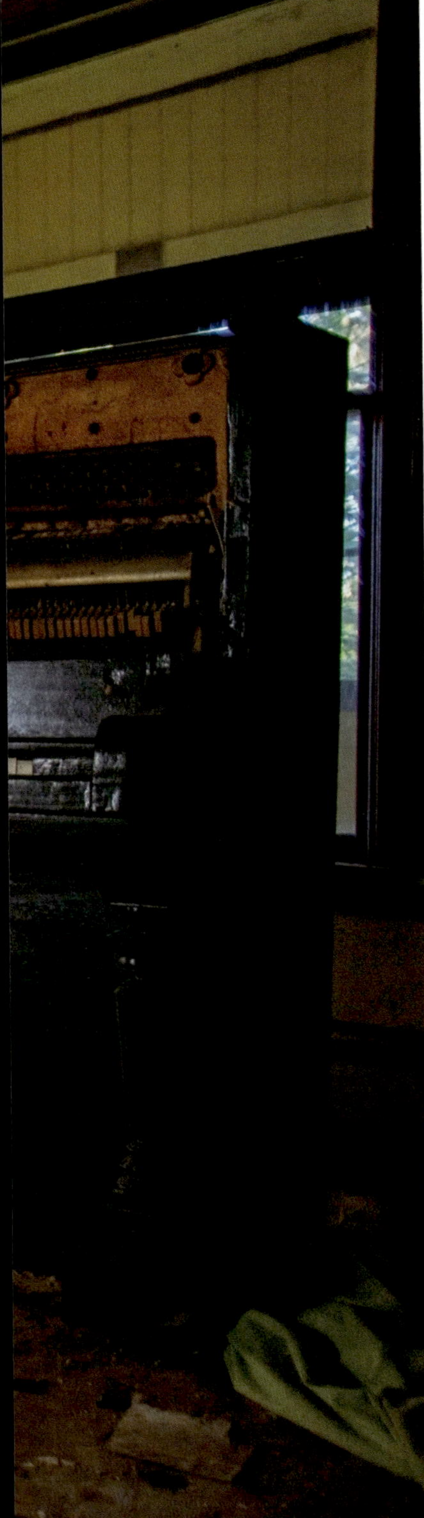

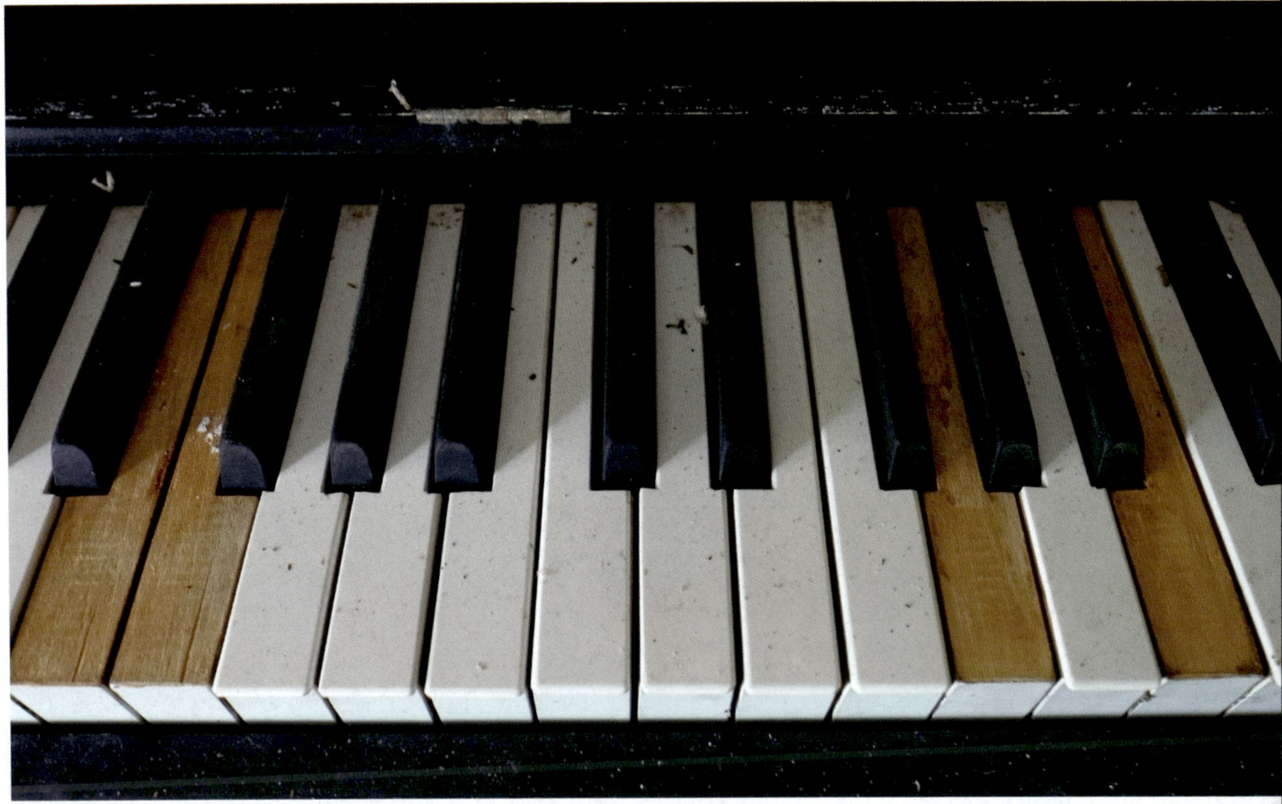

(Opposite) Continuing through the home shown on page 68, a piano has been left in what might have been the living room.

(Above) Imagine the friends and family who gathered around that piano and the hands that touched those keys.

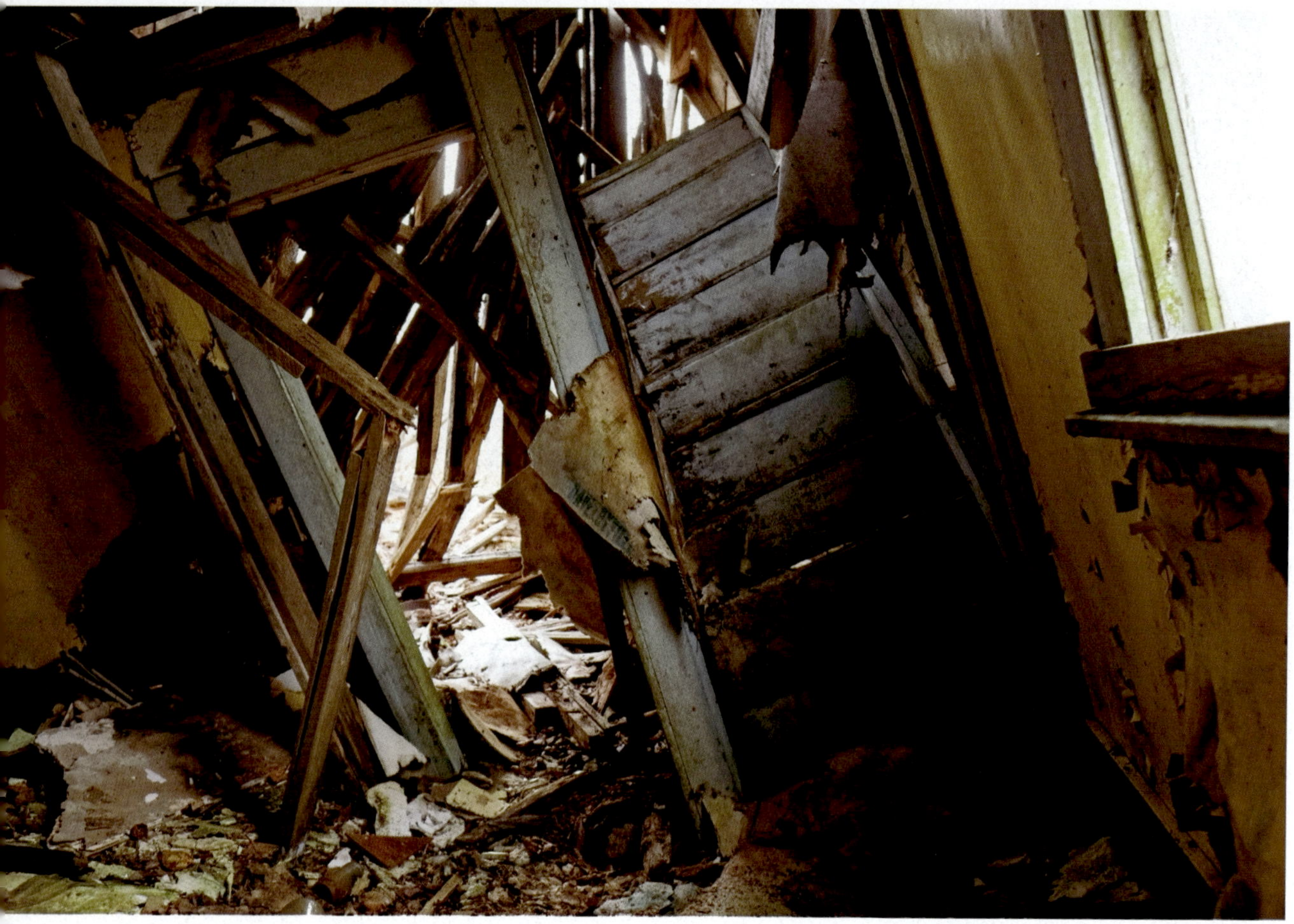

(Opposite) A drone photo shows how the roof has collapsed on this isolated home near Chester Basin on the South Shore, pulling the upper floor down with it.

(Above) Inside the Chester Basin house, a staircase is all that remains.

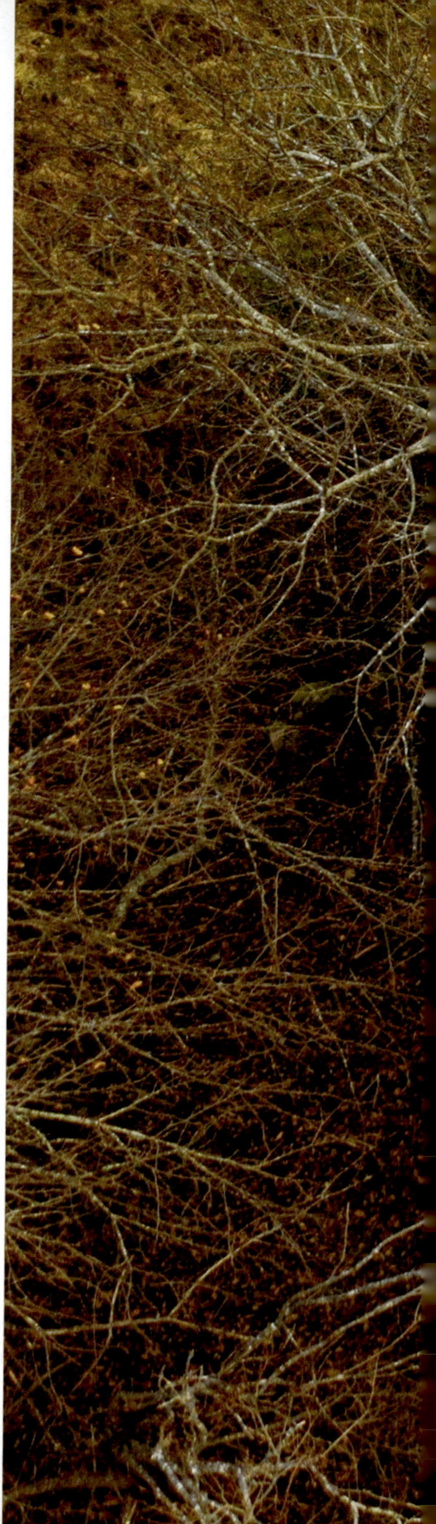

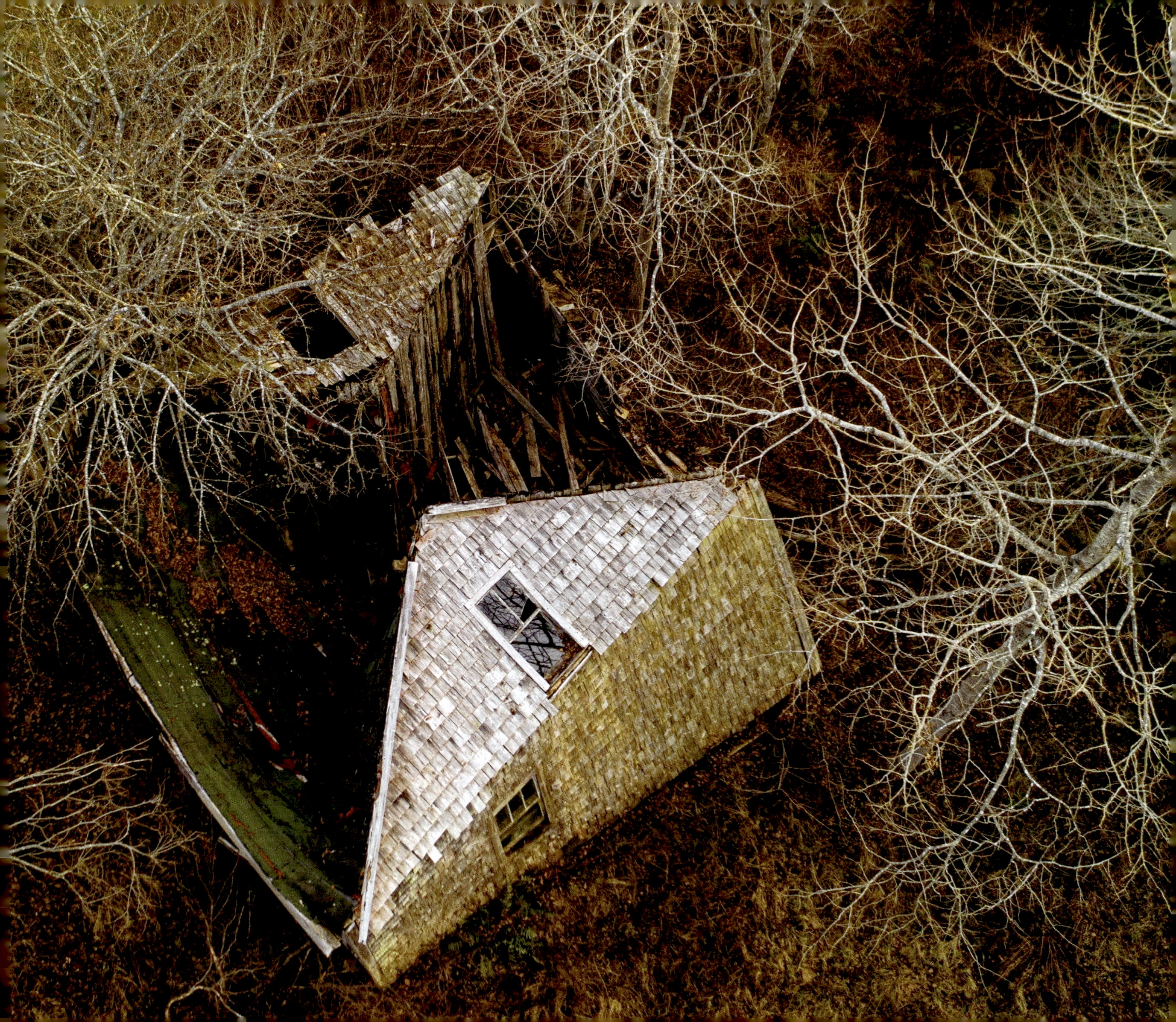

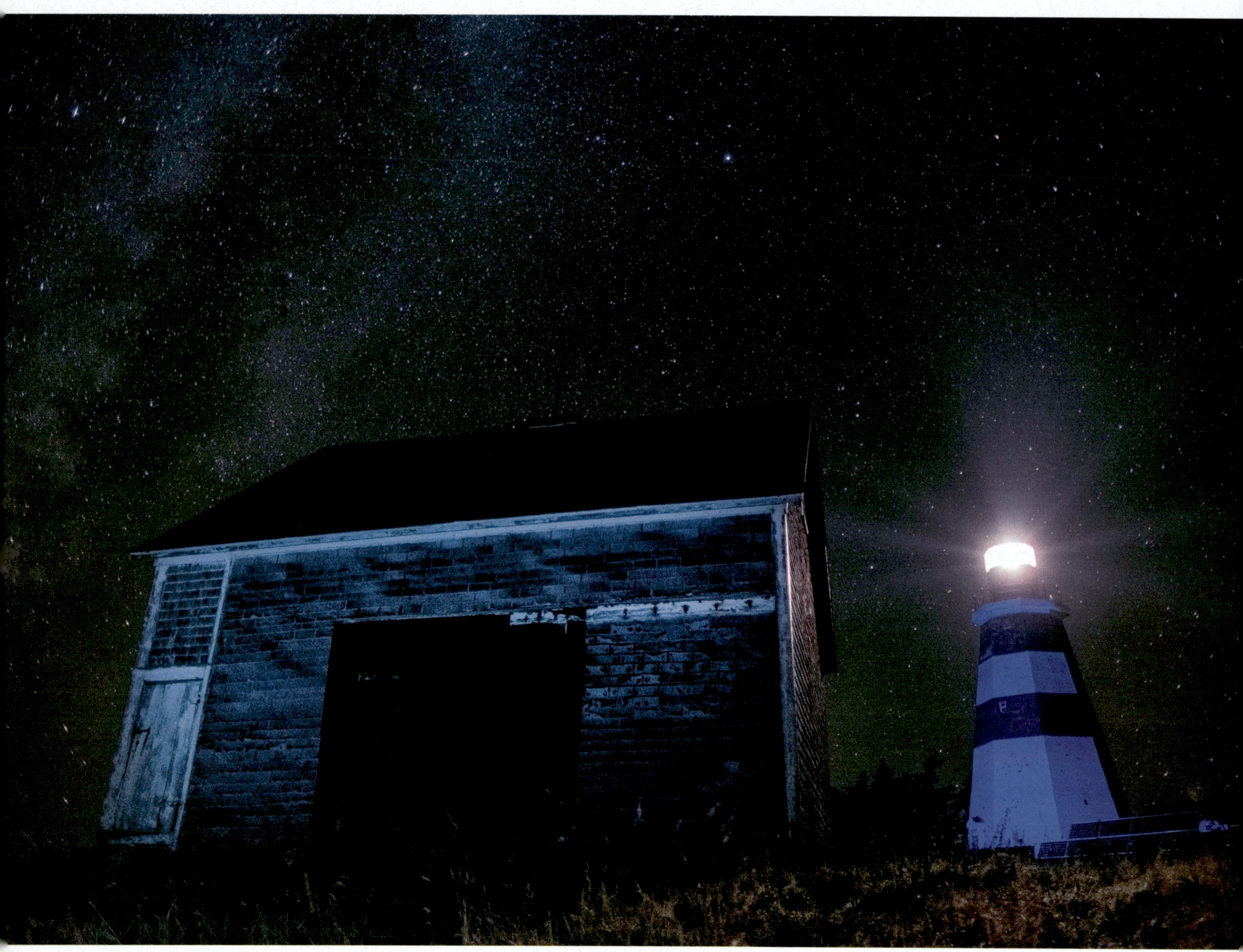

(Opposite) A small, abandoned barn next to the lighthouse on the east side of Seal Island. This lighthouse was originally built in 1830 and stands about 20 metres high.

(Right) A table and chair take the place of what appears to have been a fireplace in this house near Maitland, Hants County.

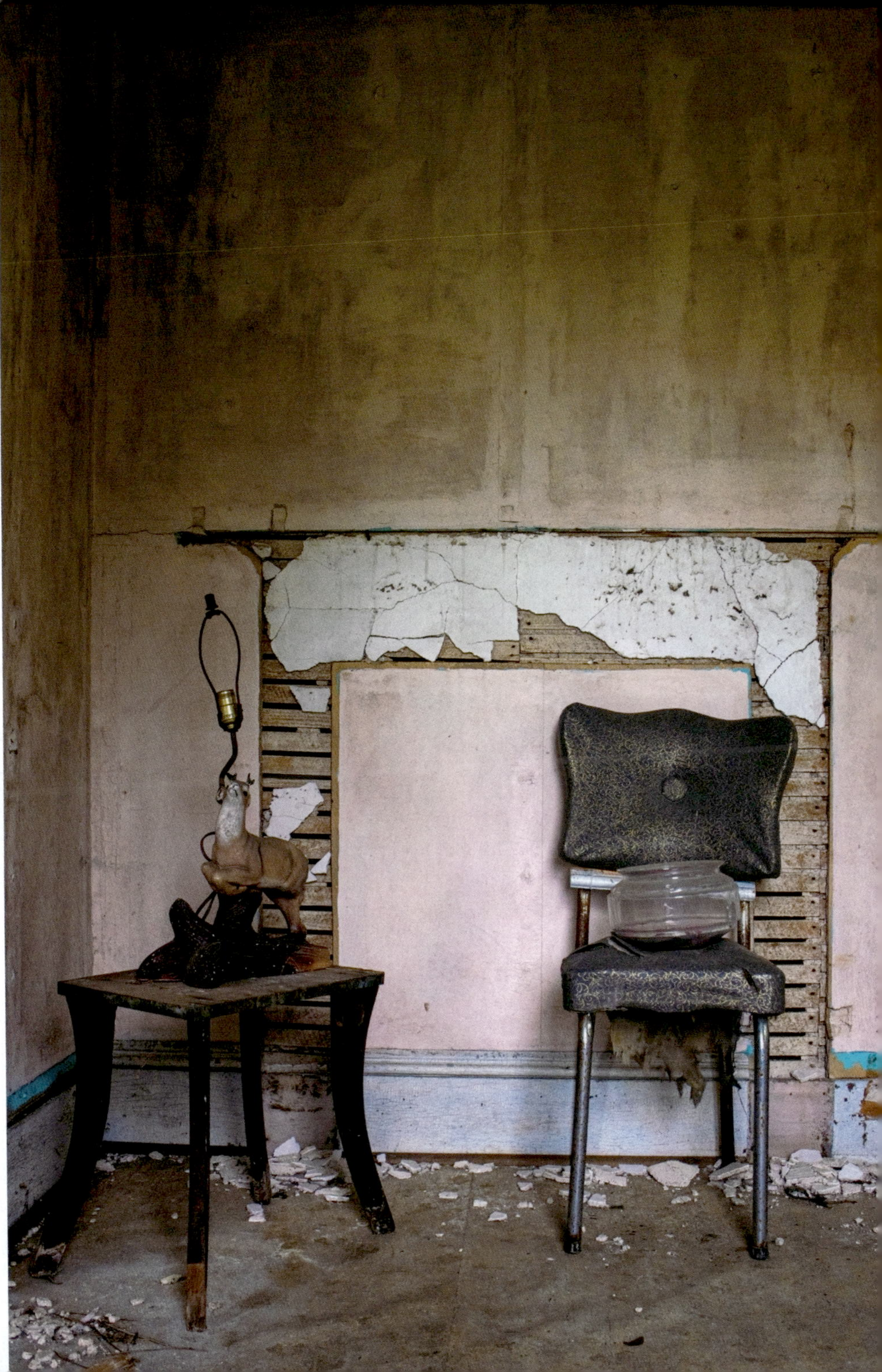

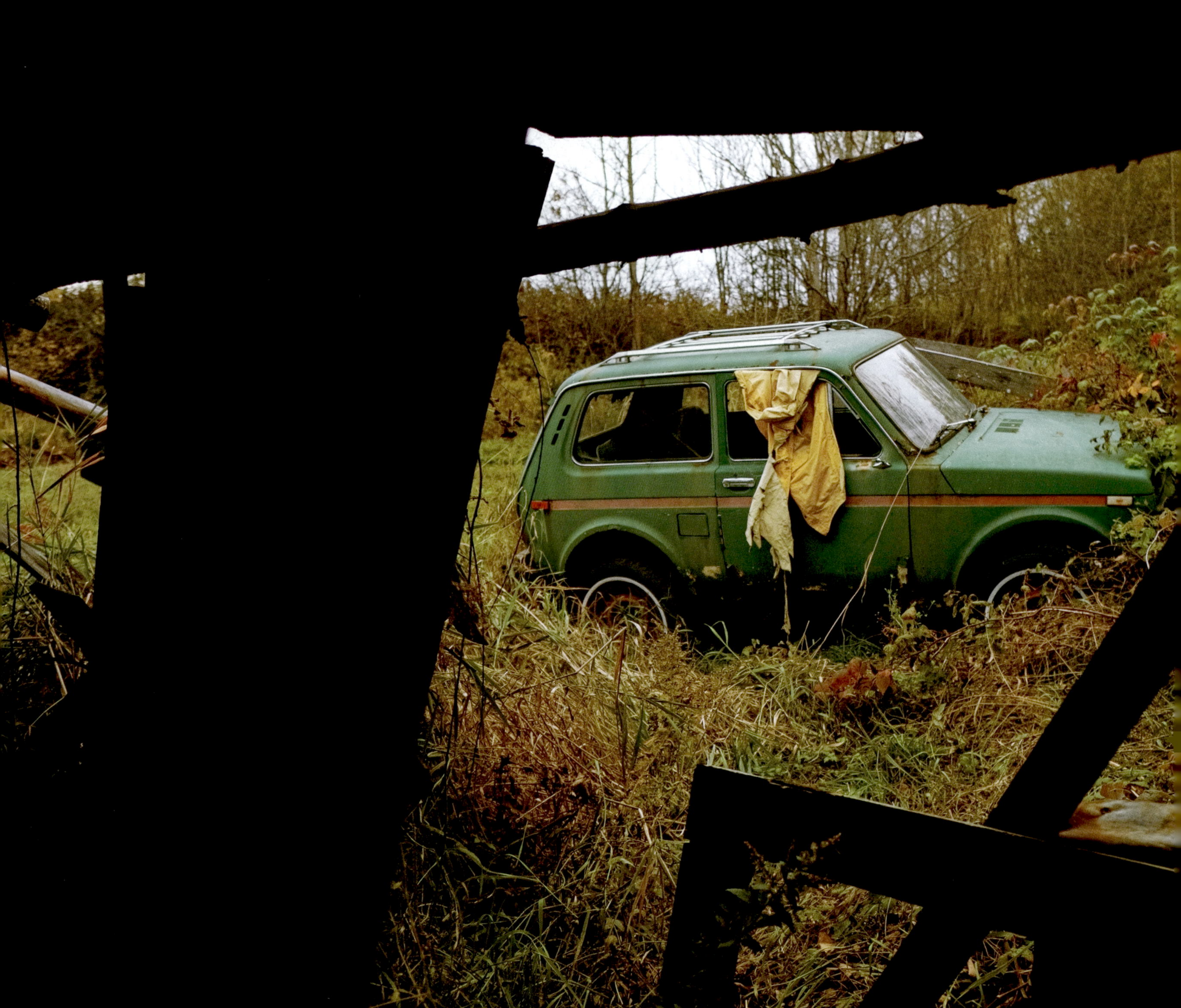

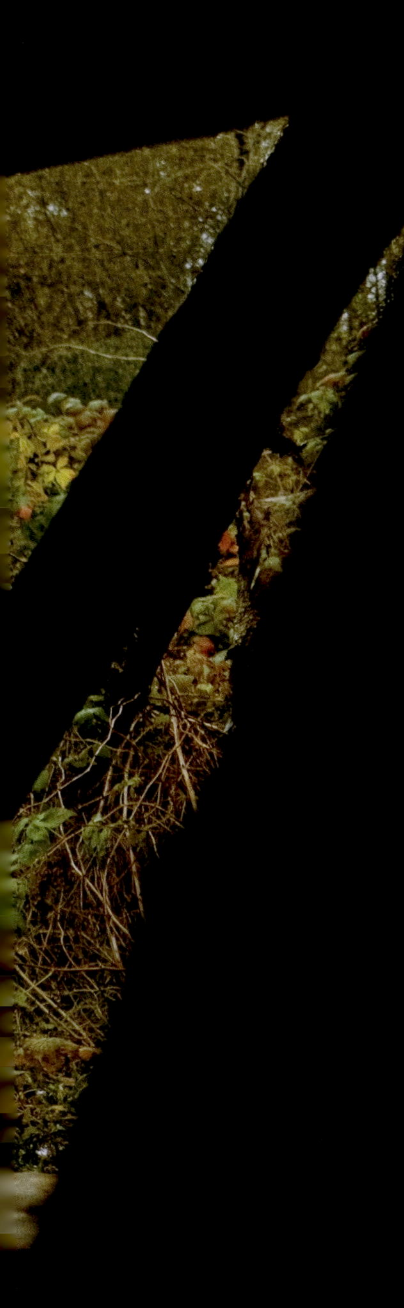

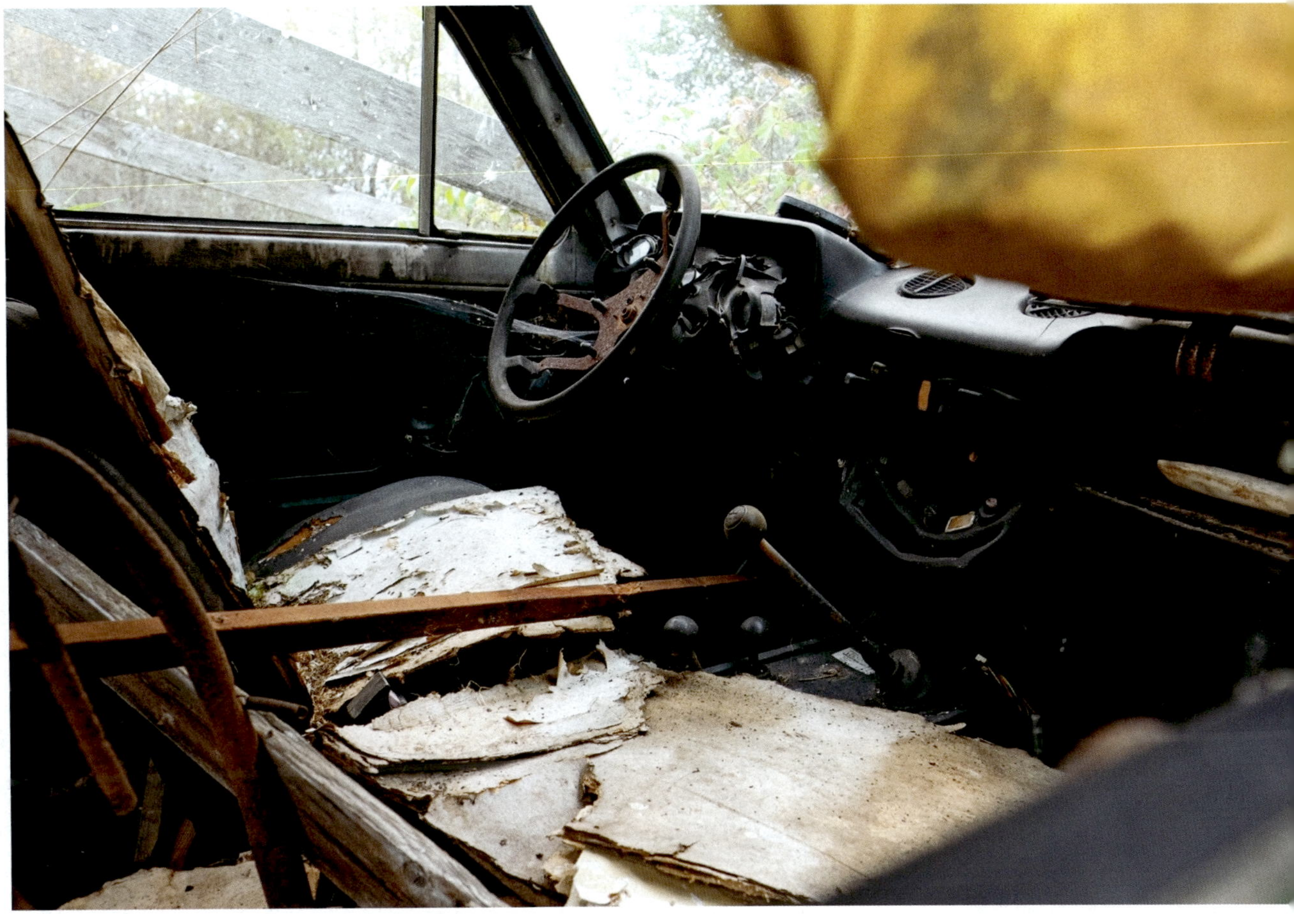

(Opposite and Above) A car lies abandoned adjacent to a dilapidated barn near the town of Hantsport, Hants County.

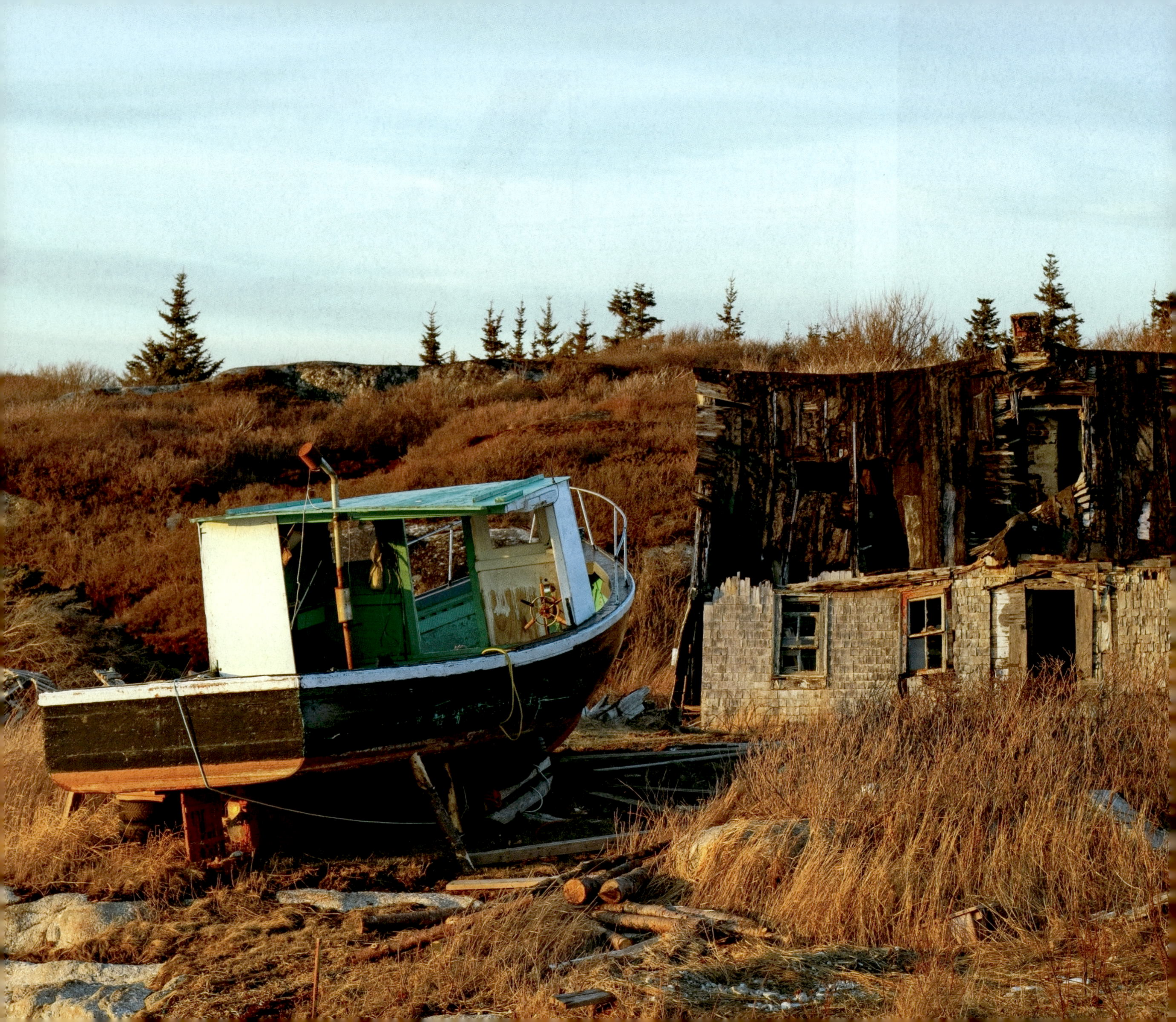

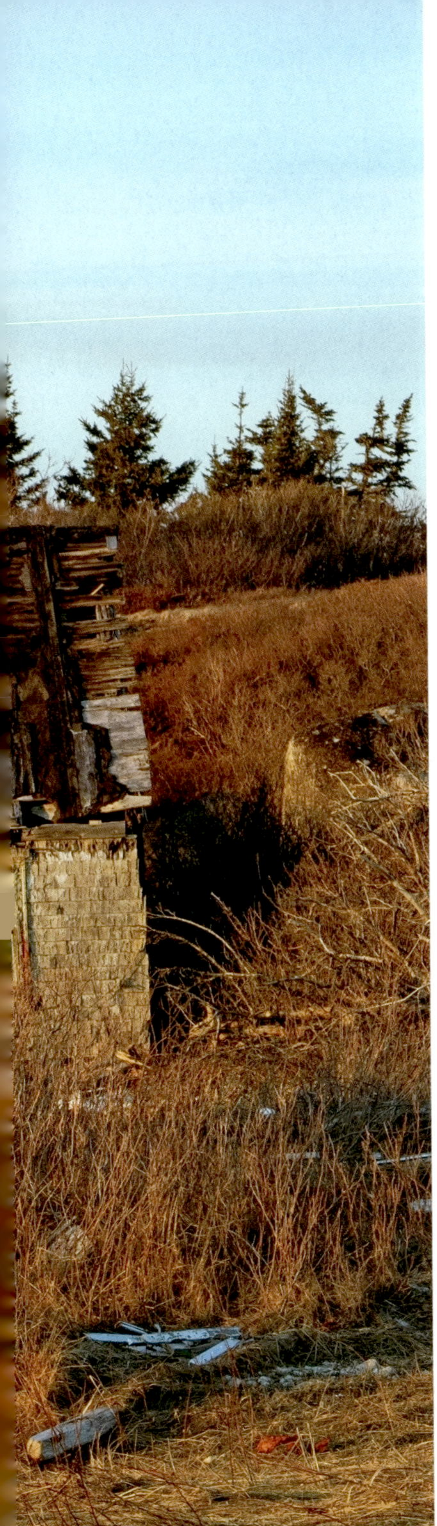

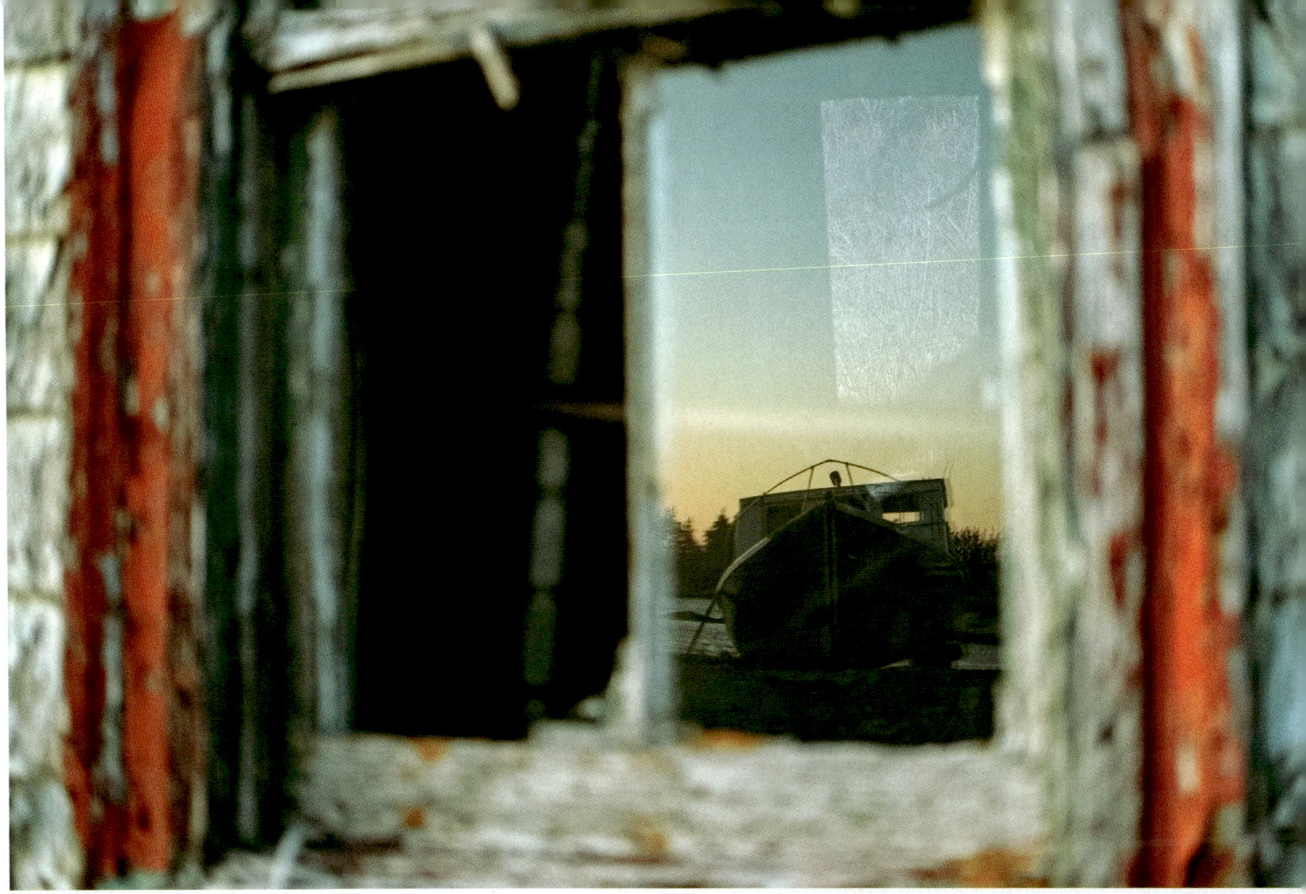

(Opposite) A fishing cottage in the final stages of decay captured in the late-day winter sun at Terence Bay. The rural fishing community is along the coast of the Chebucto Peninsula.

(Above and Right) The fishing boat is reflected in the window of the home on the opposite page. Toys are often left behind in these old homes we visited; this was one of two, almost identical dolls we found.

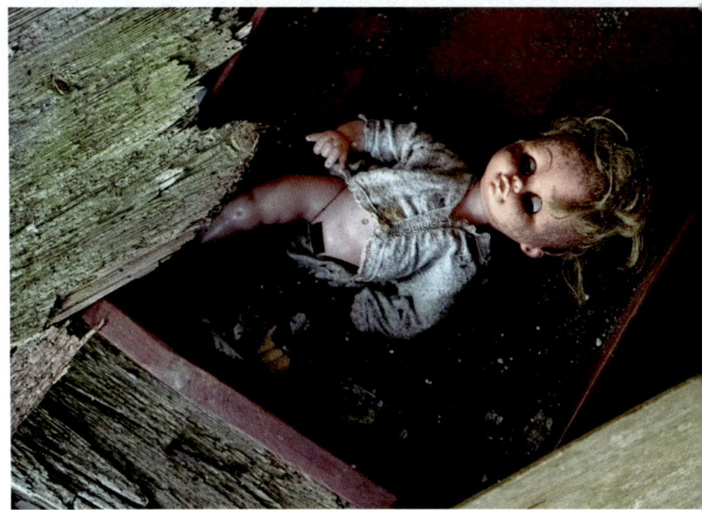

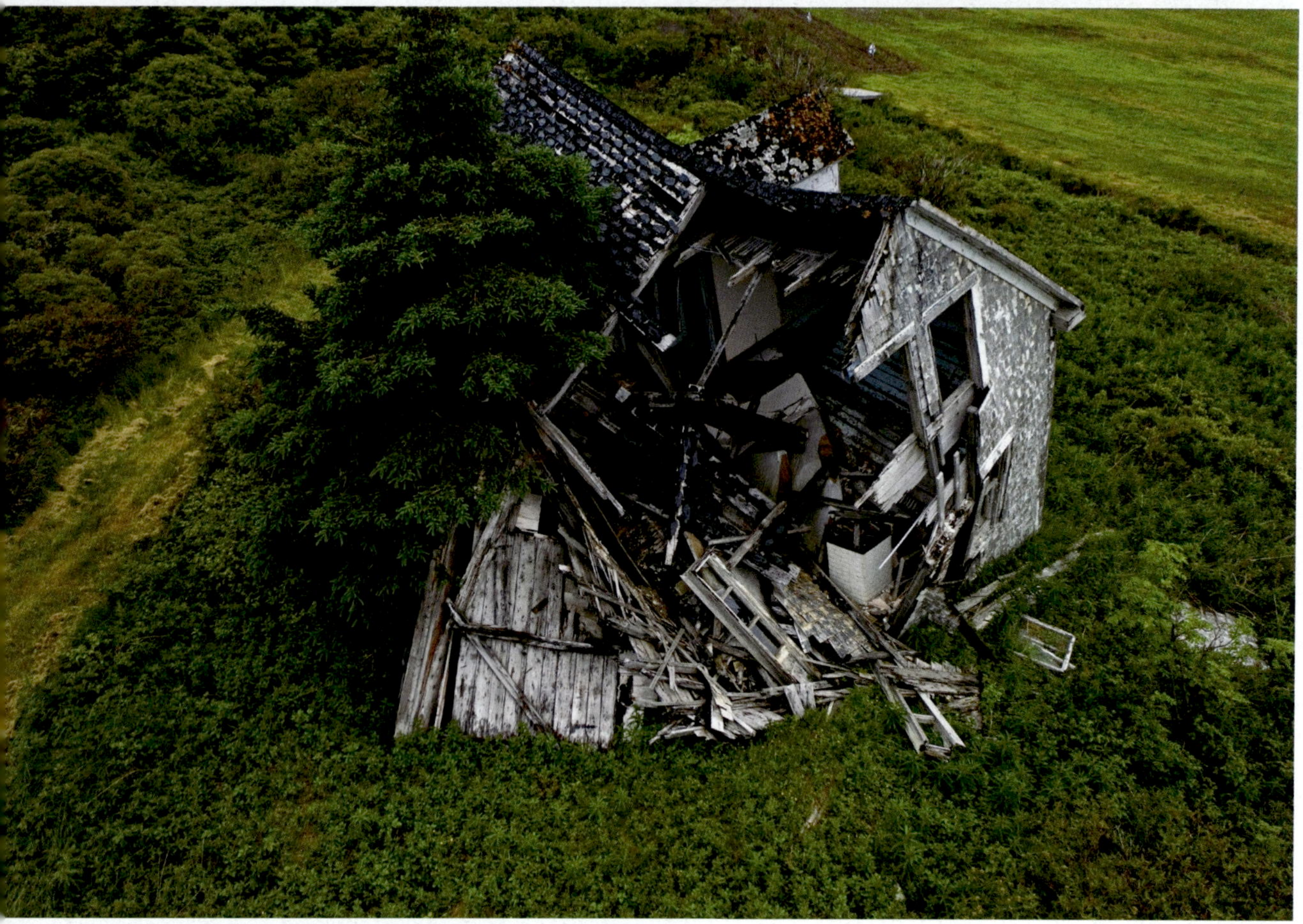

(Above) A drone view of the other side of this home (also pictured on page 59) in Whitehead, as it surrenders to gravity.

(Opposite) Pigeons have made their home in the belfry of the United Baptist Church in Goldboro. The church was built around 1899 with a seating capacity of 400. With a dwindling population in the area, the church has fallen into disrepair.

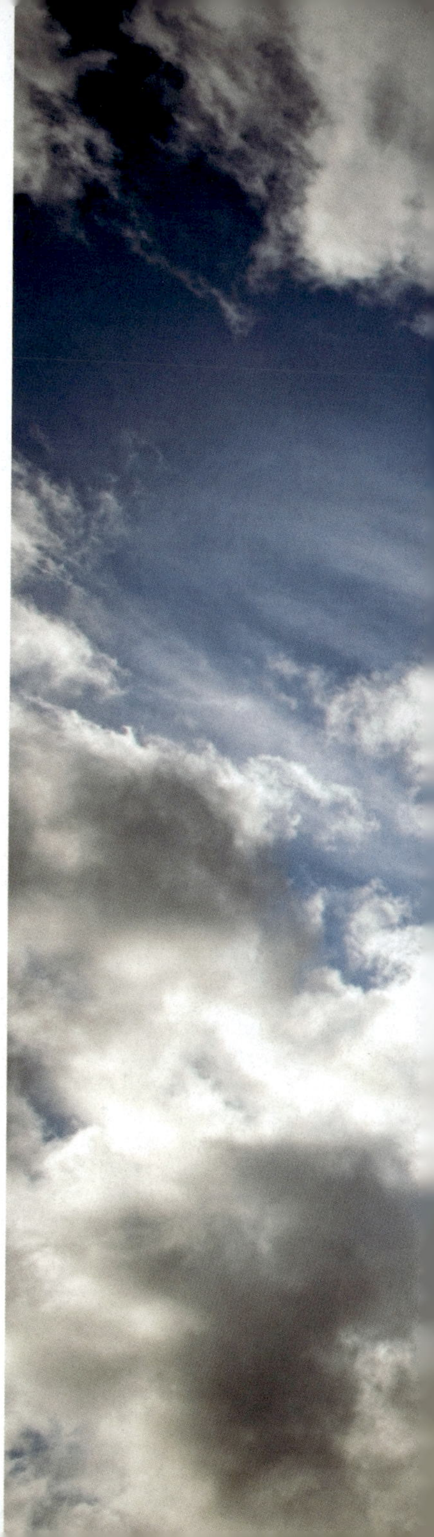

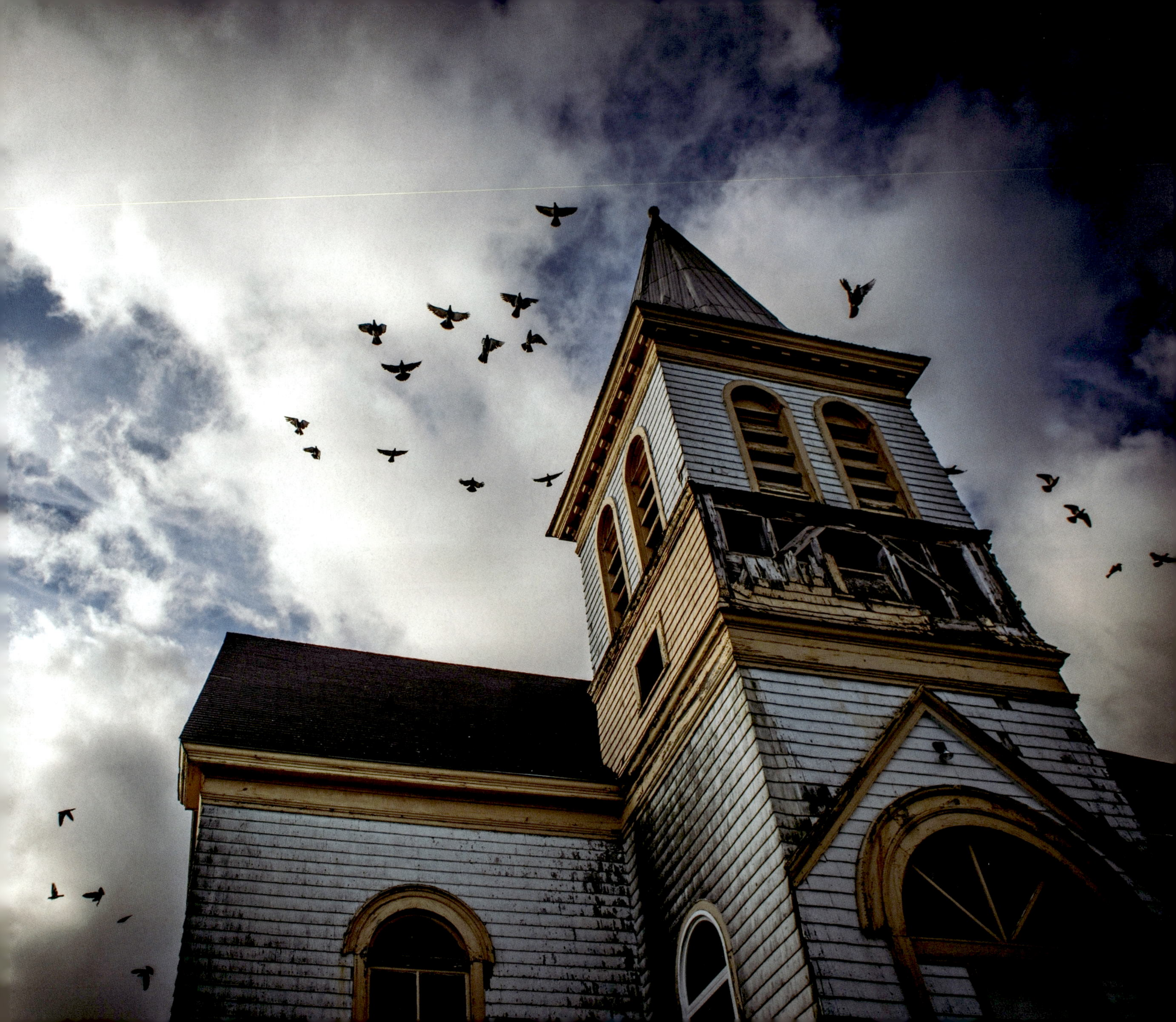

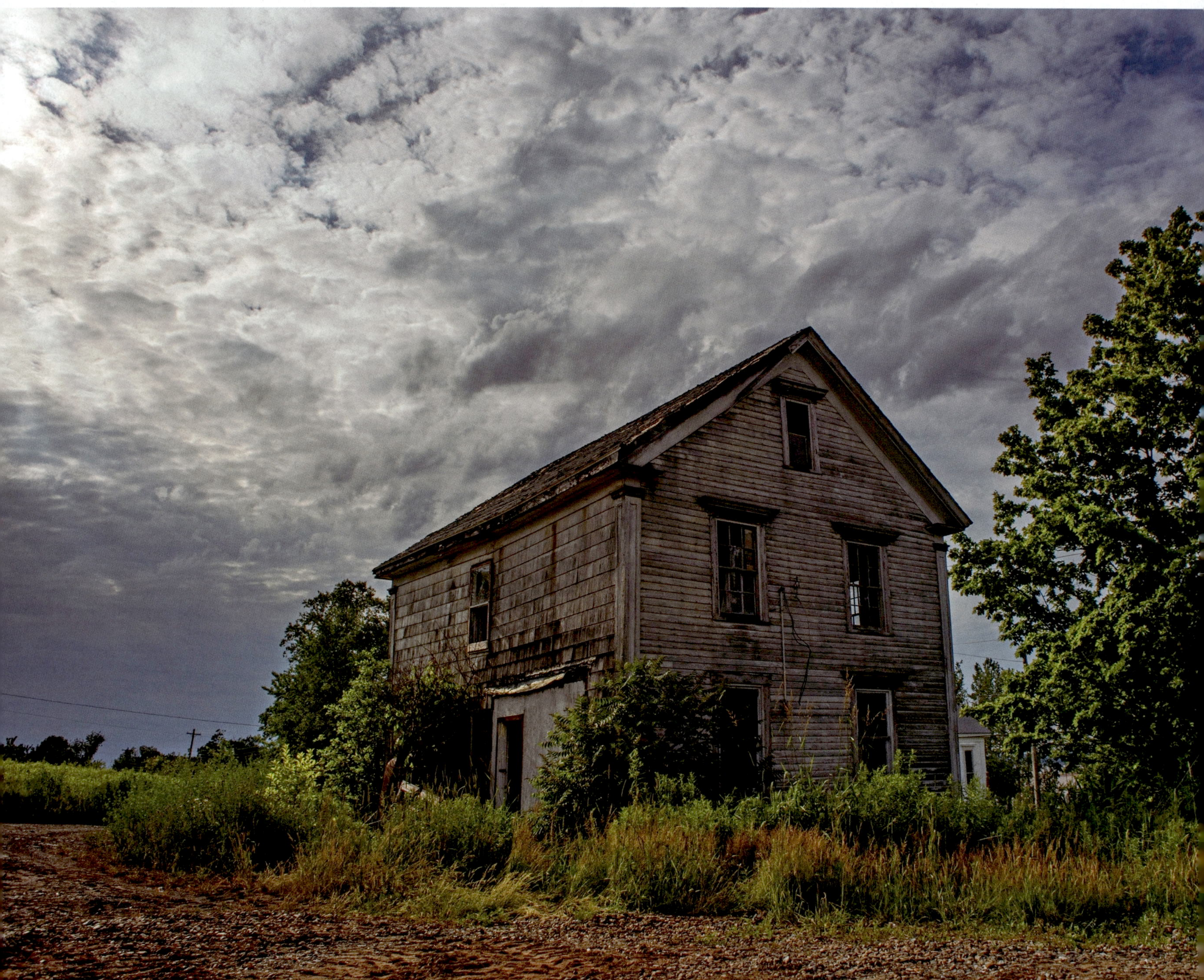

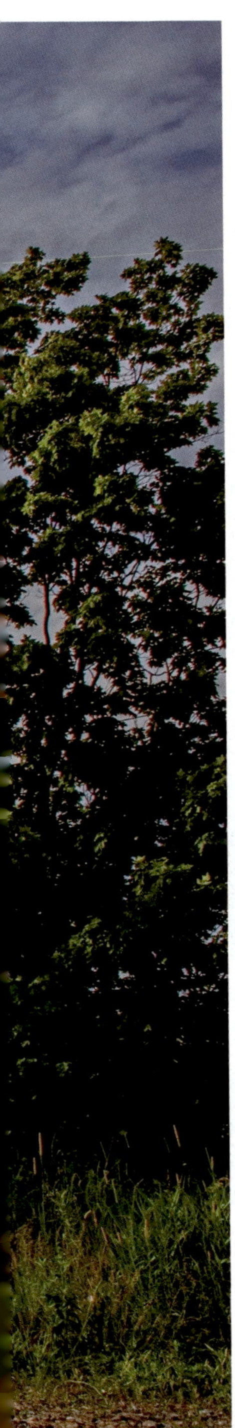

(Opposite) This house near Maitland was pretty well maintained from the outside but had clearly not been lived in for some time. The interior walls were painted in bright greens, soft pinks and bright blues, which created a welcoming atmosphere not usually experienced while exploring these homes.

(Right) The boarded entrance to the former Futures Inn turned Days Inn motel in Dartmouth. Overgrowth is starting to overtake what's left of the motel that has been scheduled for repurposing for several years but as of Spring 2021, it remains forgotten.

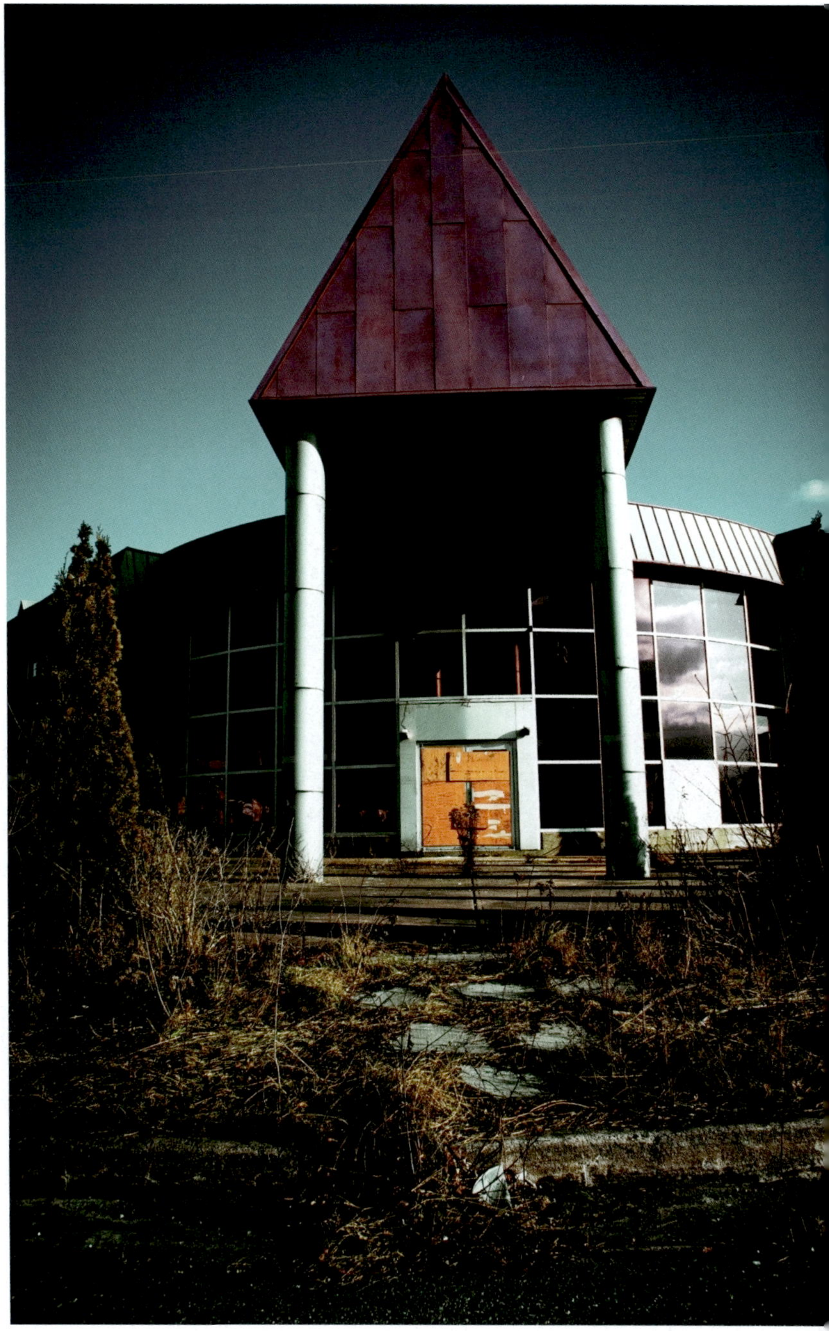

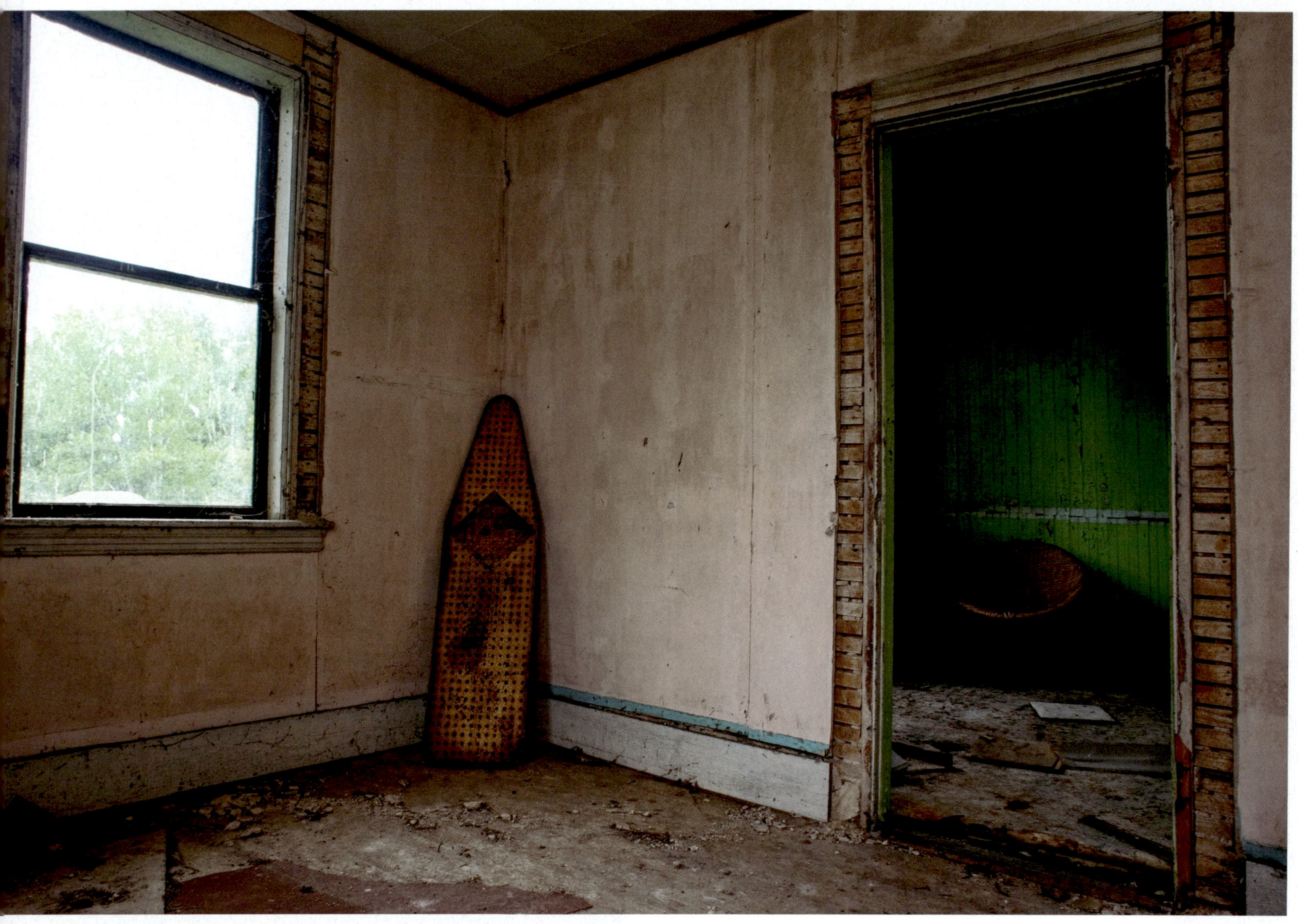

An ironing board leans against the soft pink walls of the home near Maitland (also pictured on page 82.)

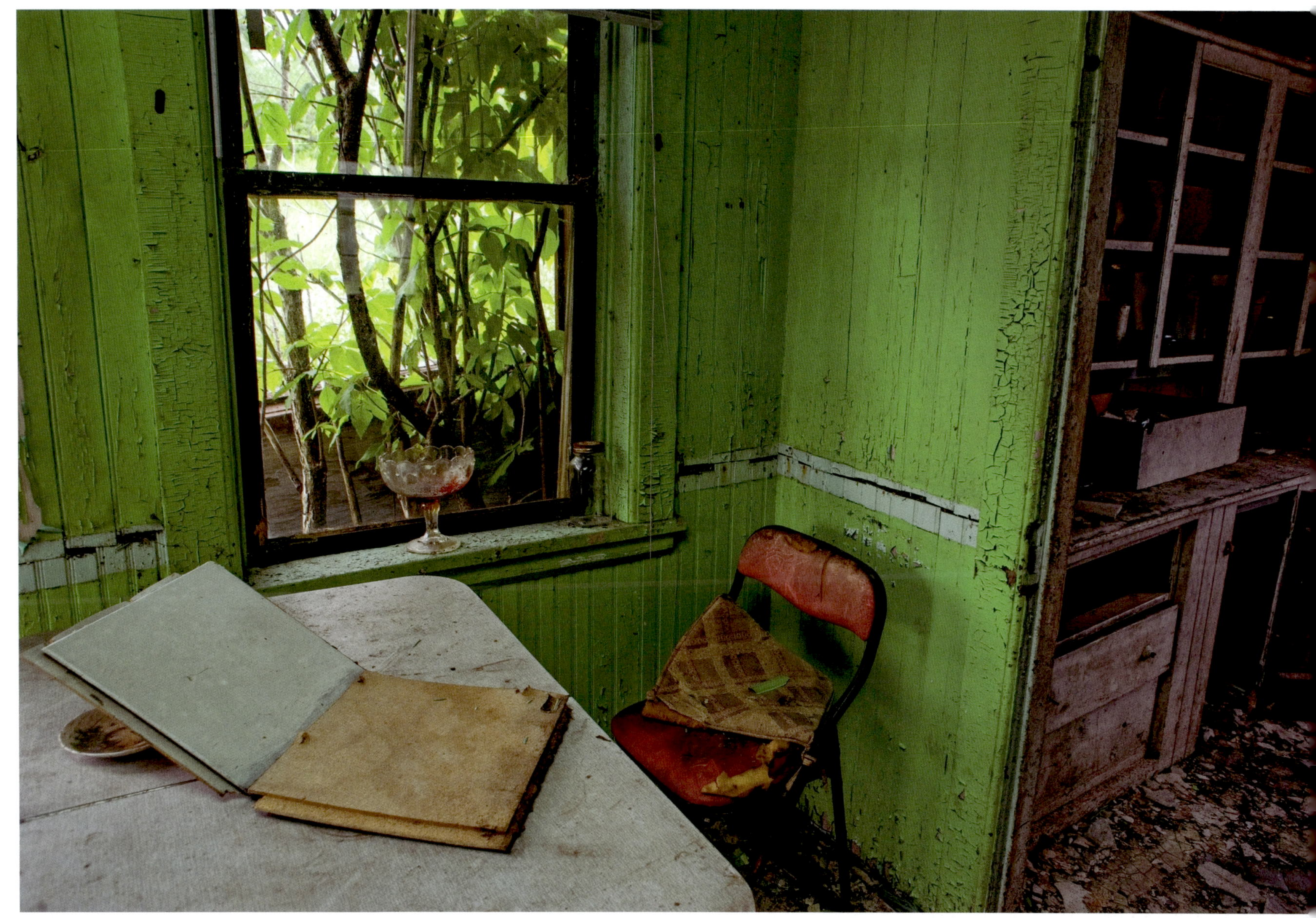

In the same home, the green walls seem to match the overgrowth of leaves in the window and those that surround the house. What appears to be an open book resting perfectly on the kitchen table are actually ceiling tiles.

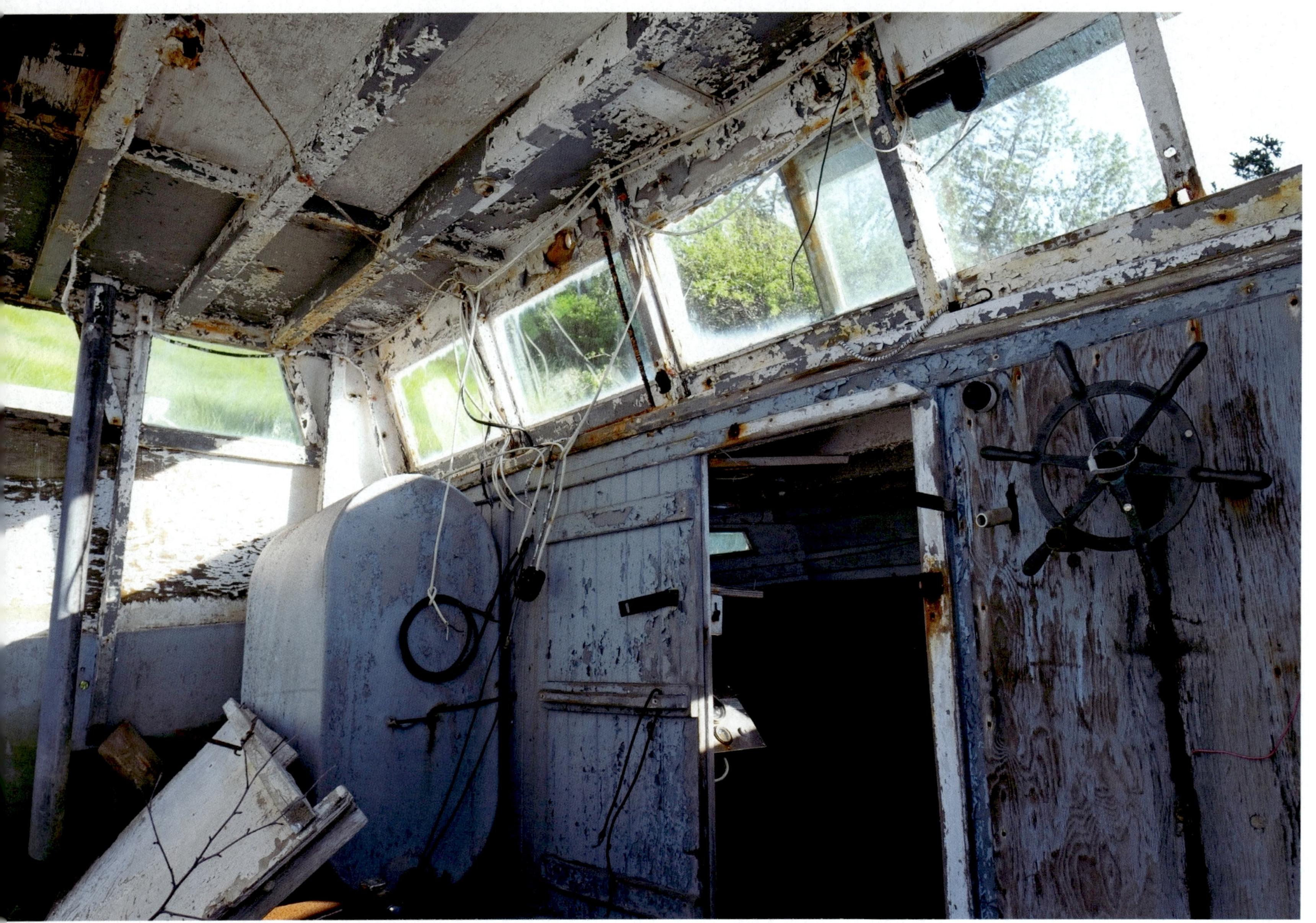

(Above and Opposite) A forlorn lobster boat taking on water along the coast in Shelburne County.

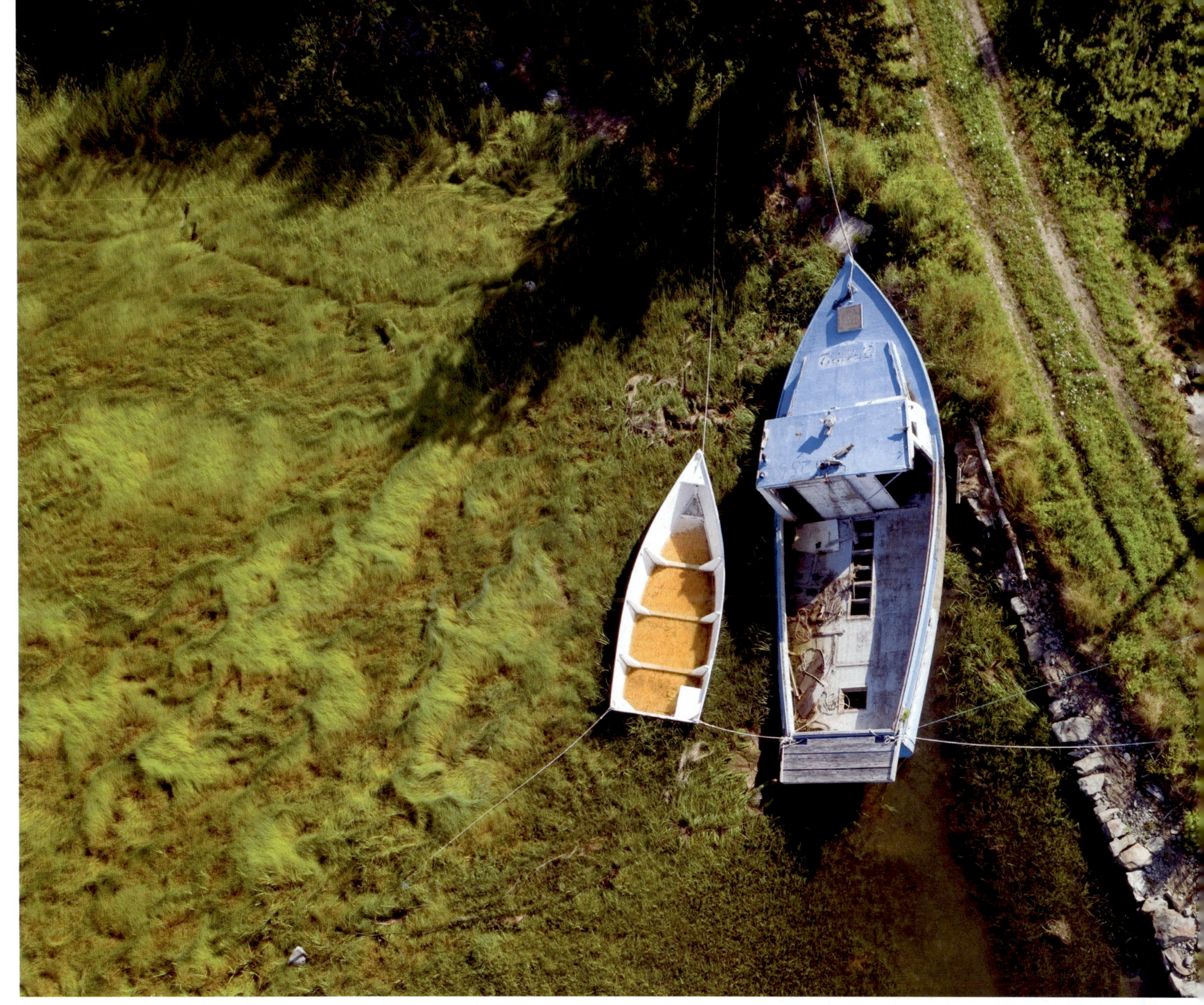

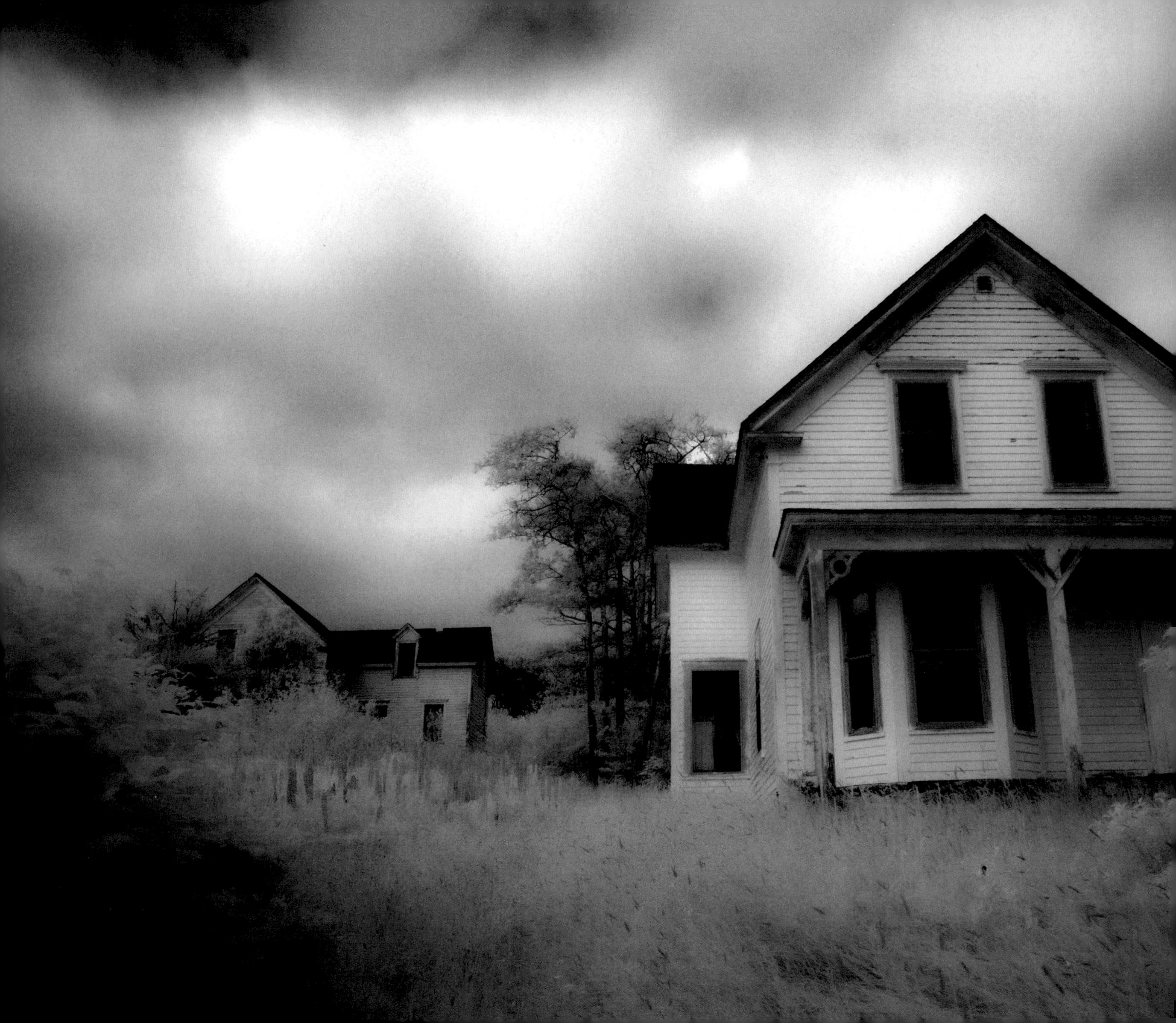

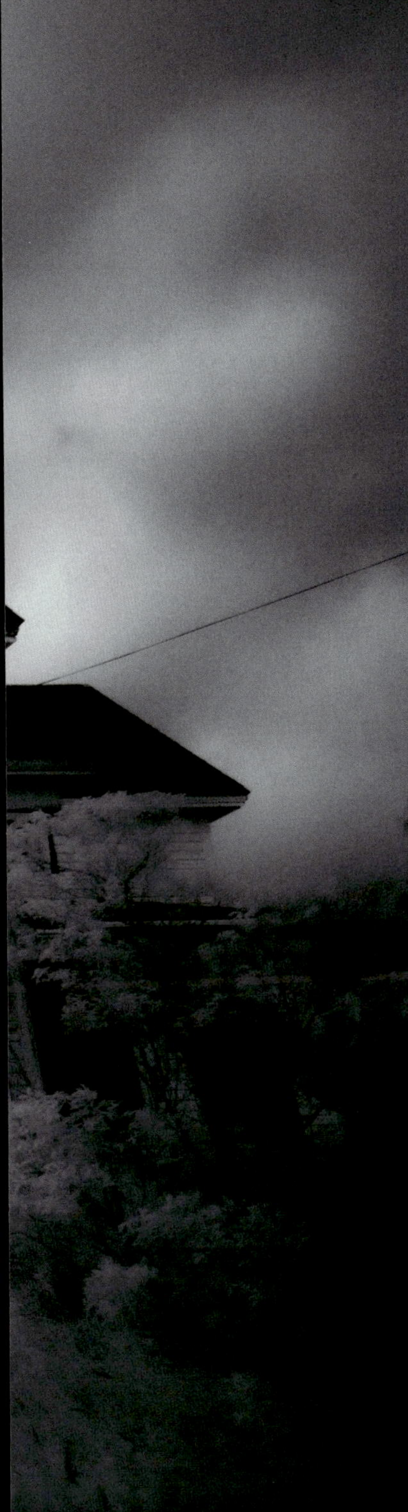

(Opposite) An infrared photo of two homes left side by side and seemingly forgotten in the scenic community of Goldboro, Gysborough County.

(Right) A rocking chair left in the back of a Goldboro home (from the opposite page.)

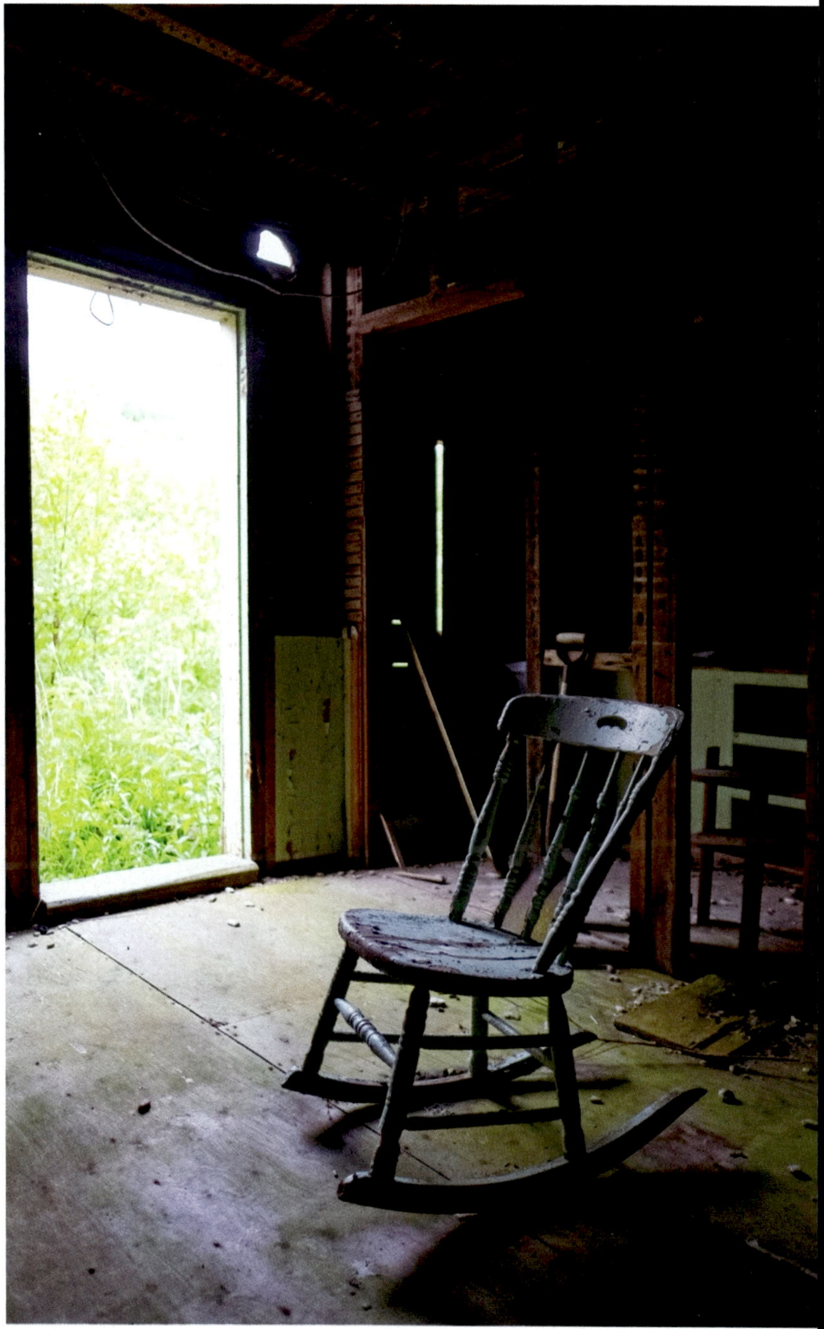

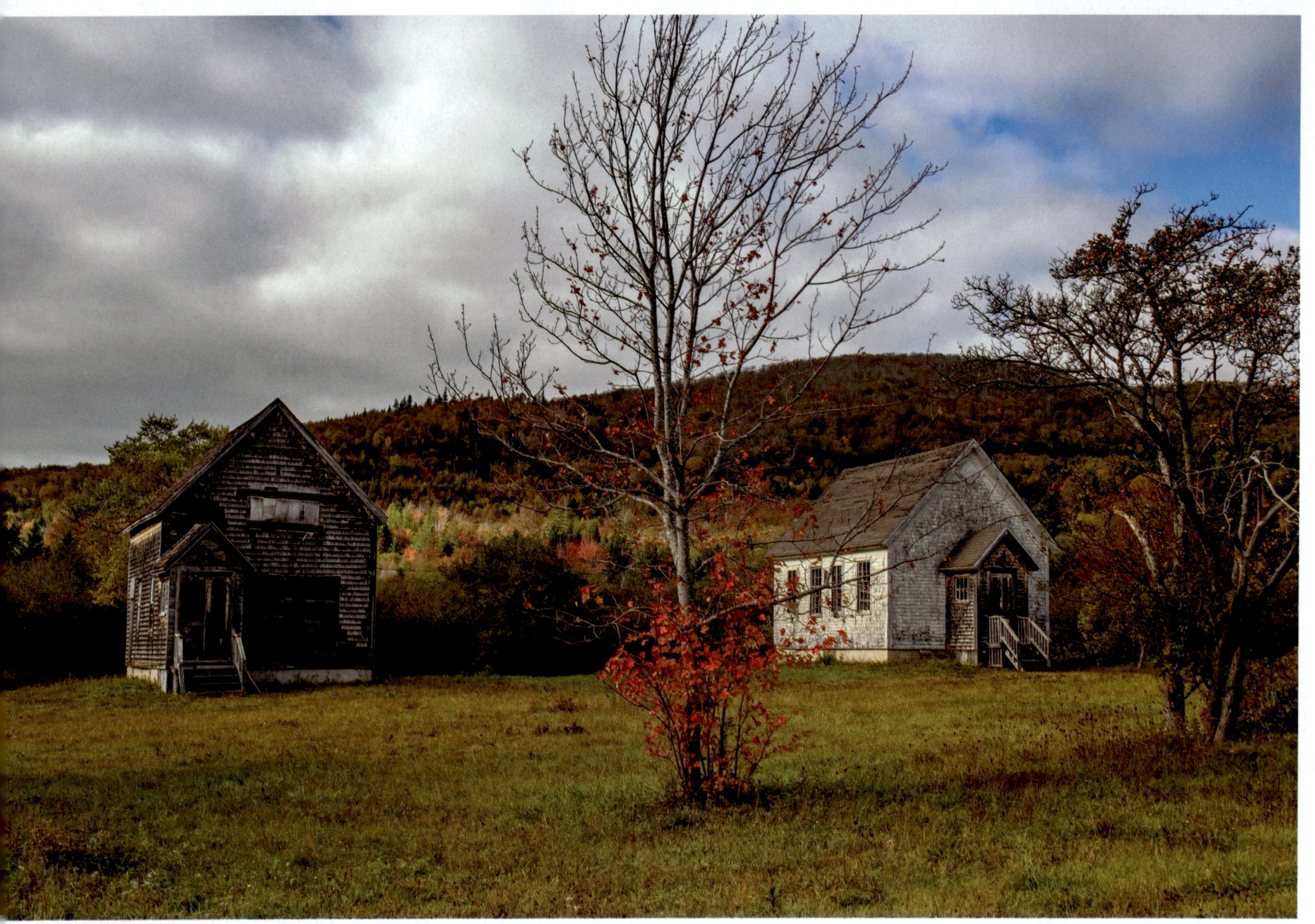

In the fall of 2020, two tiny homes near Mabou, Cape Breton Island, sit nestled among the rolling hills.

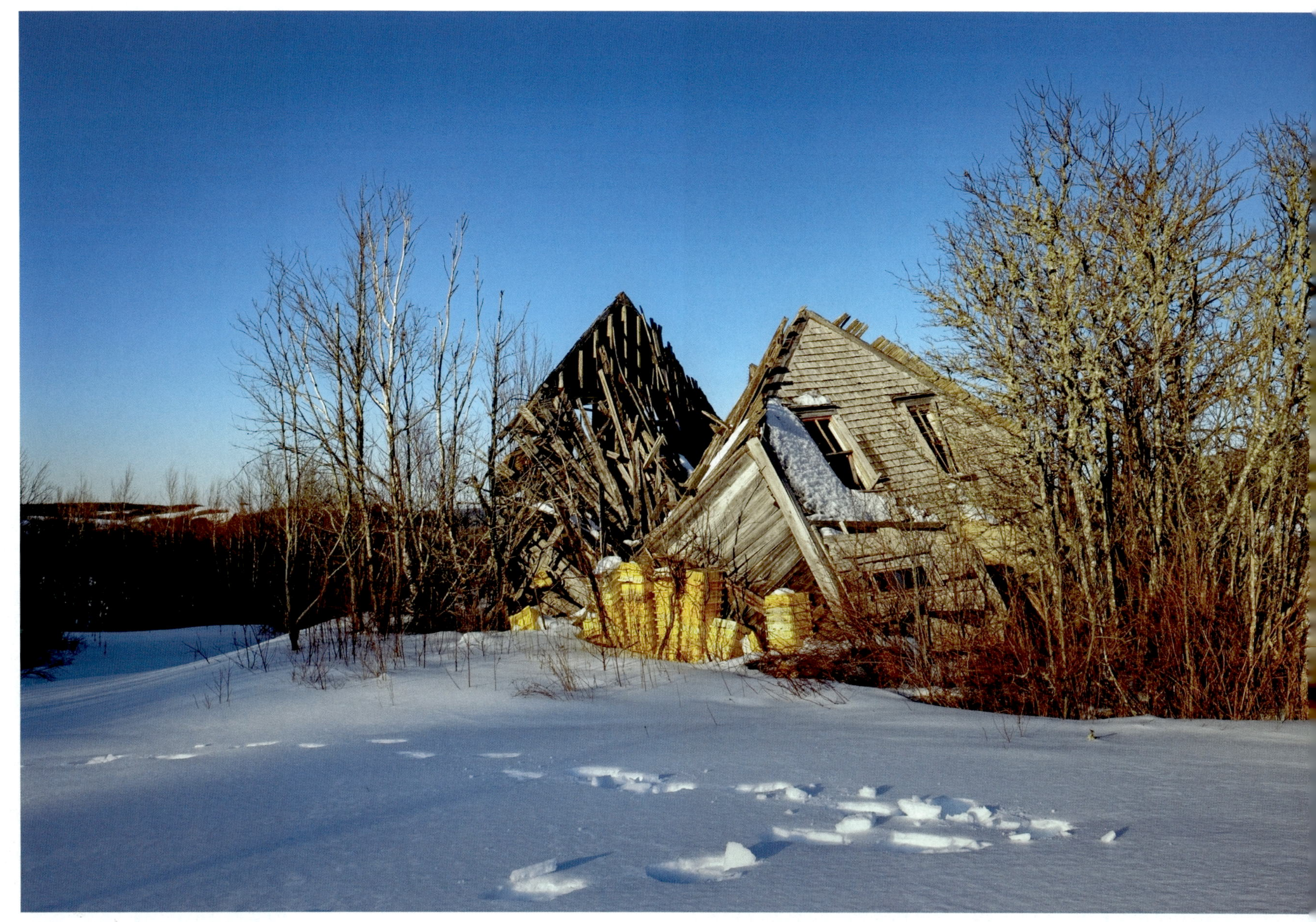

Stacked blueberry baskets remain intact as the roof of this Cumberland County home succumbs to the elements.

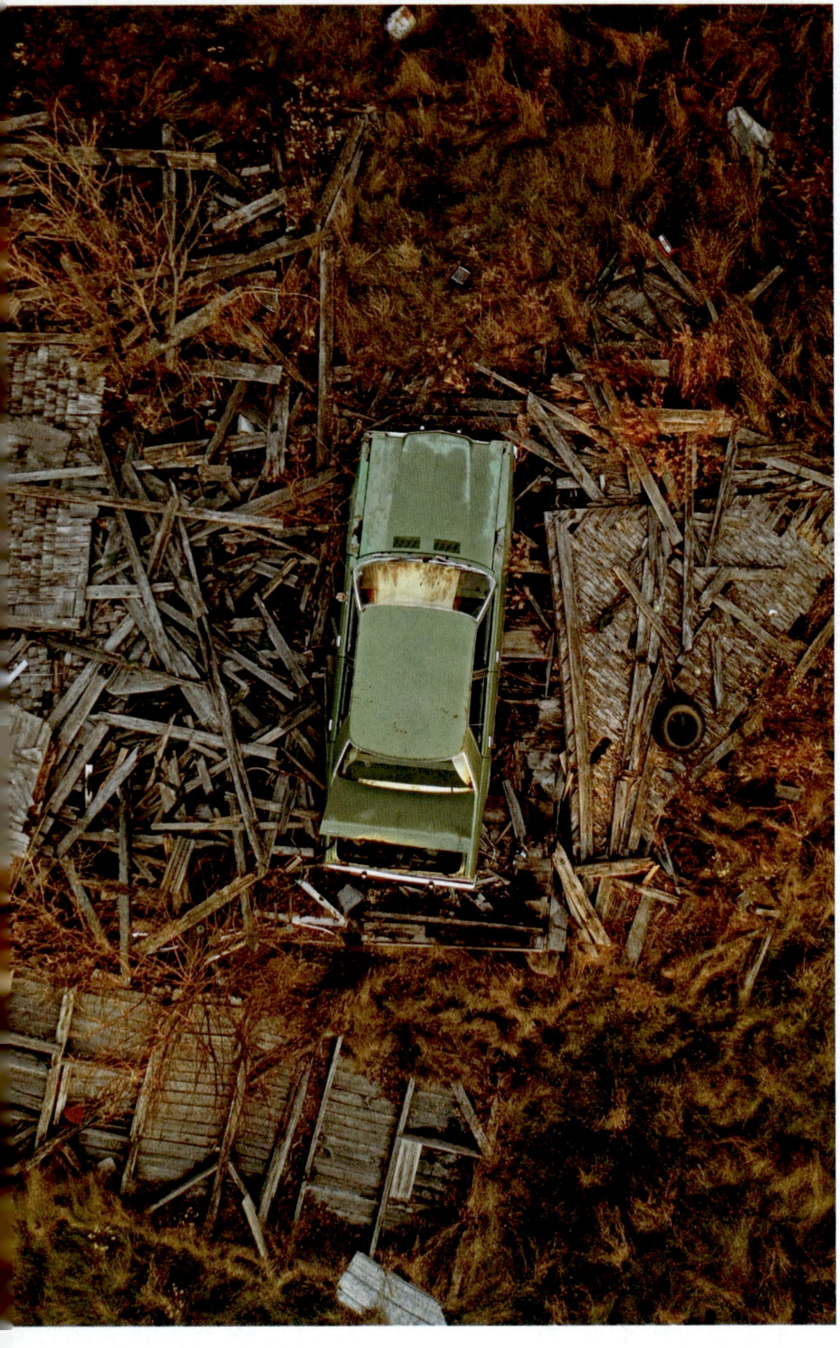

(Left) A drone photo of what appears to be a garage that simply crumbled around an old Dodge vehicle located on the Middle Economy property (featured on the opposite page.)

(Opposite) This sprawling property in Middle Economy had a majestic farmhouse, a large barn and a single, abandoned vehicle. In its day the home would have been quite lovely and secluded, surrounded by trees and blessed with a view of spectacular Nova Scotia sunsets.

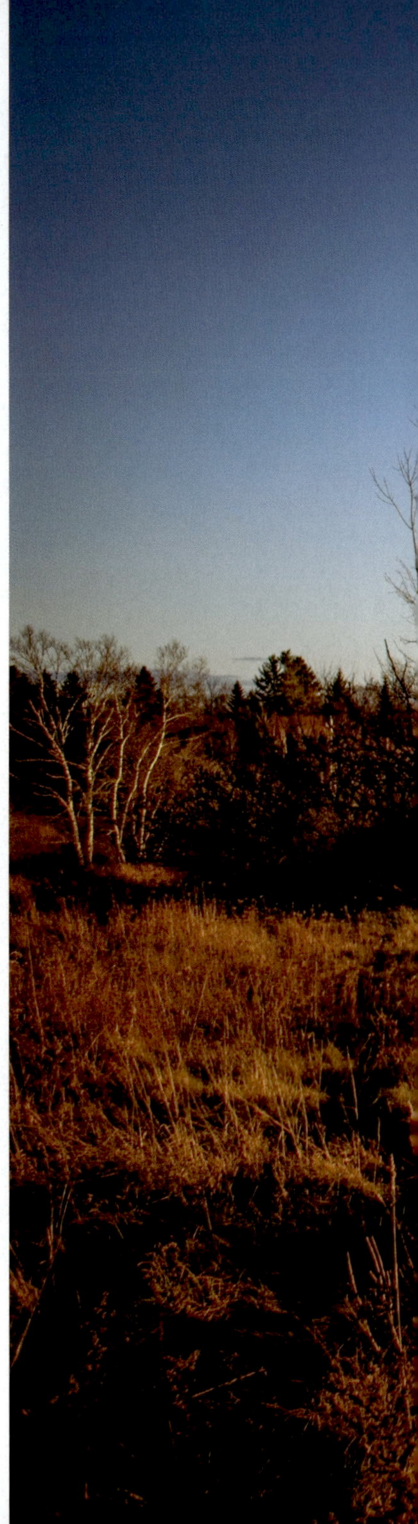

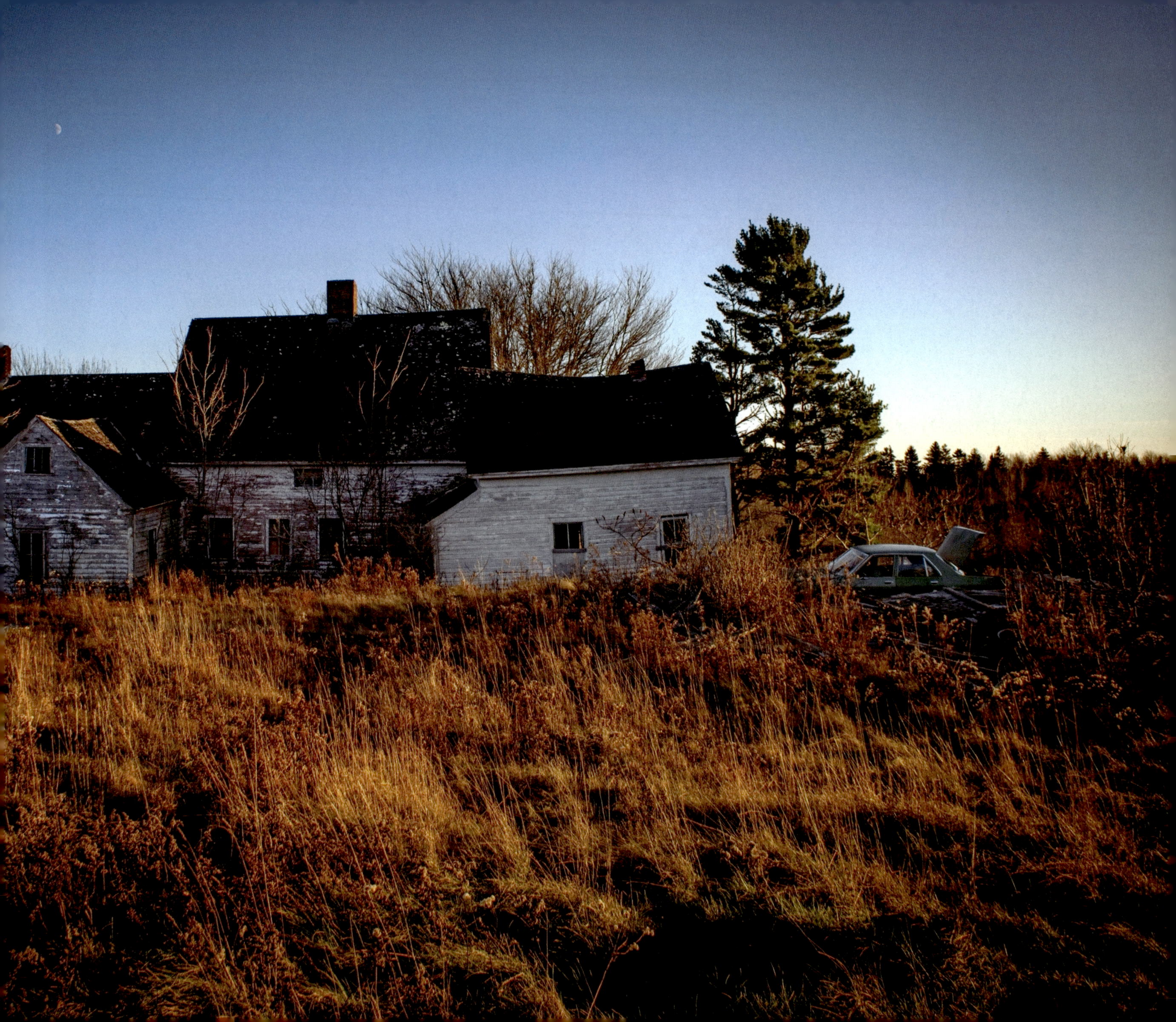

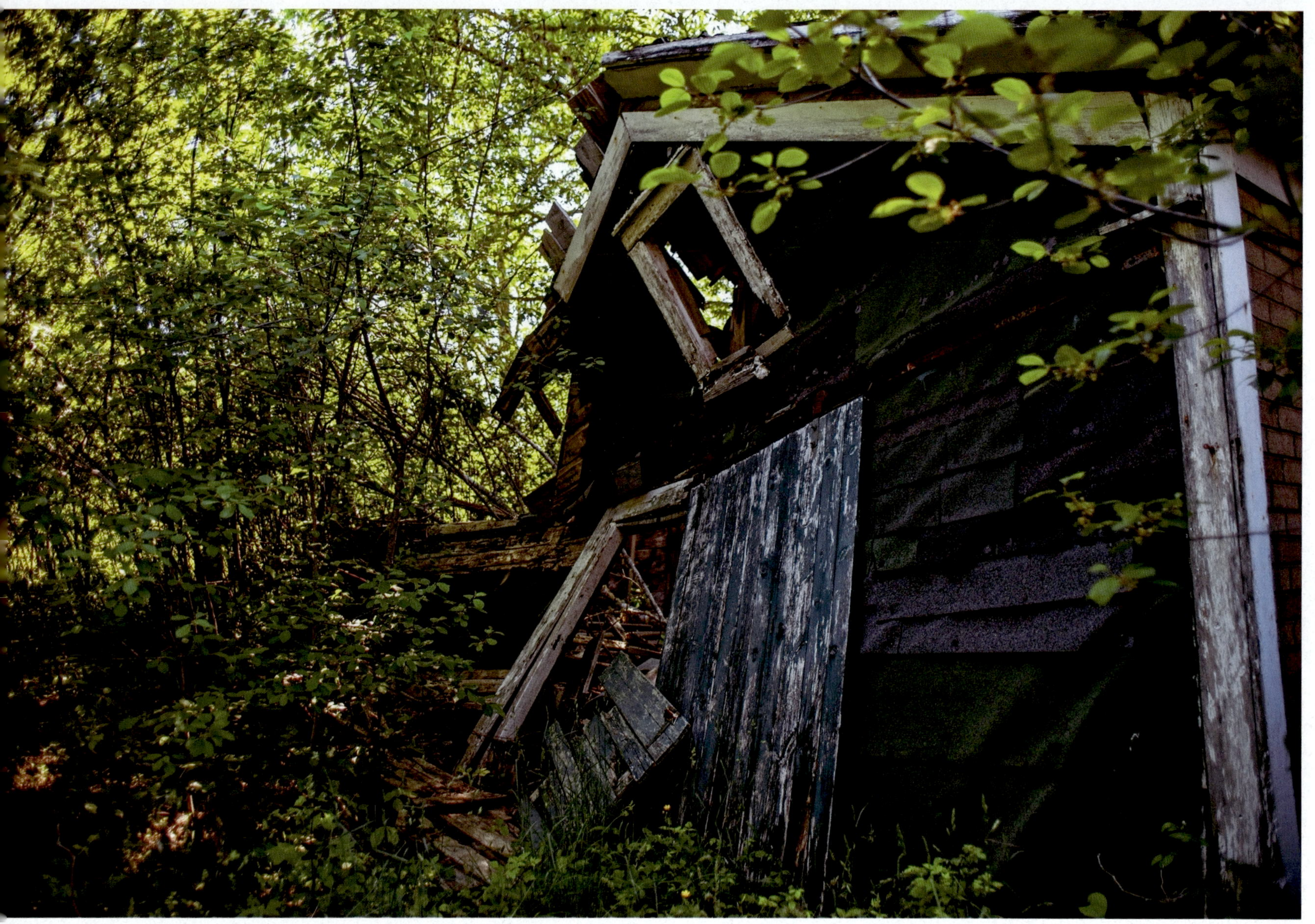

A collapsed shed sits on a hidden, abandoned property off the beaten track in Queens County.

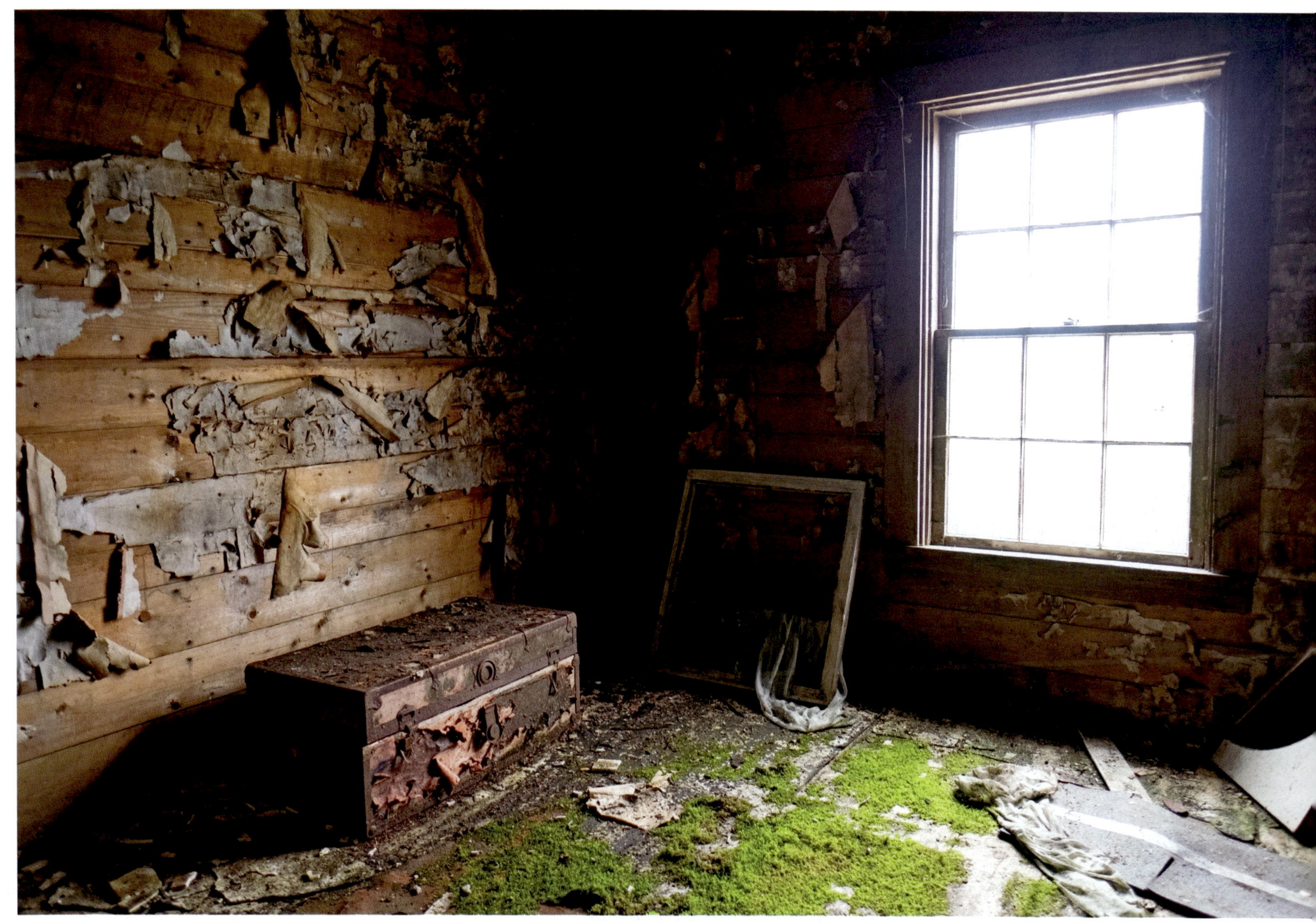

A rustic foot locker sits in a room ravaged by time in this Hants County home along the Bay of Fundy.

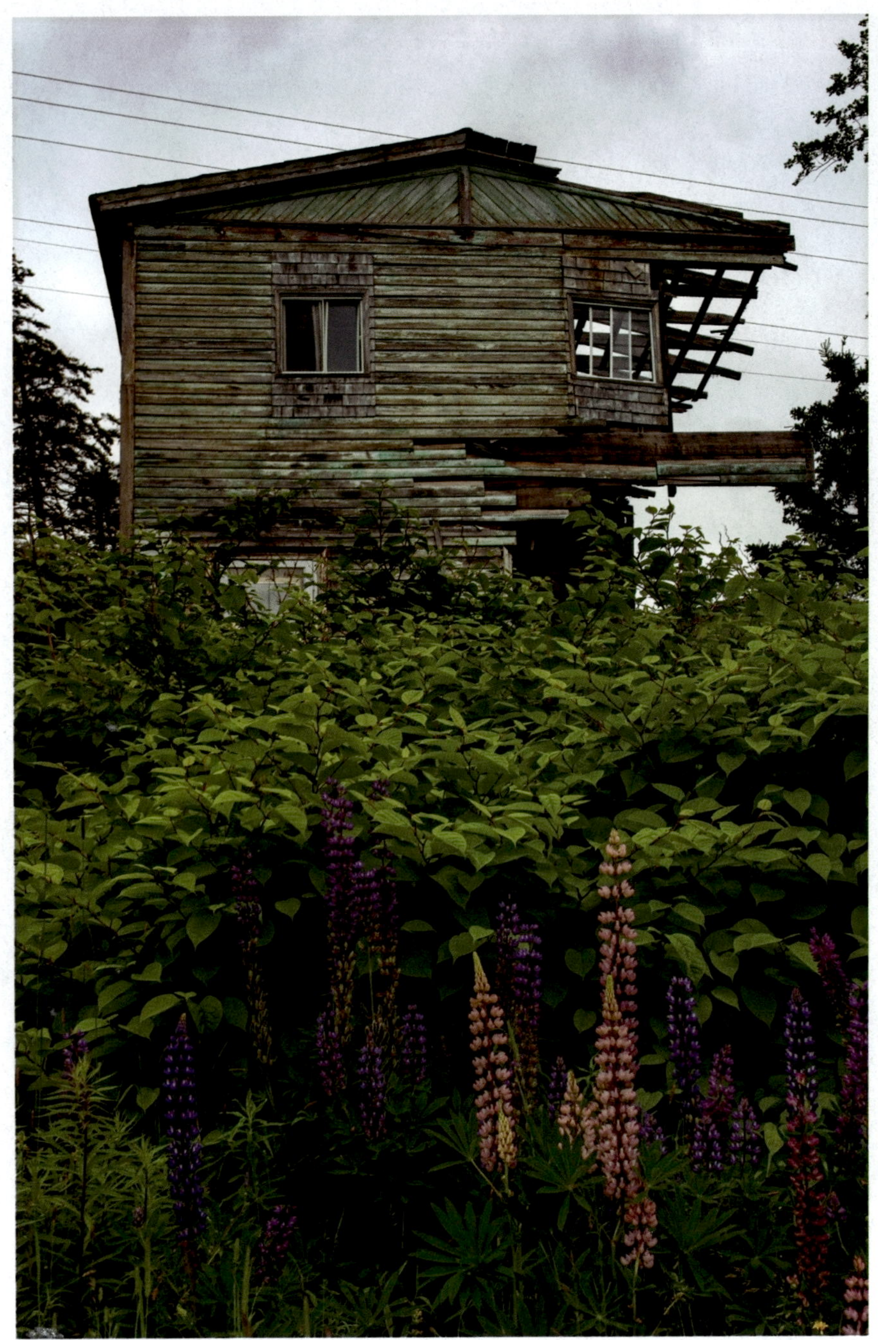

(Left) The beauty of nature is juxtaposed against this deteriorating home in Goldboro. Driving along the winding coastal route, this house stood out because of its shocking structural damage. Without knowing how old it is or how long it has been abandoned, we can only guess what happened.

(Opposite) A detail shot of what's left of the home on the opposite page. Peeling wallpaper reveals coral-coloured walls and bright green paint peeks through the white door.

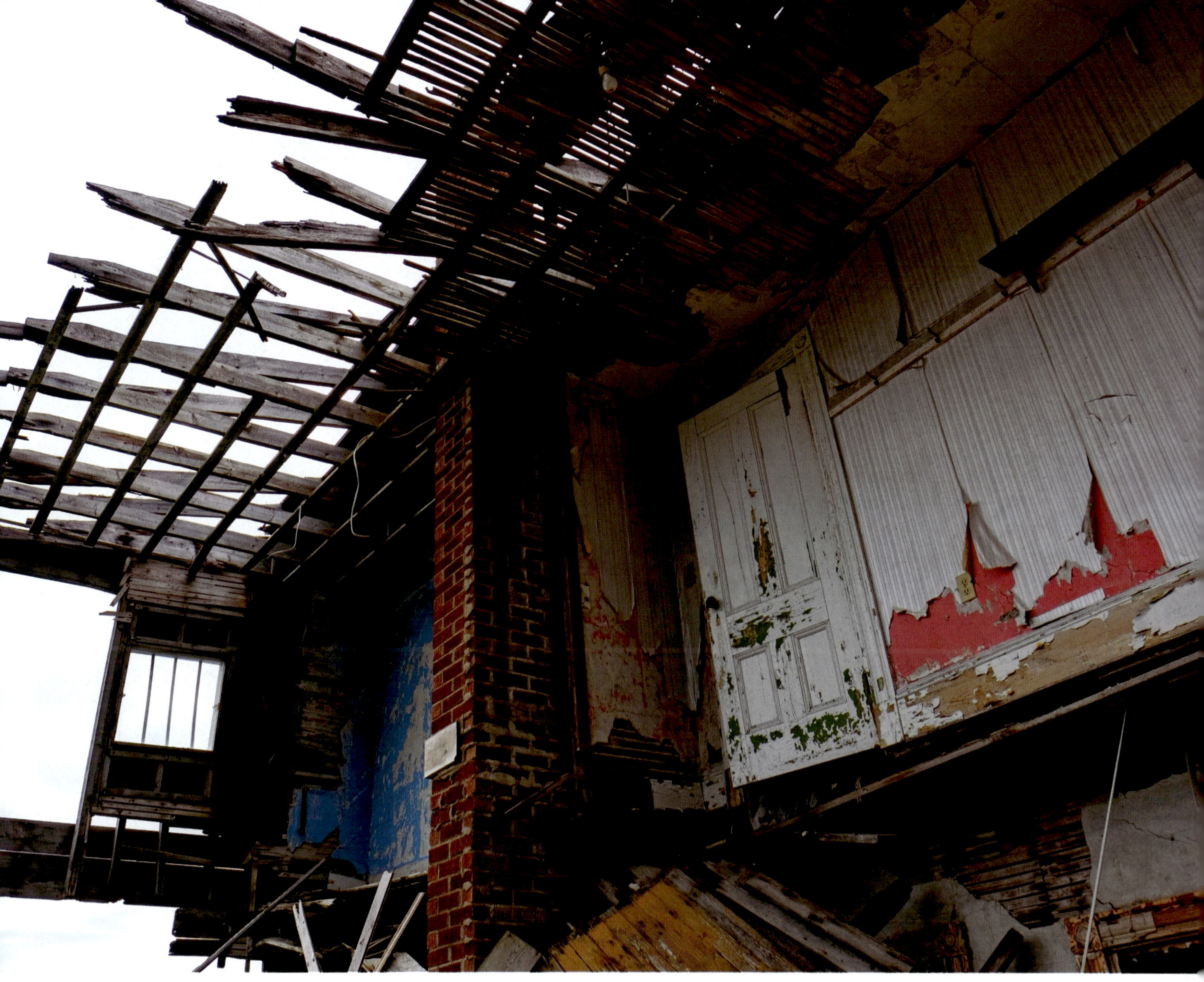

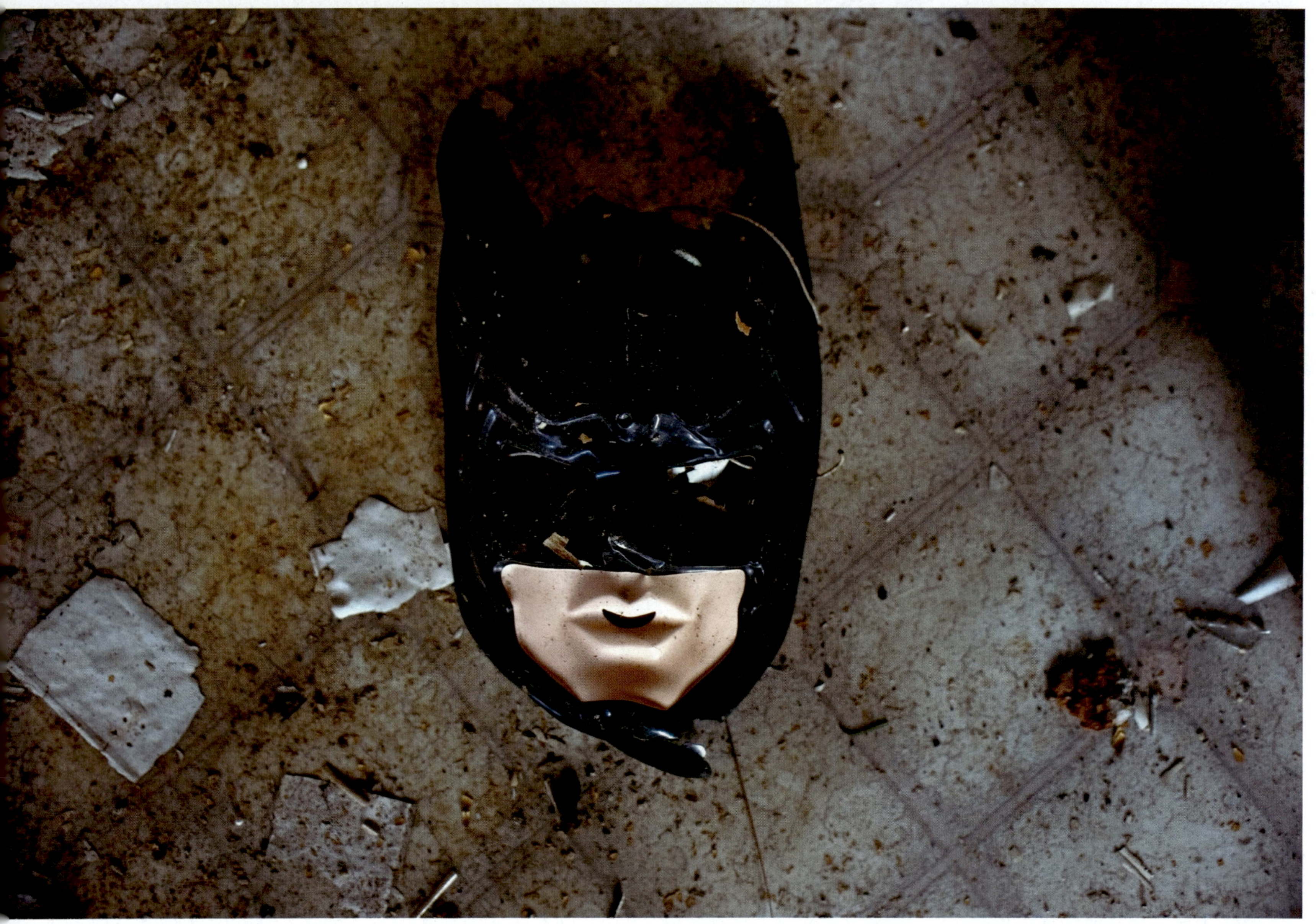

A Batman mask lies discarded on the floor of an abandoned property at Bear Point in Shelburne County. The detritus of life abounds in many of these places, as diverse as the many owners who once filled these rooms with life.

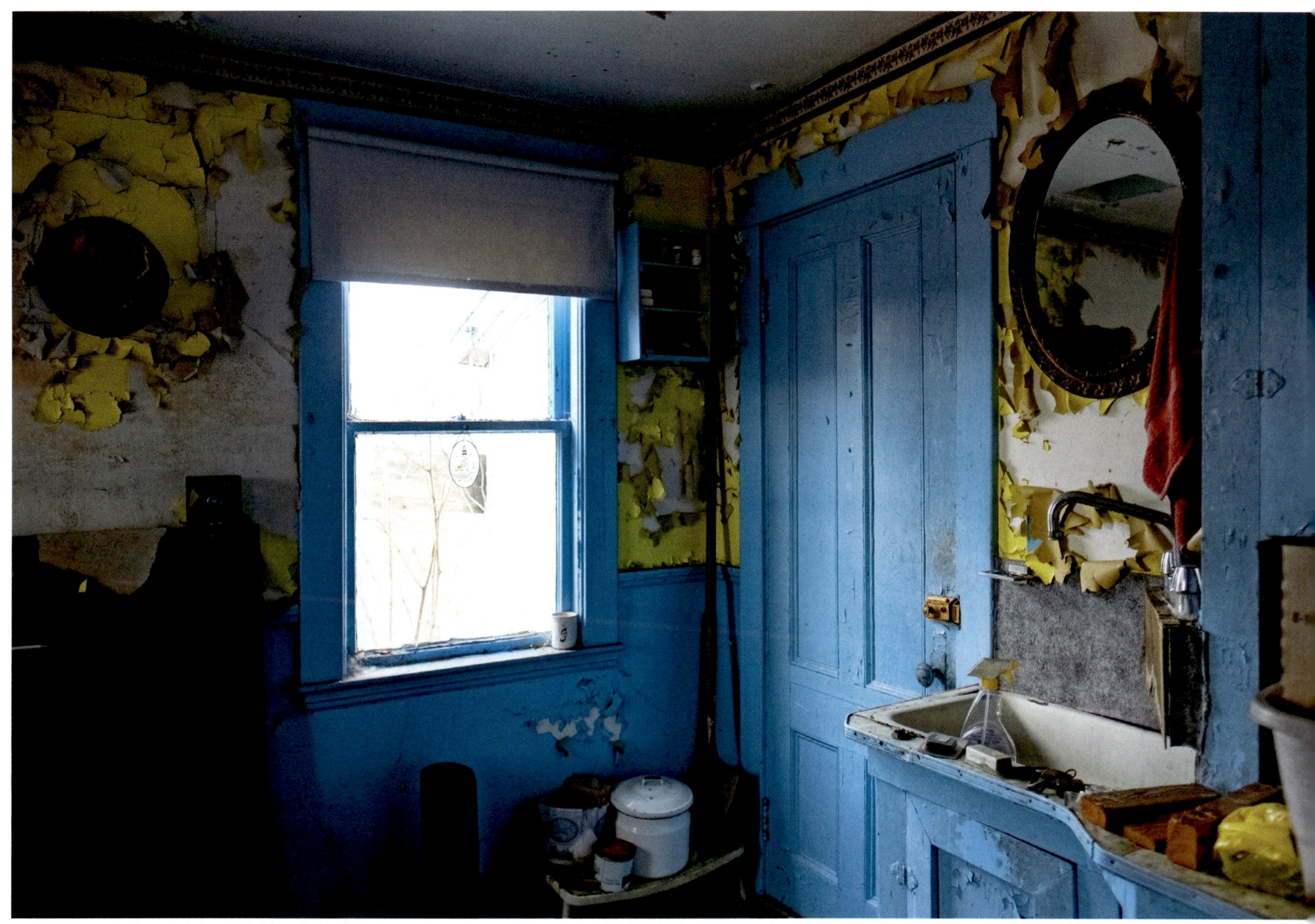

Inside a still-colourful kitchen of a forlorn property near Bridgetown, Annapolis County, along the Annapolis River. Vivid colours often remain in many abandoned properties long after the effects of desolation have begun.

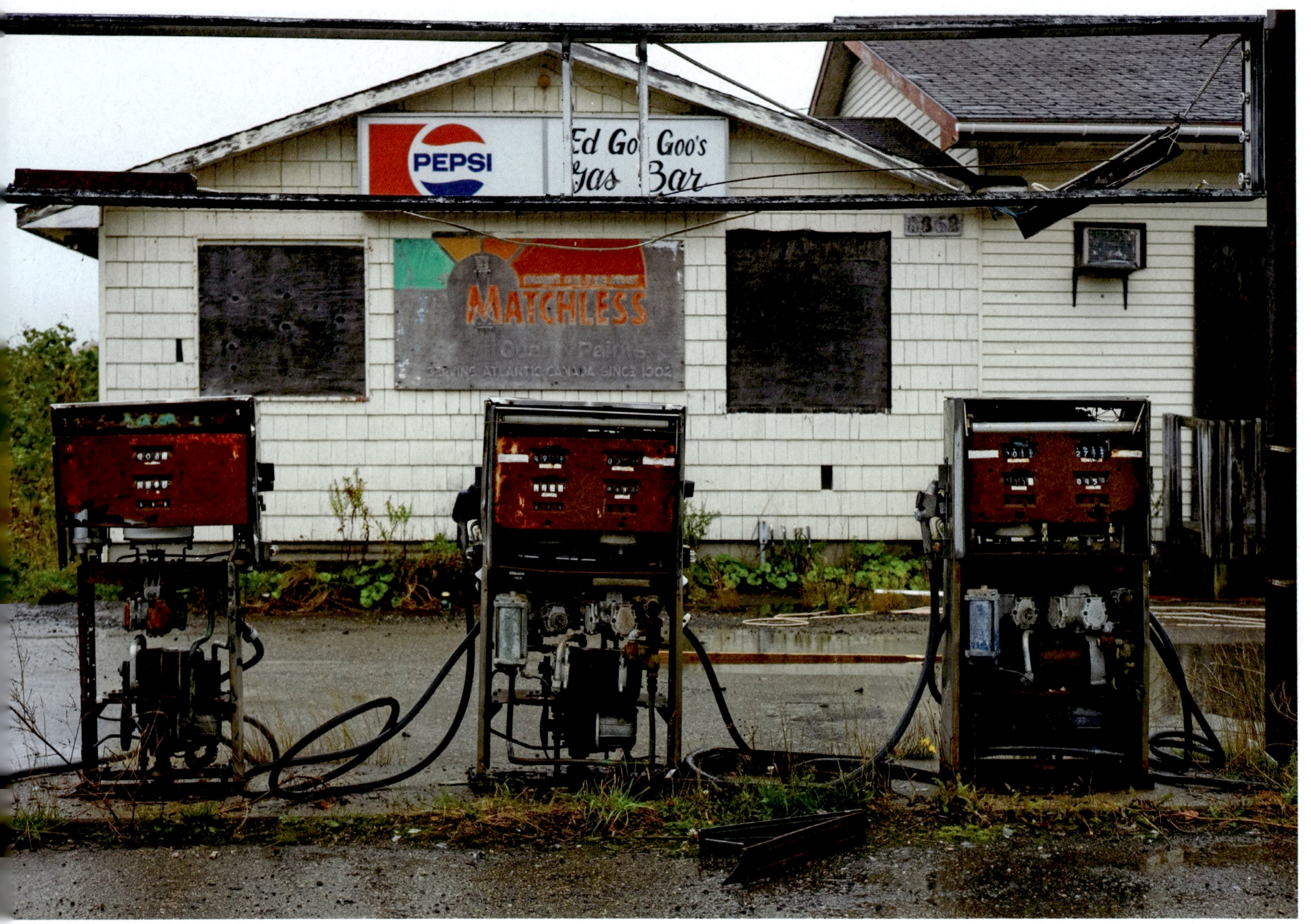

Rusted gas pumps at Ed Goo Goo's Gas Bar along the Trans-Canada Highway in Whycocomagh on Cape Breton Island. This abandoned gas bar is a popular attraction for tourists and photographers visiting the area.

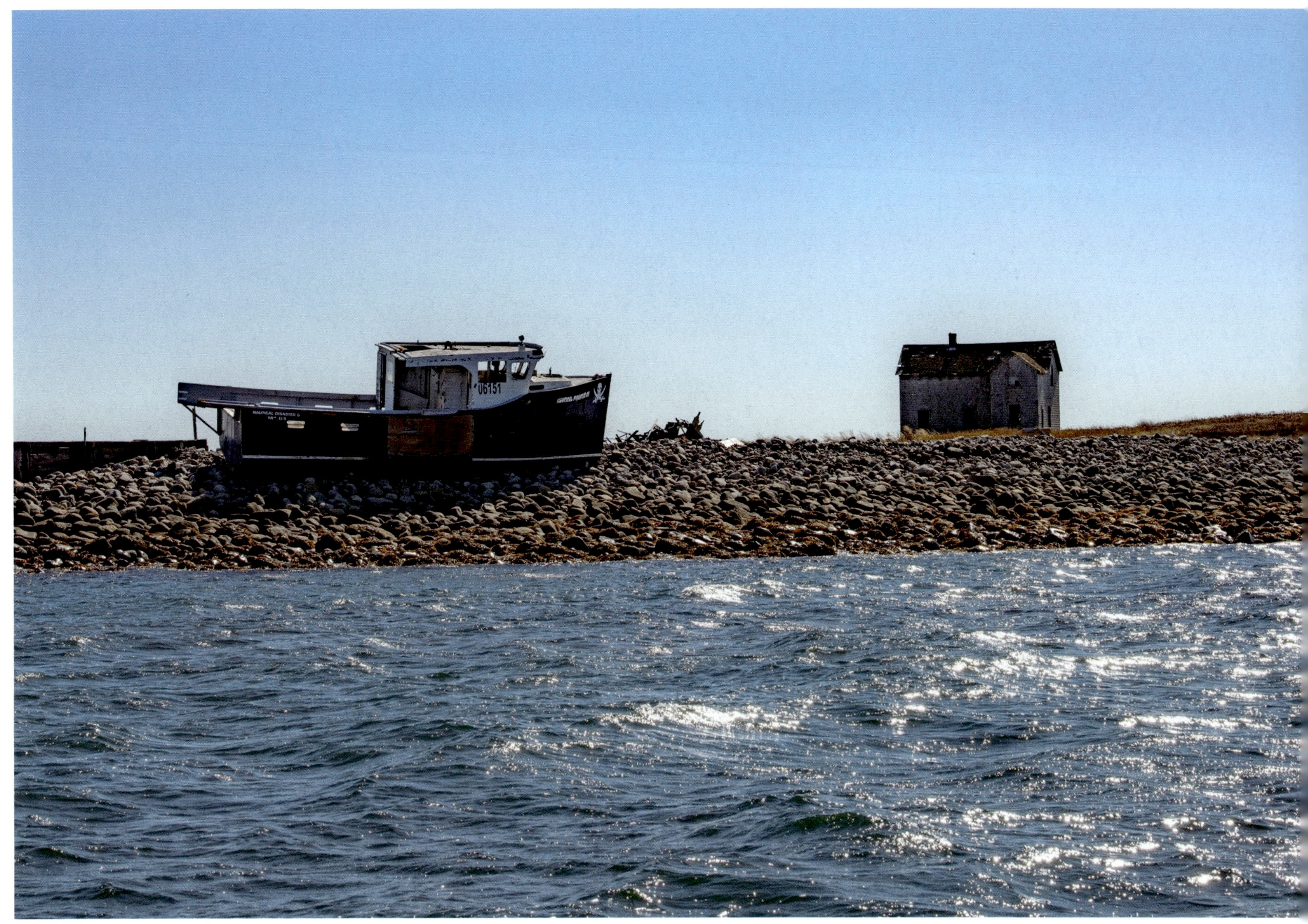

The Lobster boat *Nautical Disaster* sits beached and abandoned on the shores of Flat Island off the southern coast of Nova Scotia.

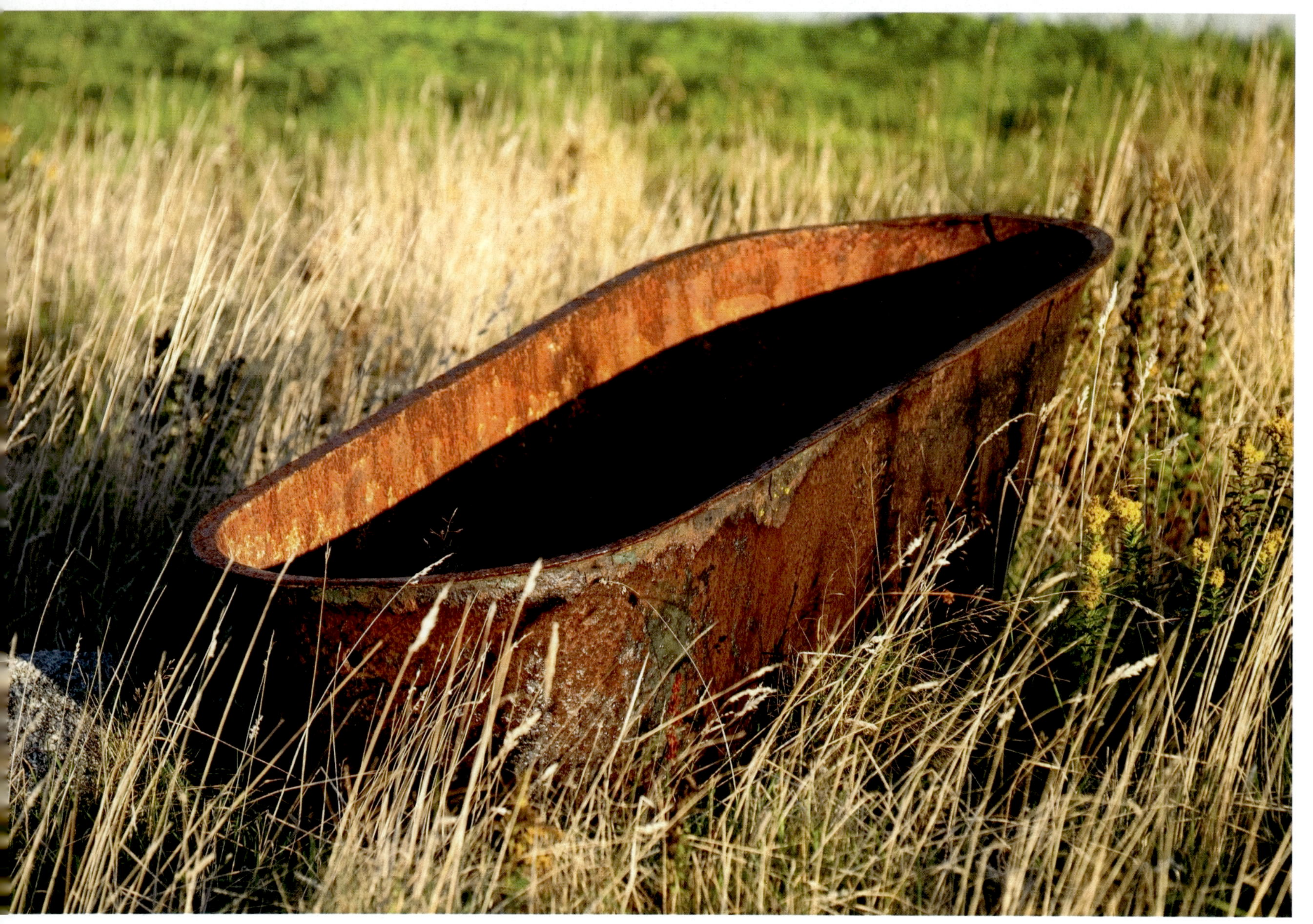

A rusted bathtub sits in a field of tall grass on Seal Island off the southern coast of Nova Scotia. Isolated and uninhabited most of the year, the island is left to hardy populations of sheep and hare.

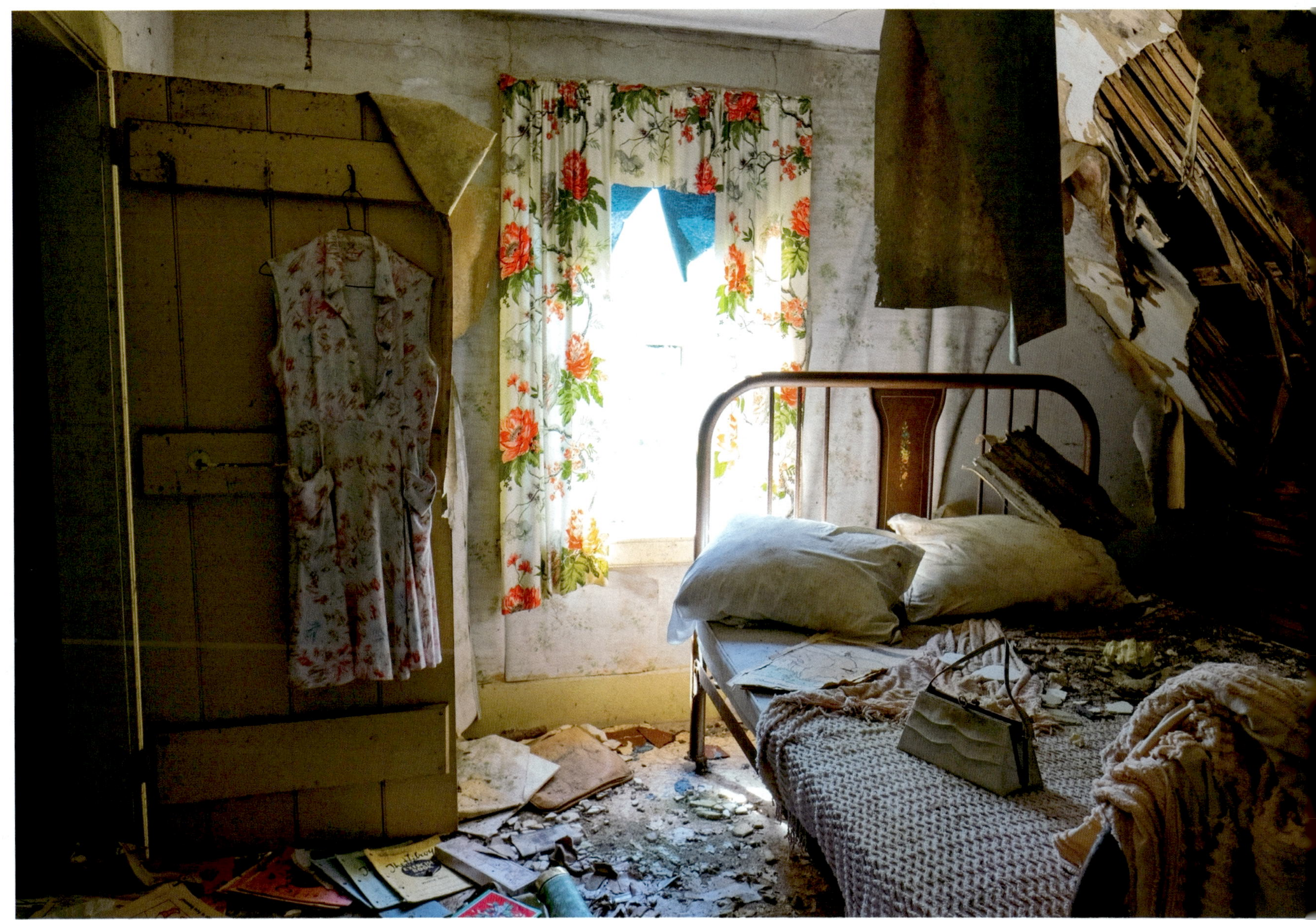

A dress hangs on a closet door of the second-floor bedroom in an abandoned property in Queens County, in the south-central region of the province.

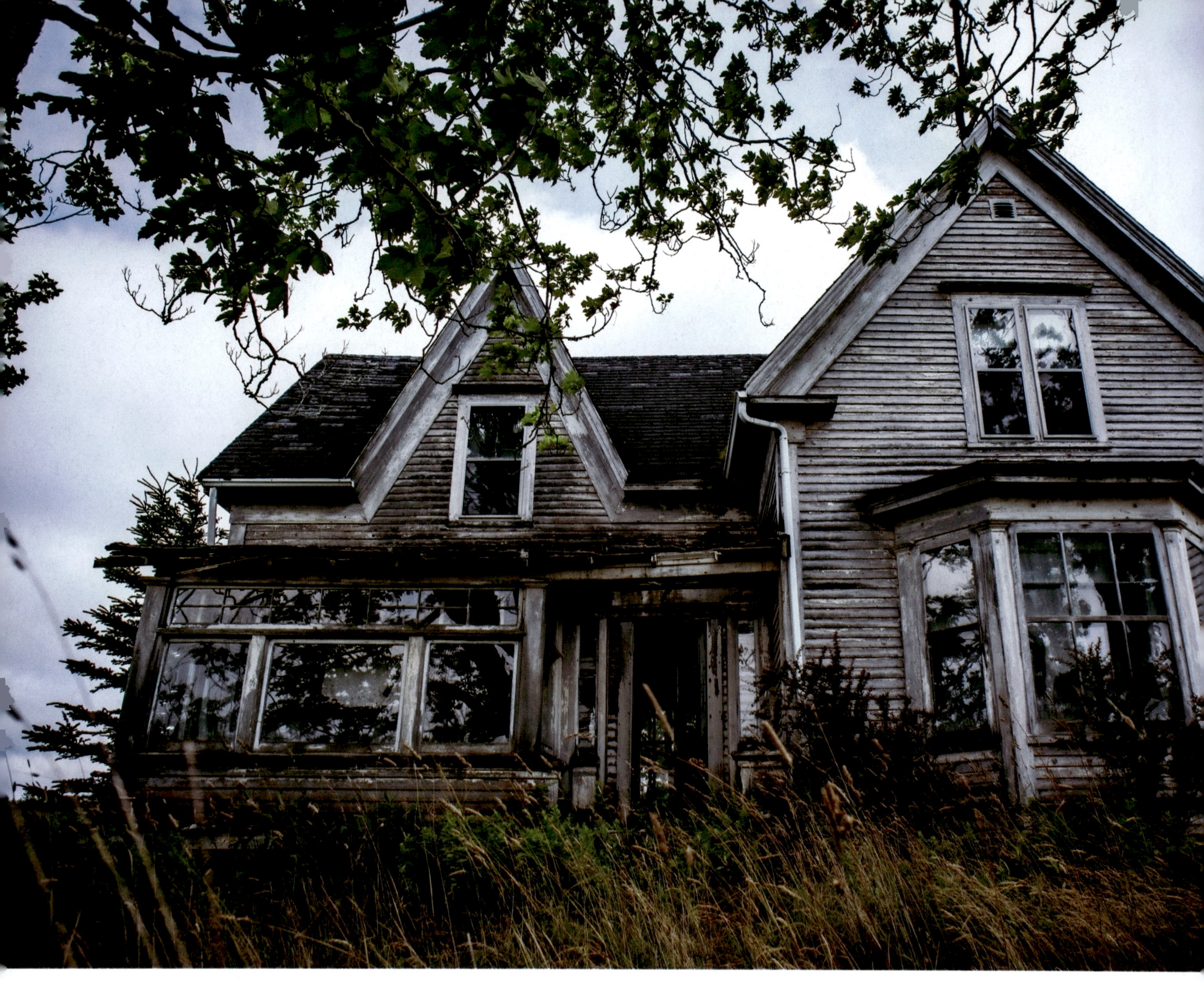

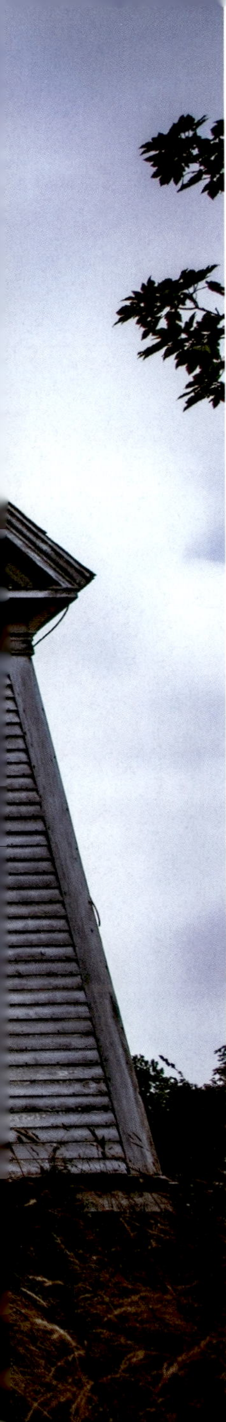

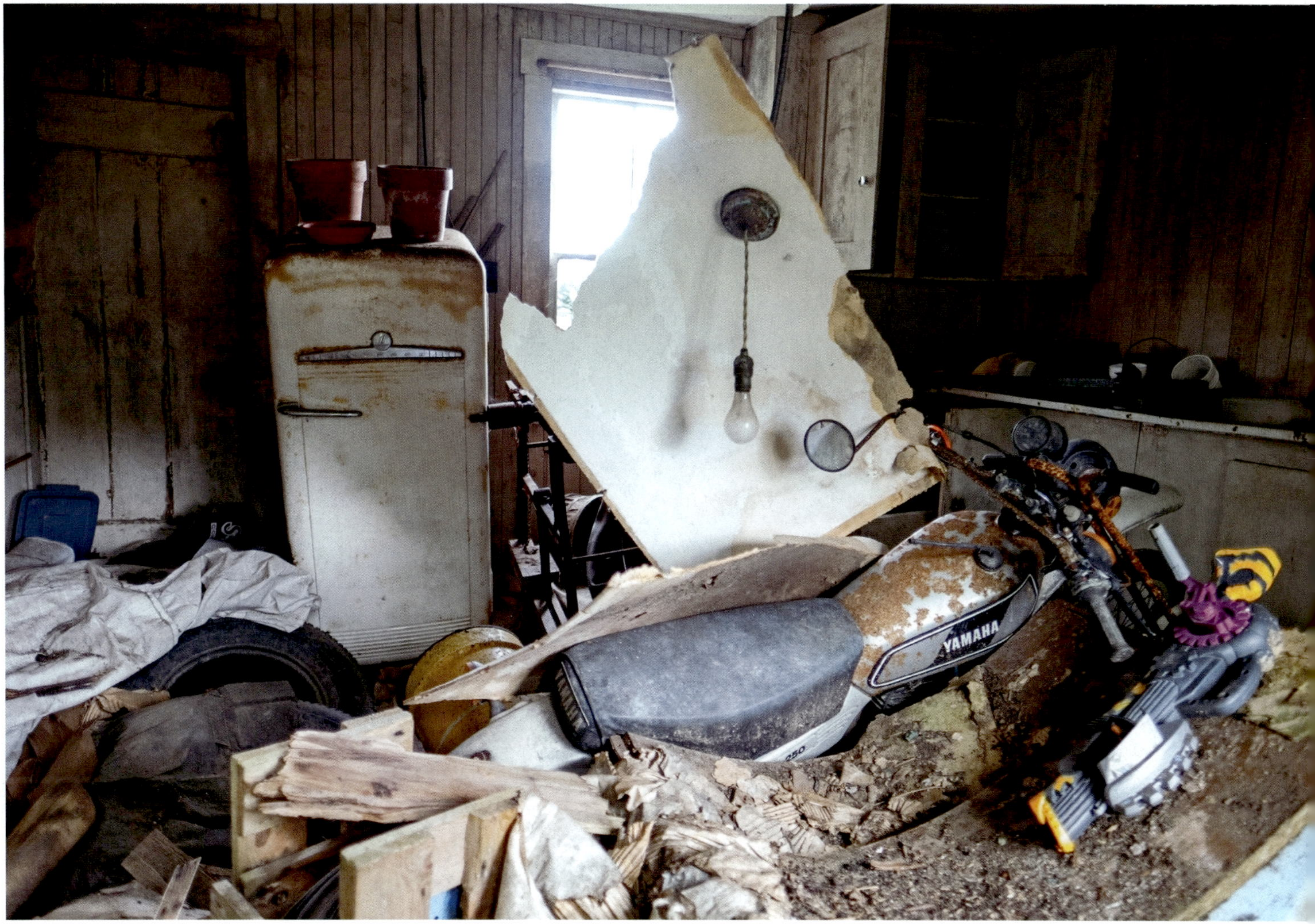

(Opposite and Above) Exterior and interior detail of an abandoned home in the Acadian community of Belliveaus Cove, Digby County, on the Bay of Fundy.

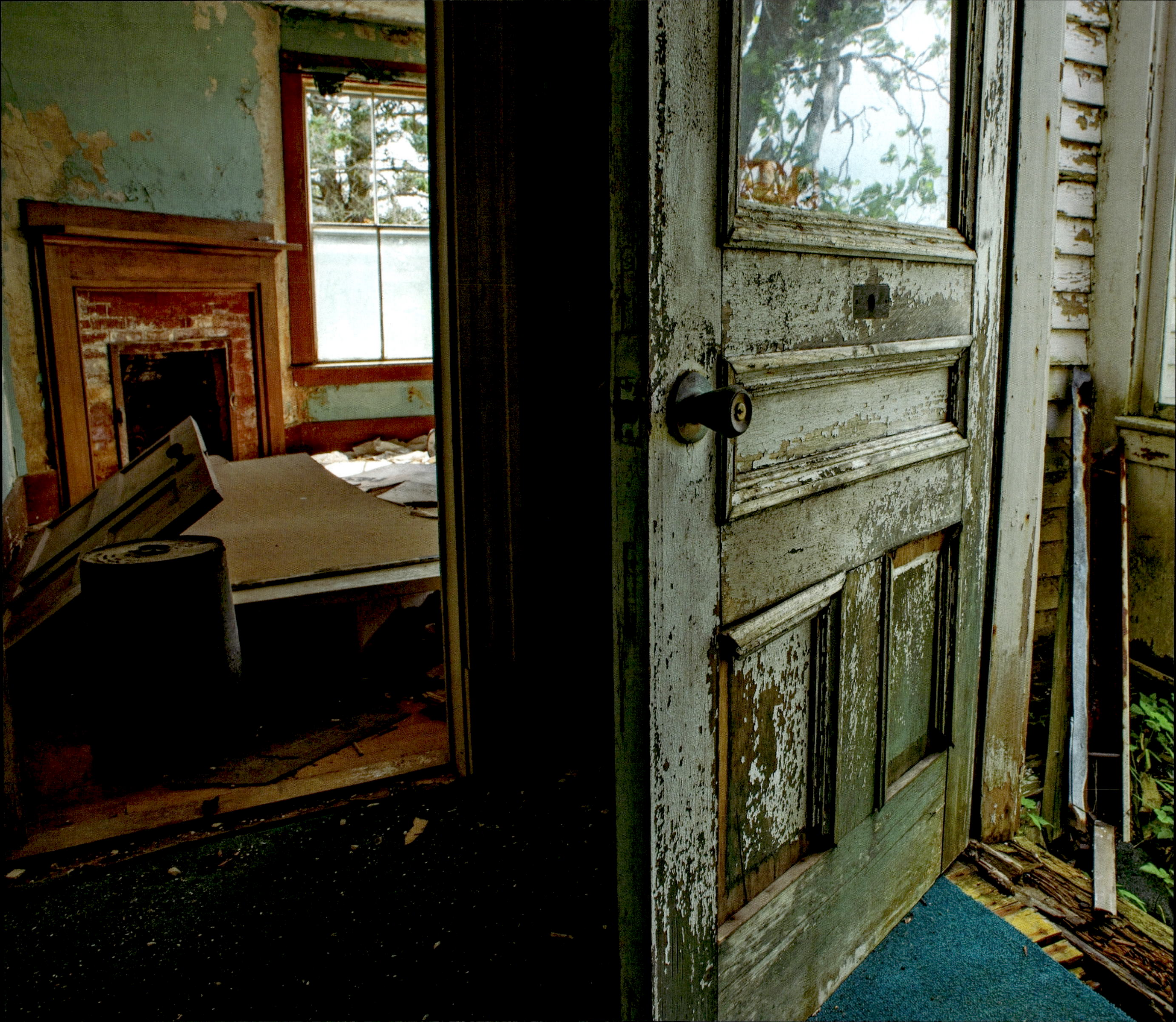

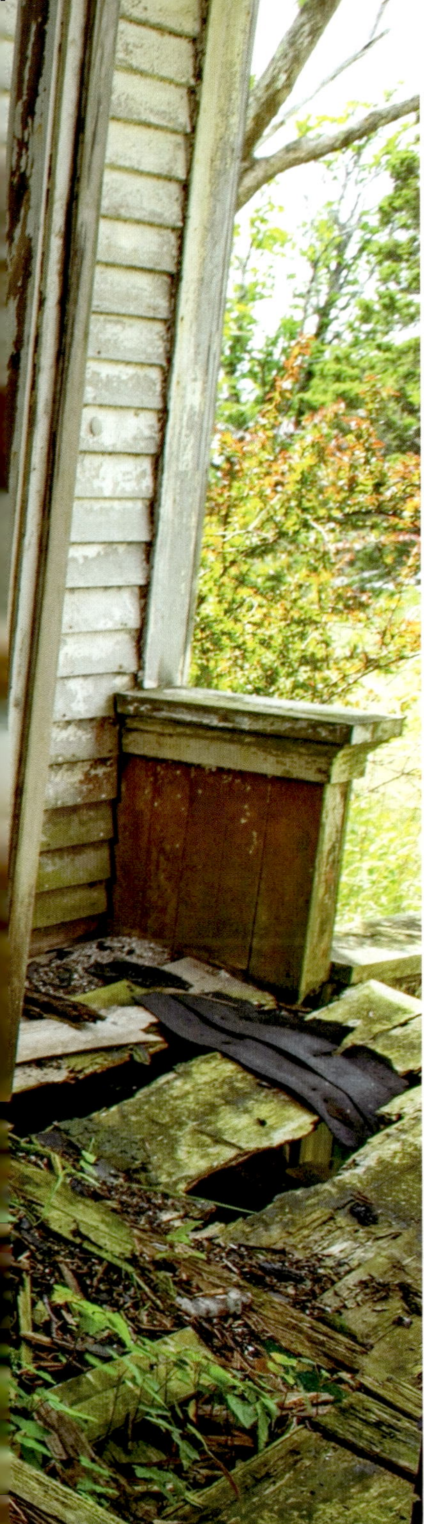

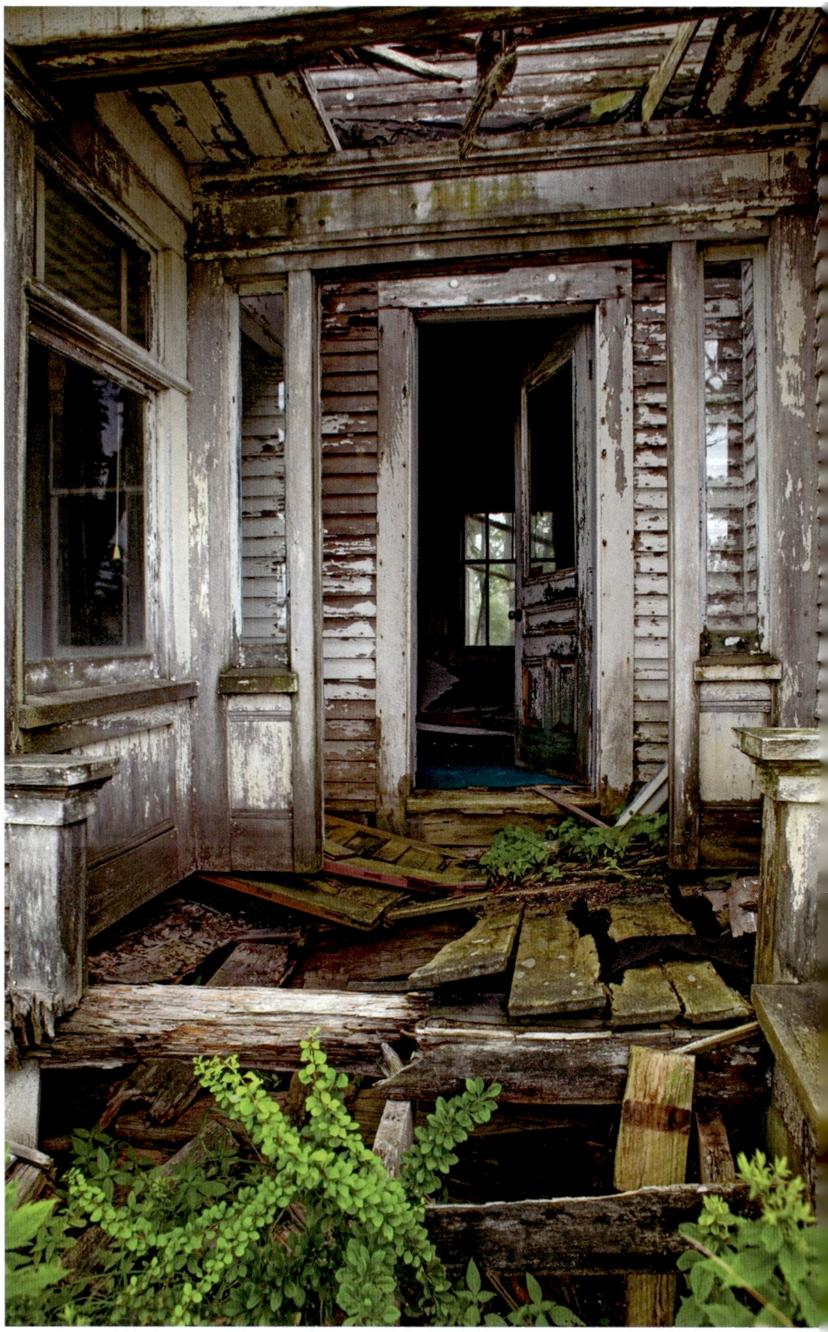

(Opposite and Right) The Belliveaus Cove home welcomed us with an open door but the rotting porch floor and steps quickly dampened any feeling of conviviality.

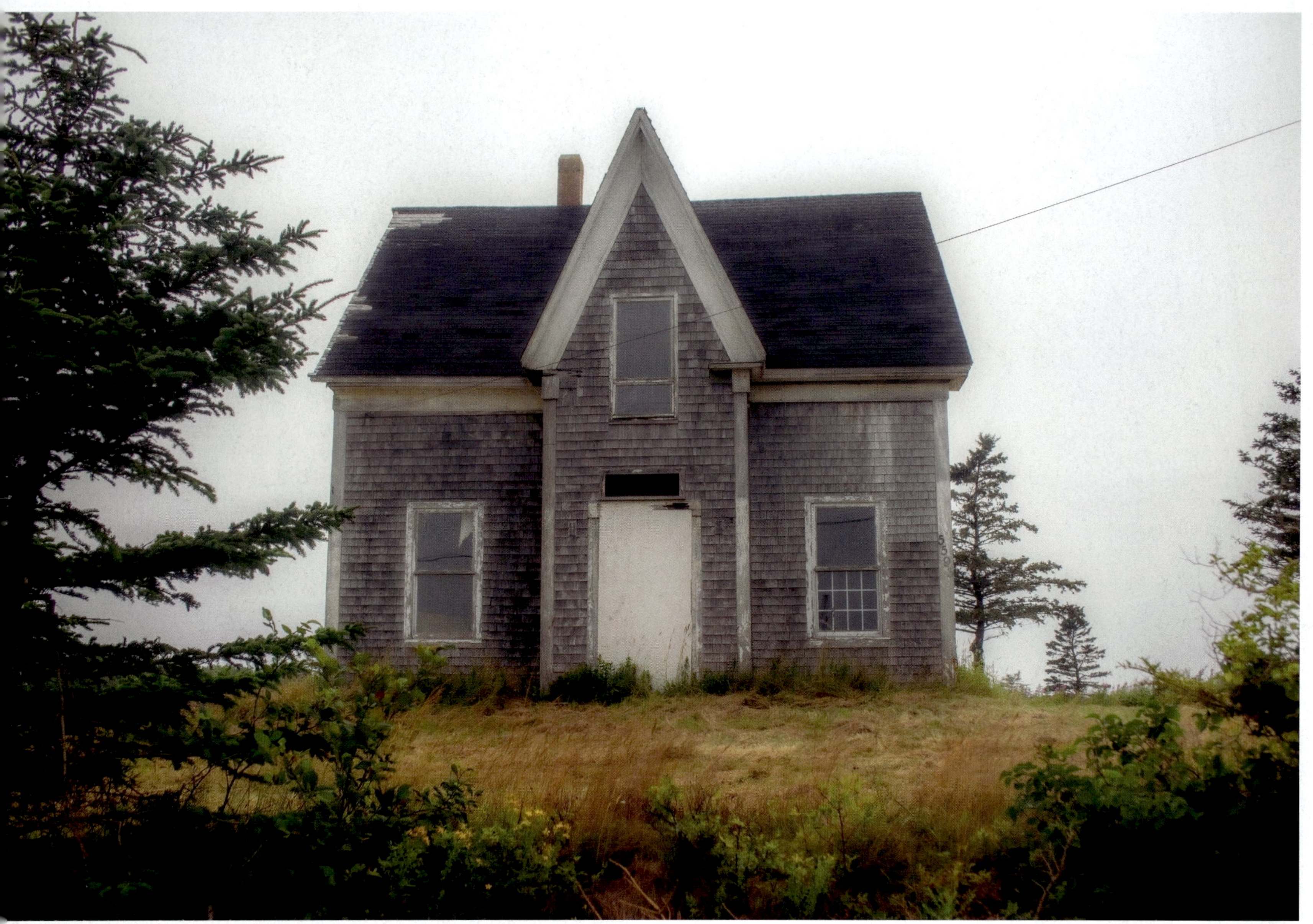

Just before the fog started to roll in, we captured this little home in Bear Cove, Digby County.

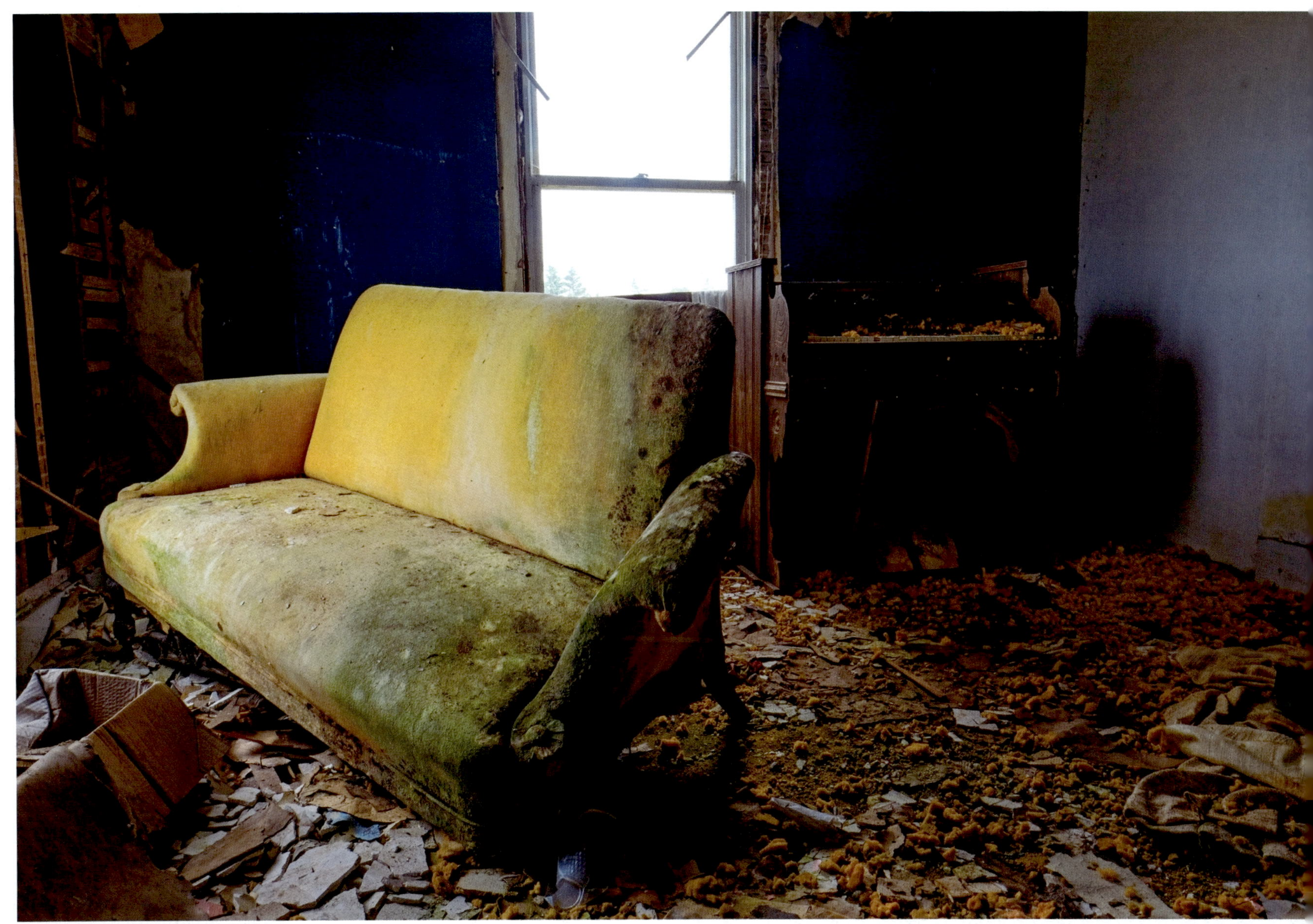

A striking yellow sofa is contrasted by the royal blue walls in this Bear Cove home.

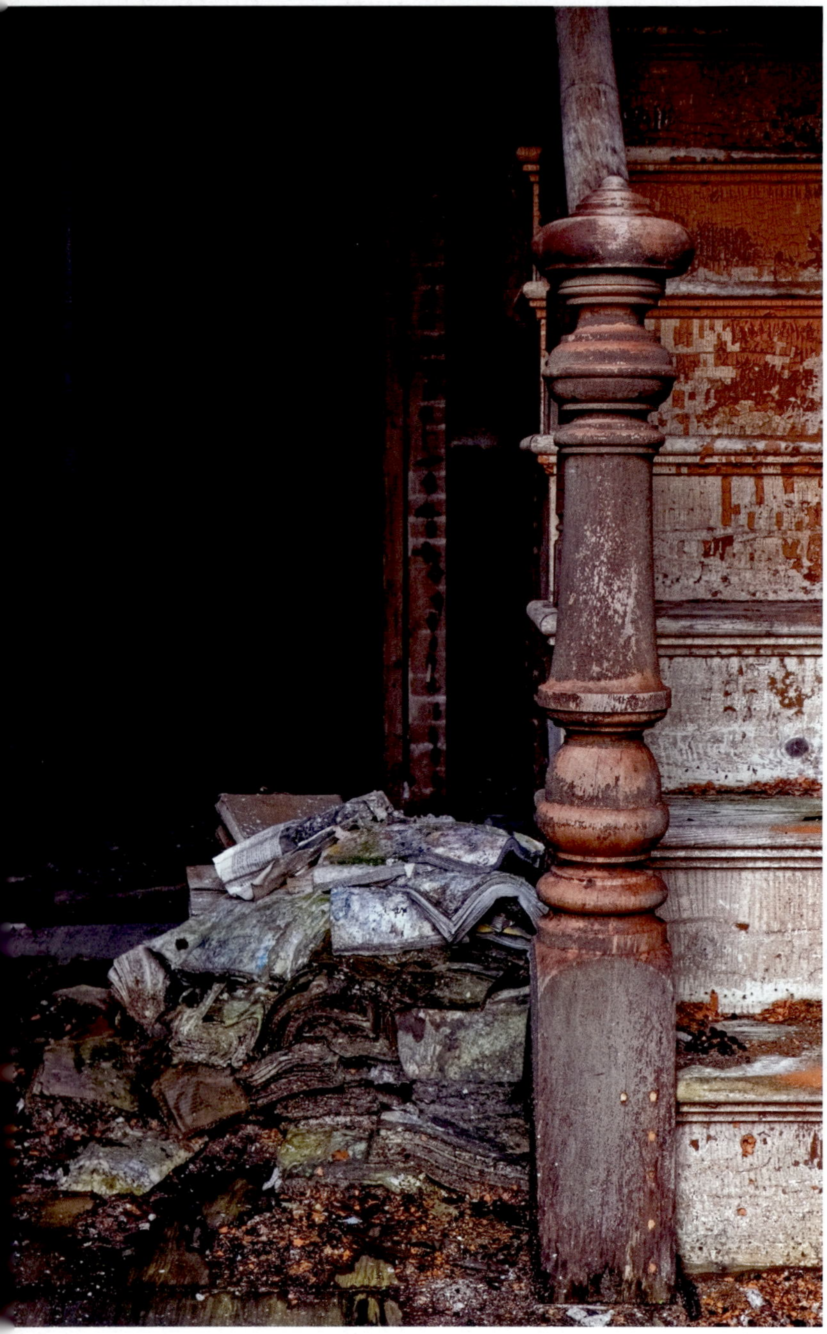

(Left) A weathered stair banister stands up to the decay of a Goldboro home. Sadly, many homes in the area have been left abandoned, but perhaps not really forgotten.

(Opposite) A shed tilts on its side behind an abandoned house in Goldboro.

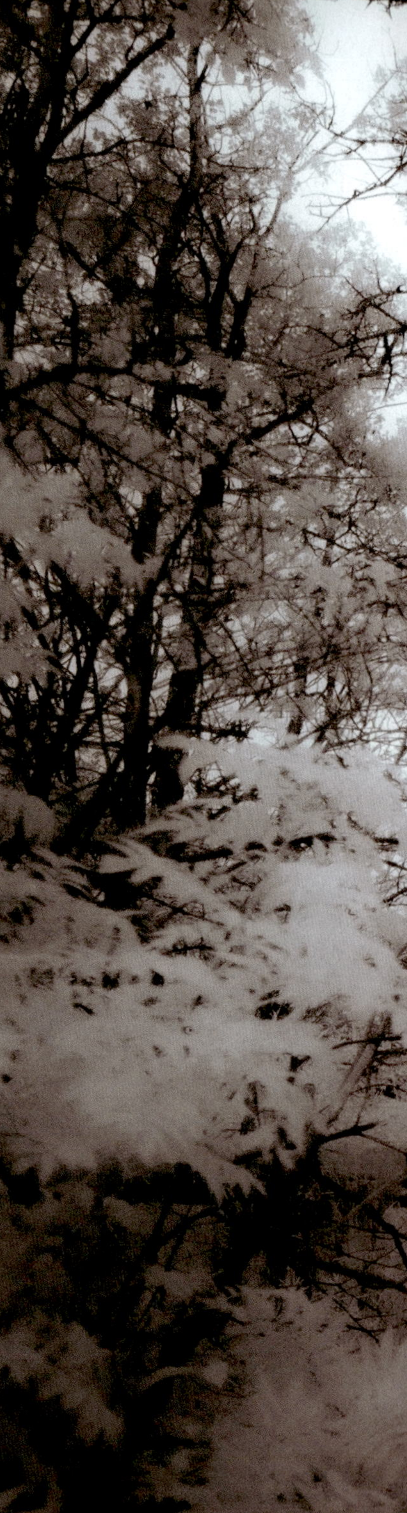

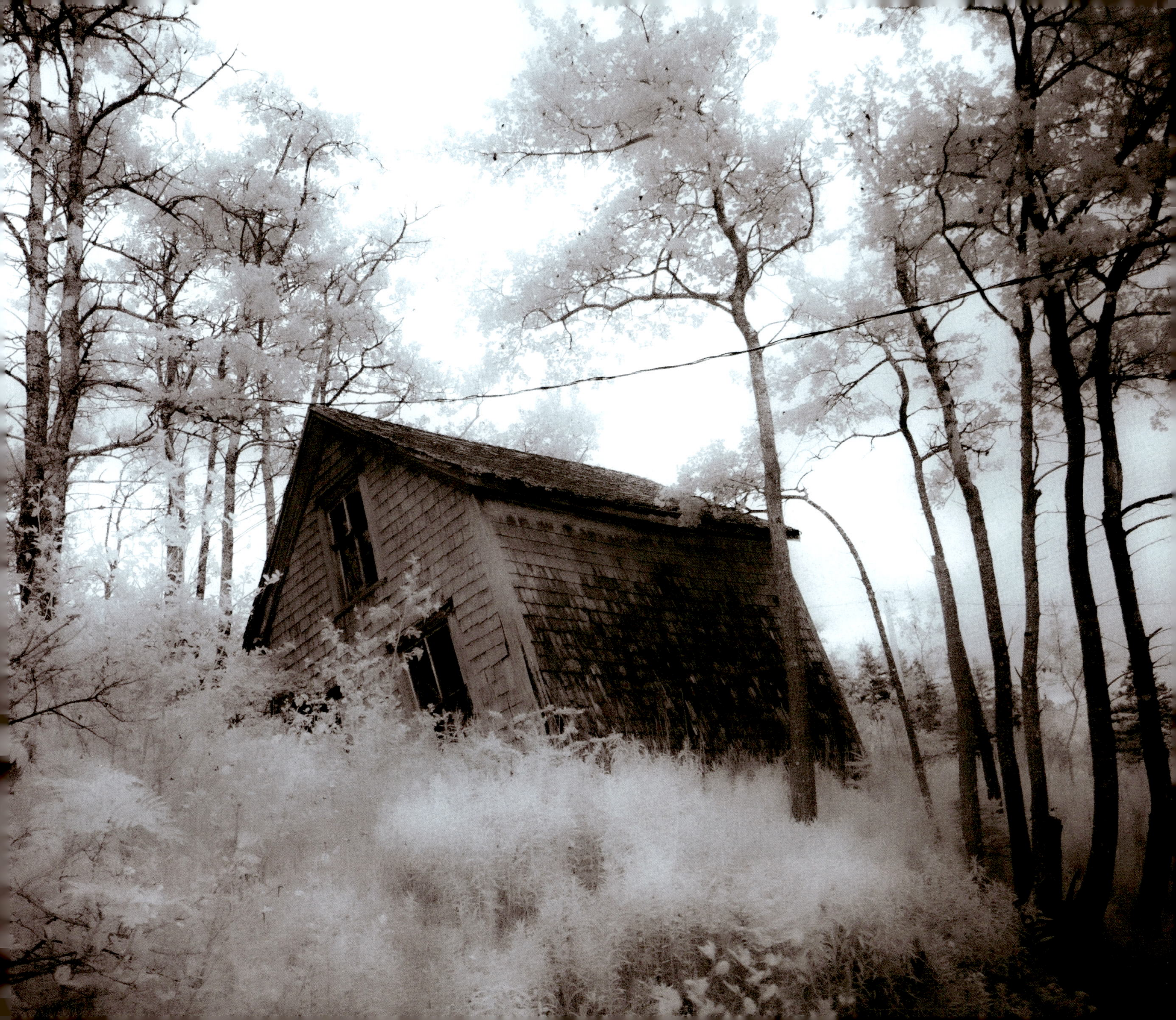

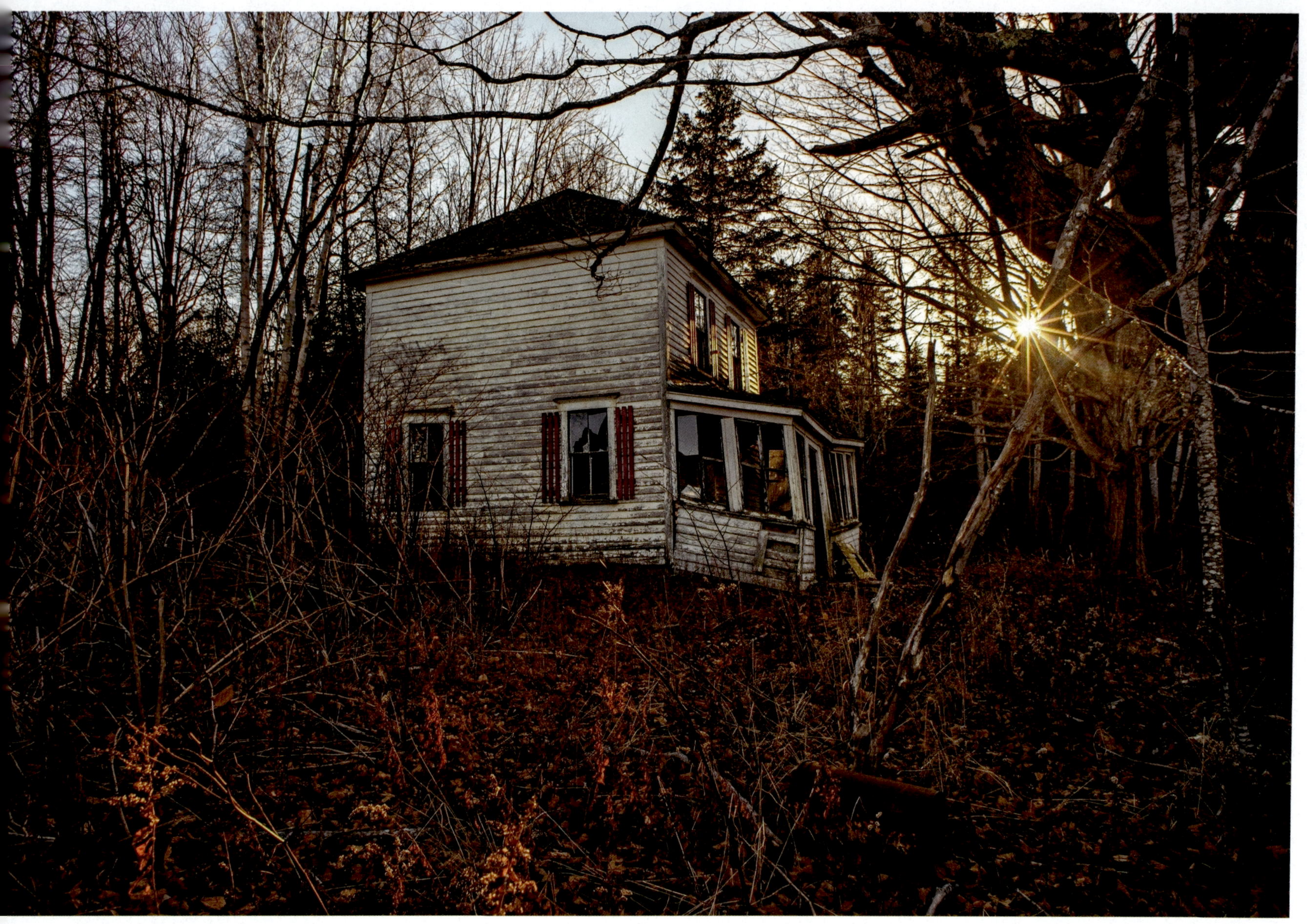

This home in Bass River, Colchester County, is tucked away behind another abandoned property. There were no obvious signs of how anyone living there was able to come and go. The house had no driveway and was perched close to a steep embankment about 10 metres from the front door.

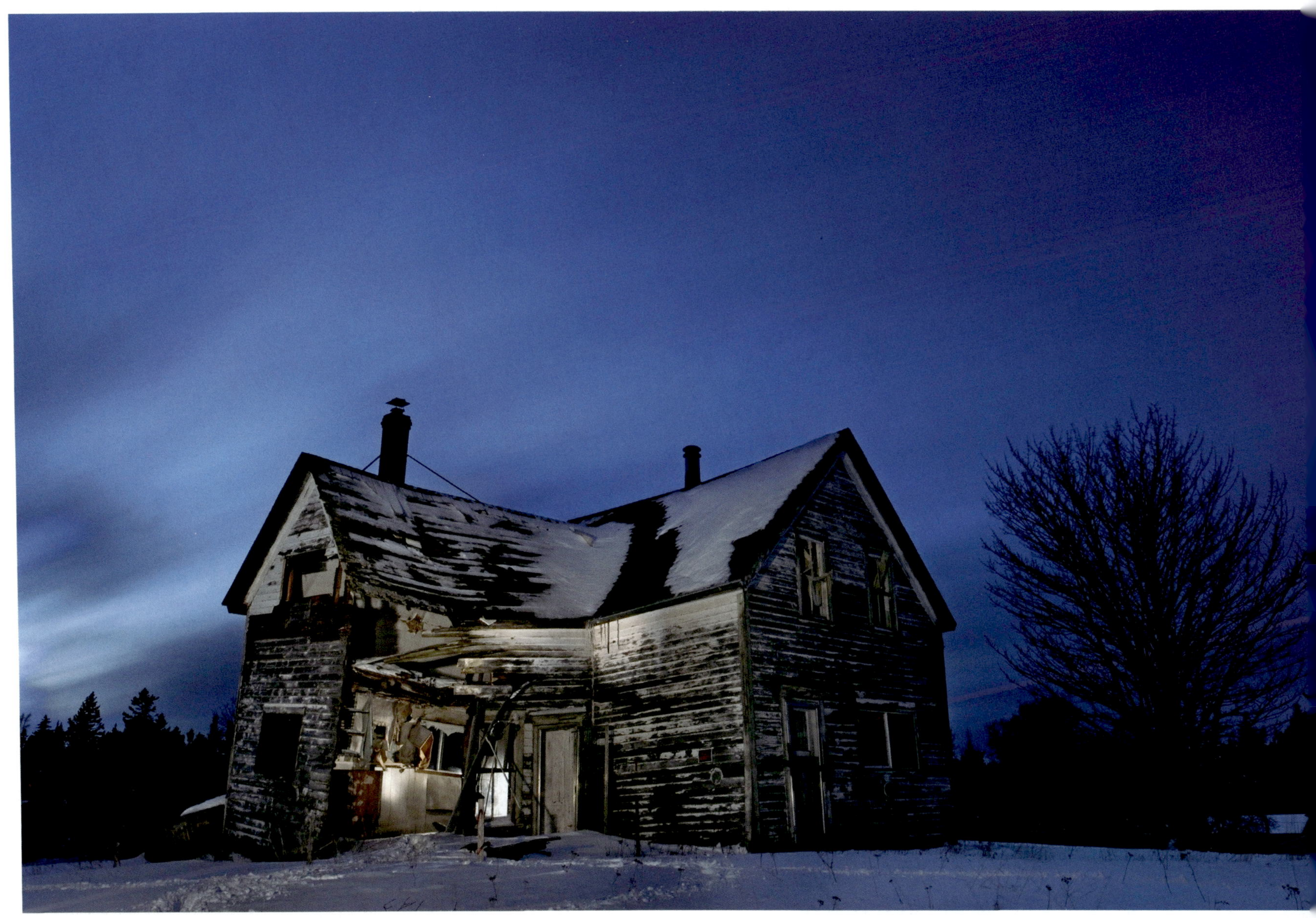

This photo of a home near Folly Mountain, Colchester County, was shot just after sunset with the use of handheld strobes.

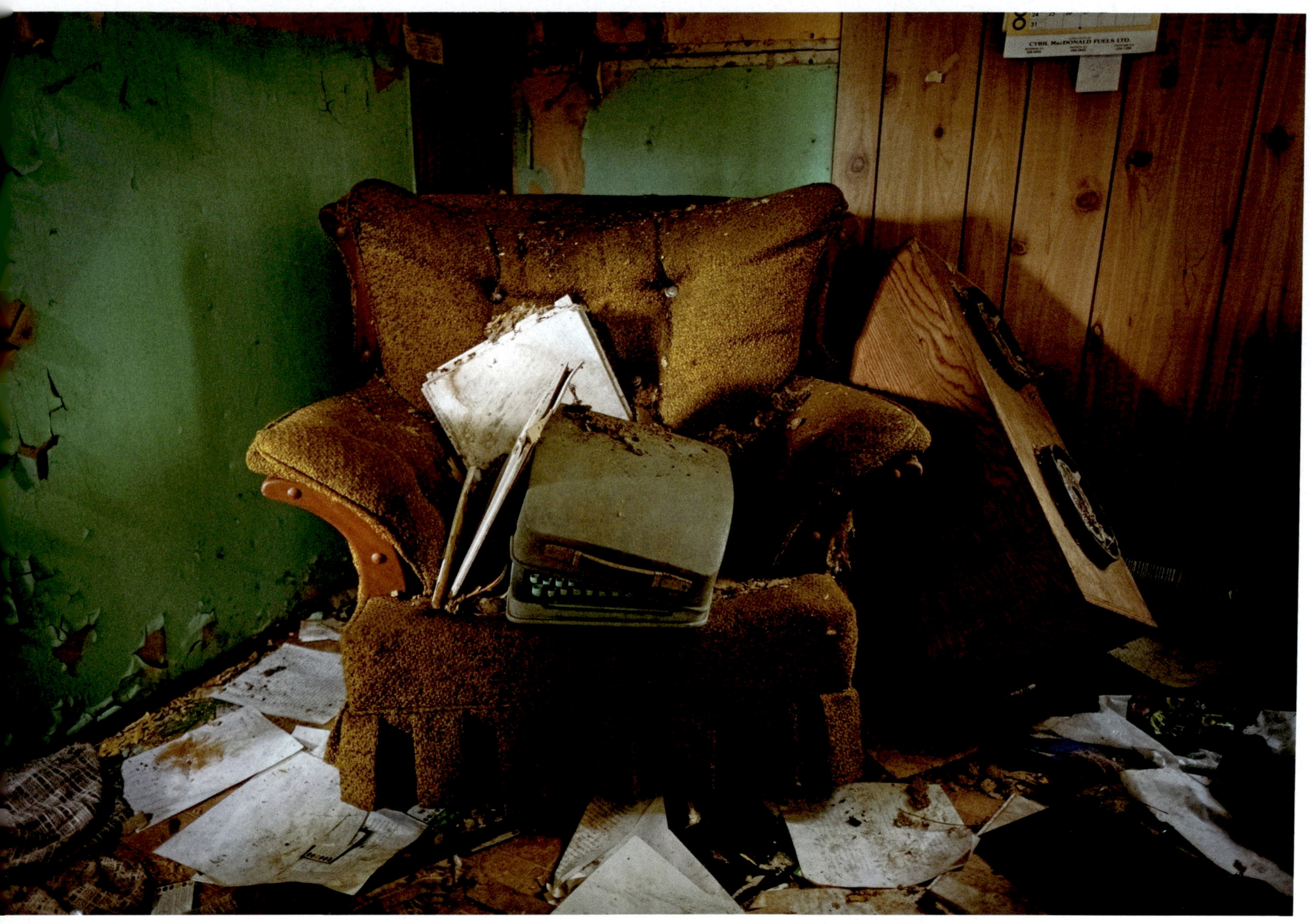

A typewriter sits on a chair inside the living room of an abandoned home on the outskirts of Inverness, Cape Breton Island.

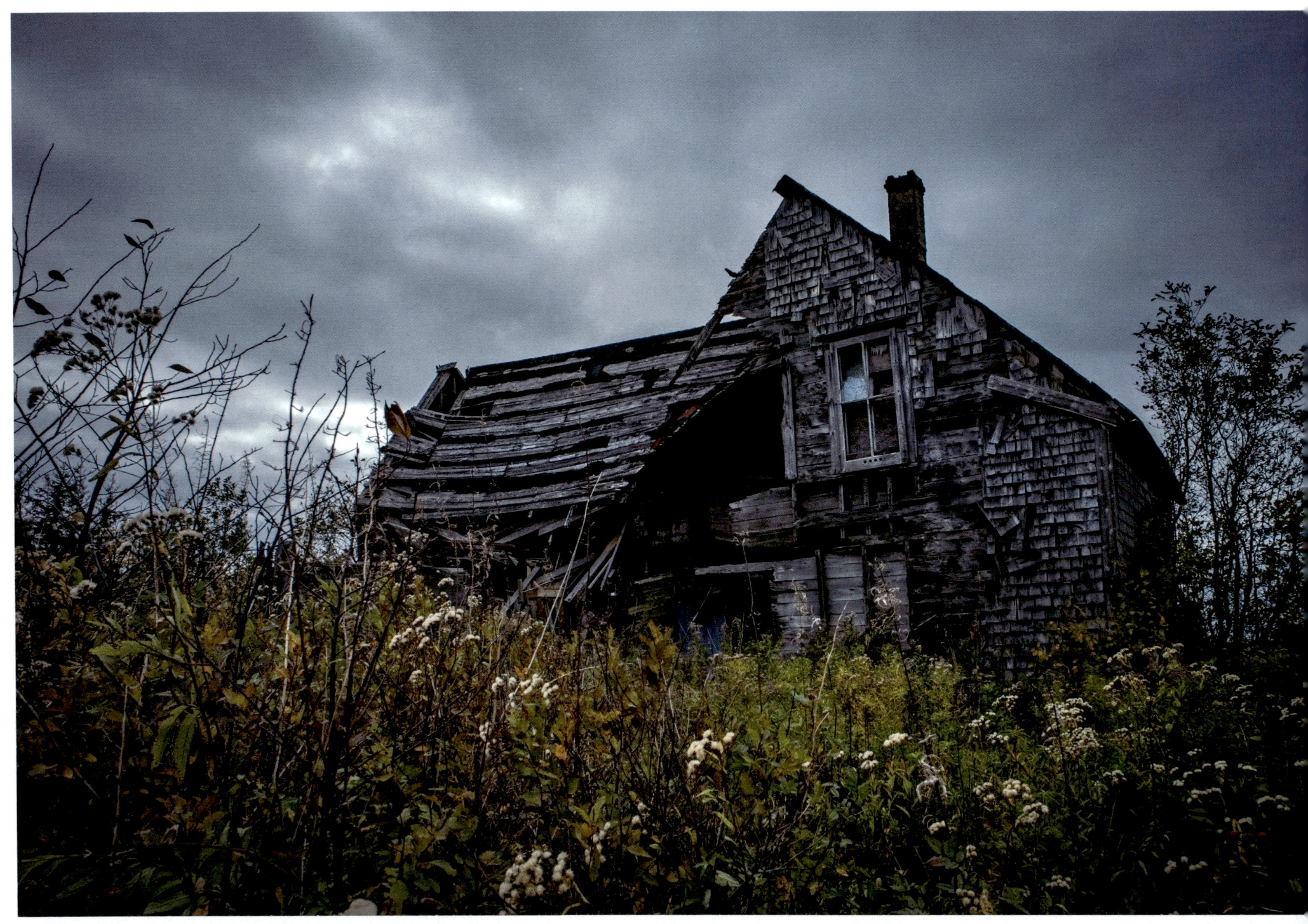

An old farmhouse in Little Judique, Cape Breton Island, starts to crumble as it makes its last stand.

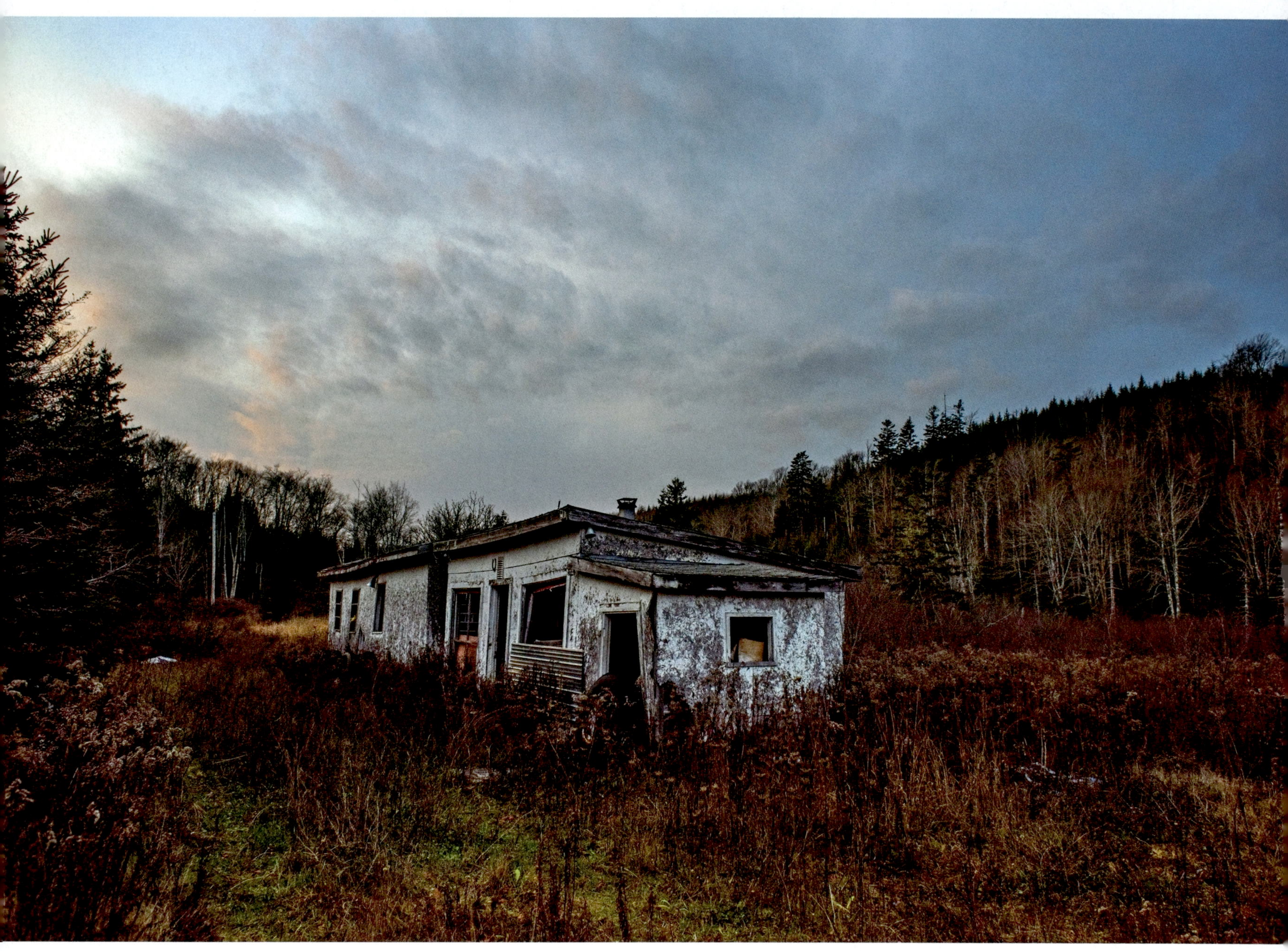

In Salt Springs, Pictou County, the sun sets on a dilapidated garage filled with unwanted items.

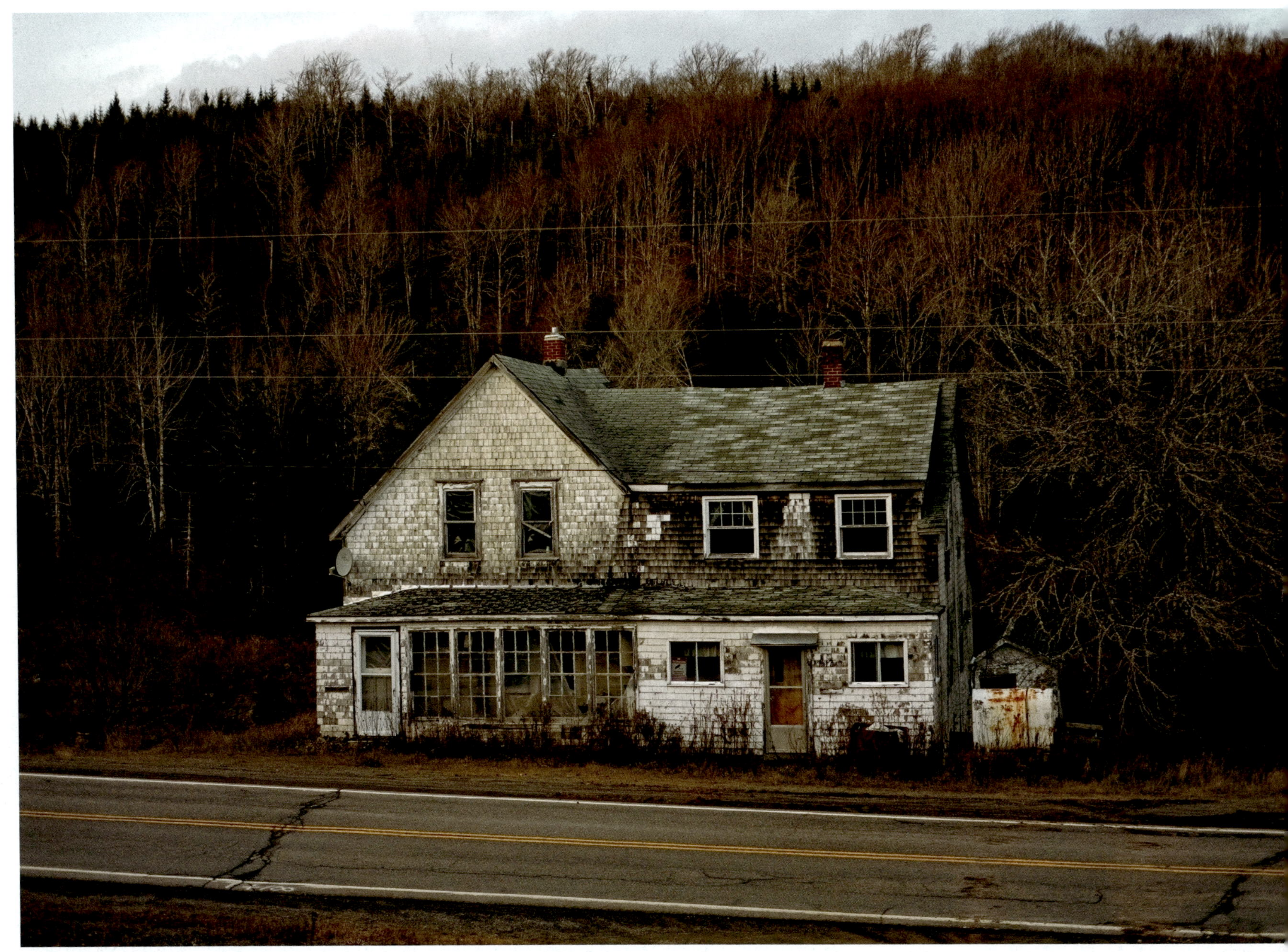

This unique home in Salt Springs, Pictou County, was home to two brothers who each lived on one side of the home. A neighbour explained that the brothers were less than thrilled to share their old homestead and rarely spoke to one another. Sadly, both men passed away and the home remains vacant.

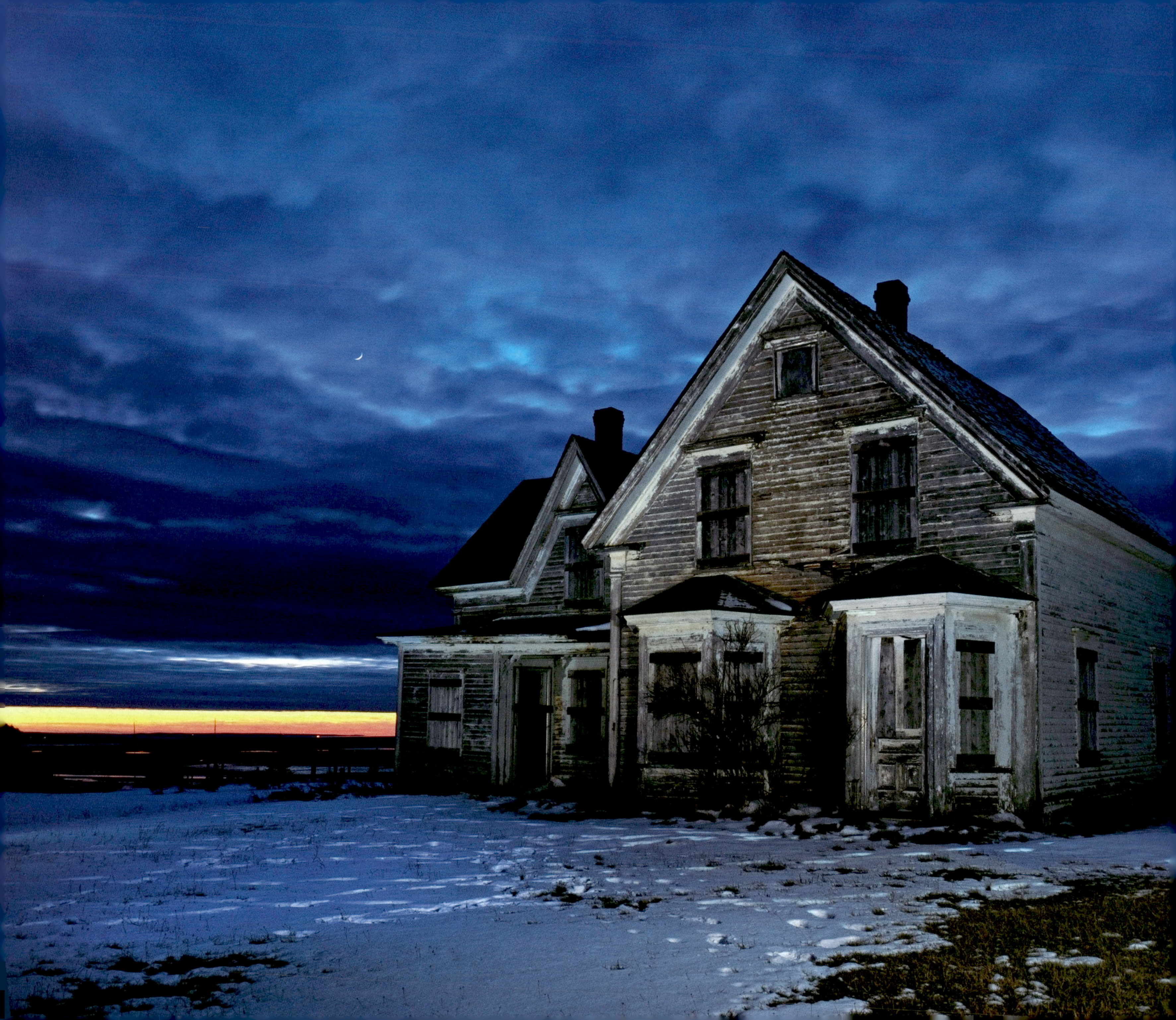

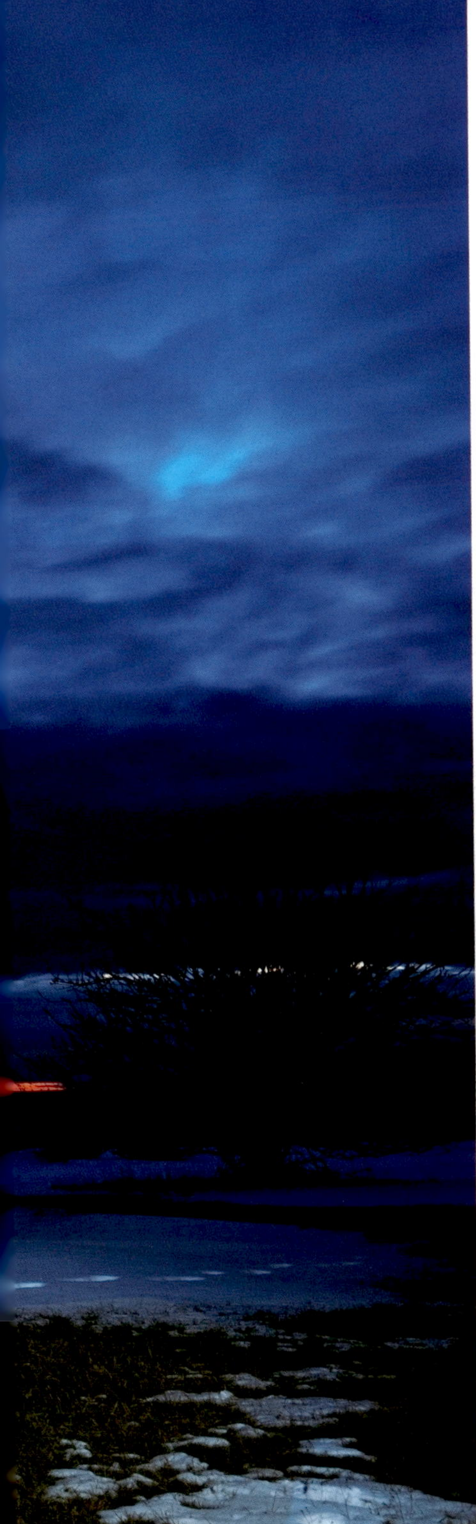

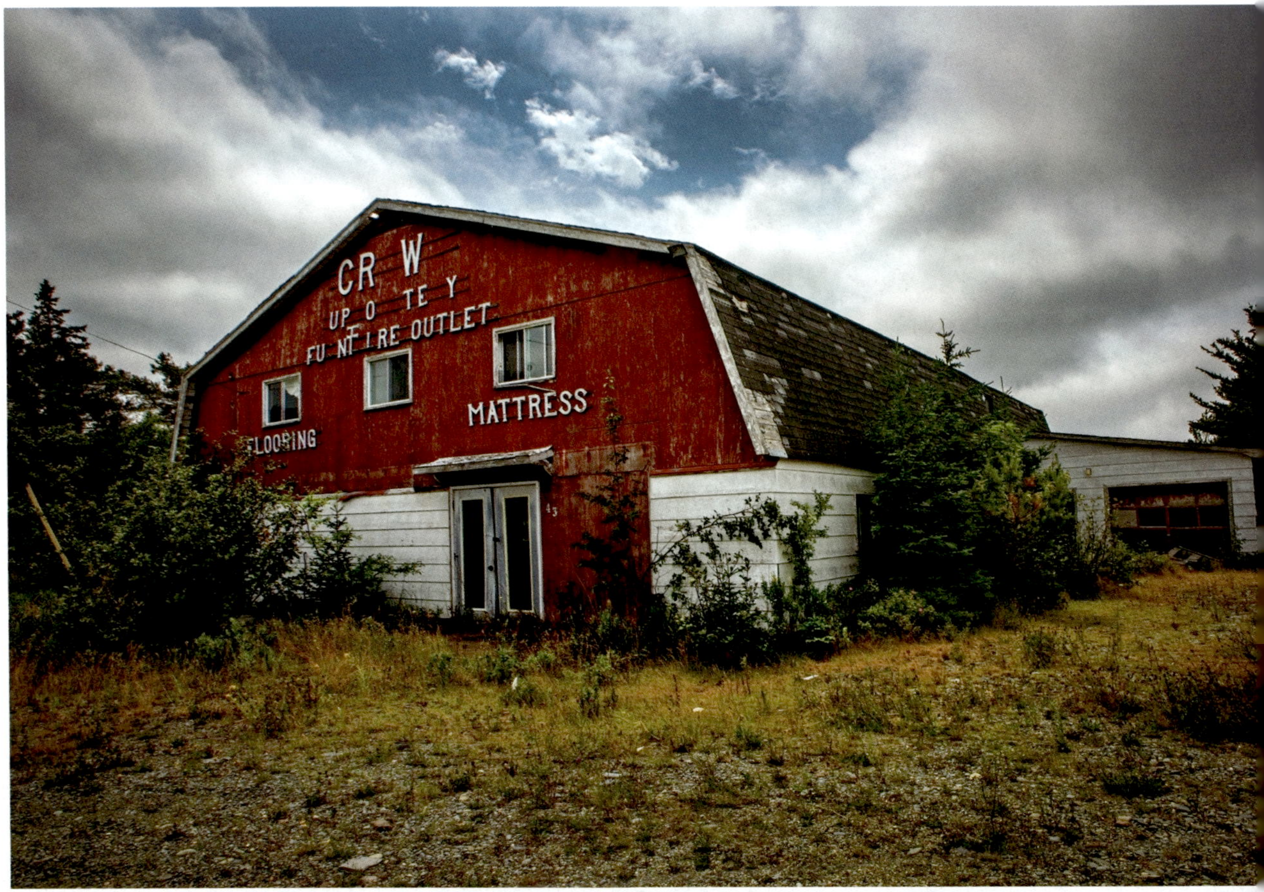

(Opposite) The sun sets on this home in Advocate Harbour, Cumberland County.

(Above) An abandoned upholstery warehouse in Belliveaus Cove, near the community's waterfront. Homes are not the only places that can become forsaken and forlorn. No community is immune to such losses.

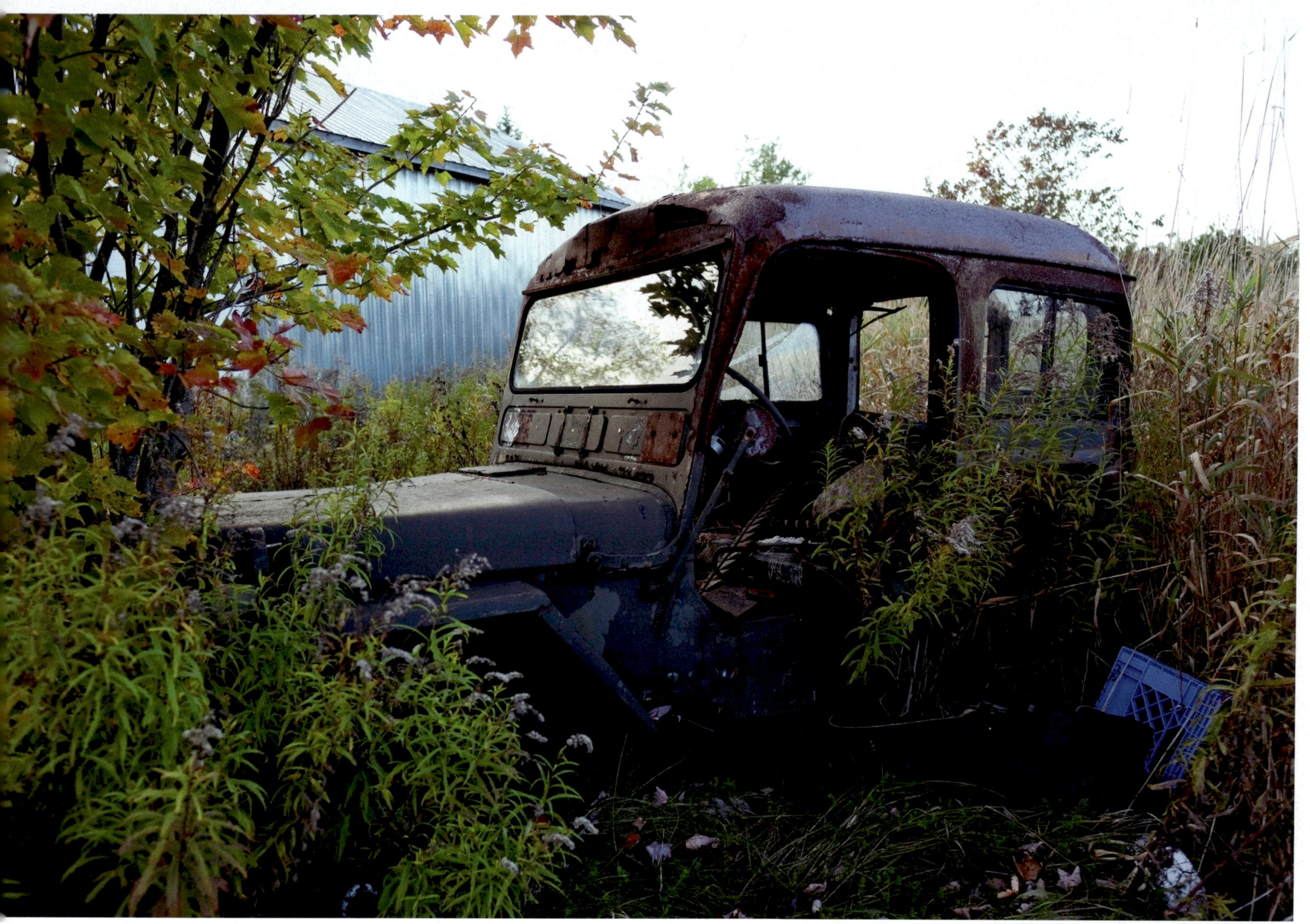

An abandoned vehicle sits in a field outside the town of Stellerton, Pictou County.

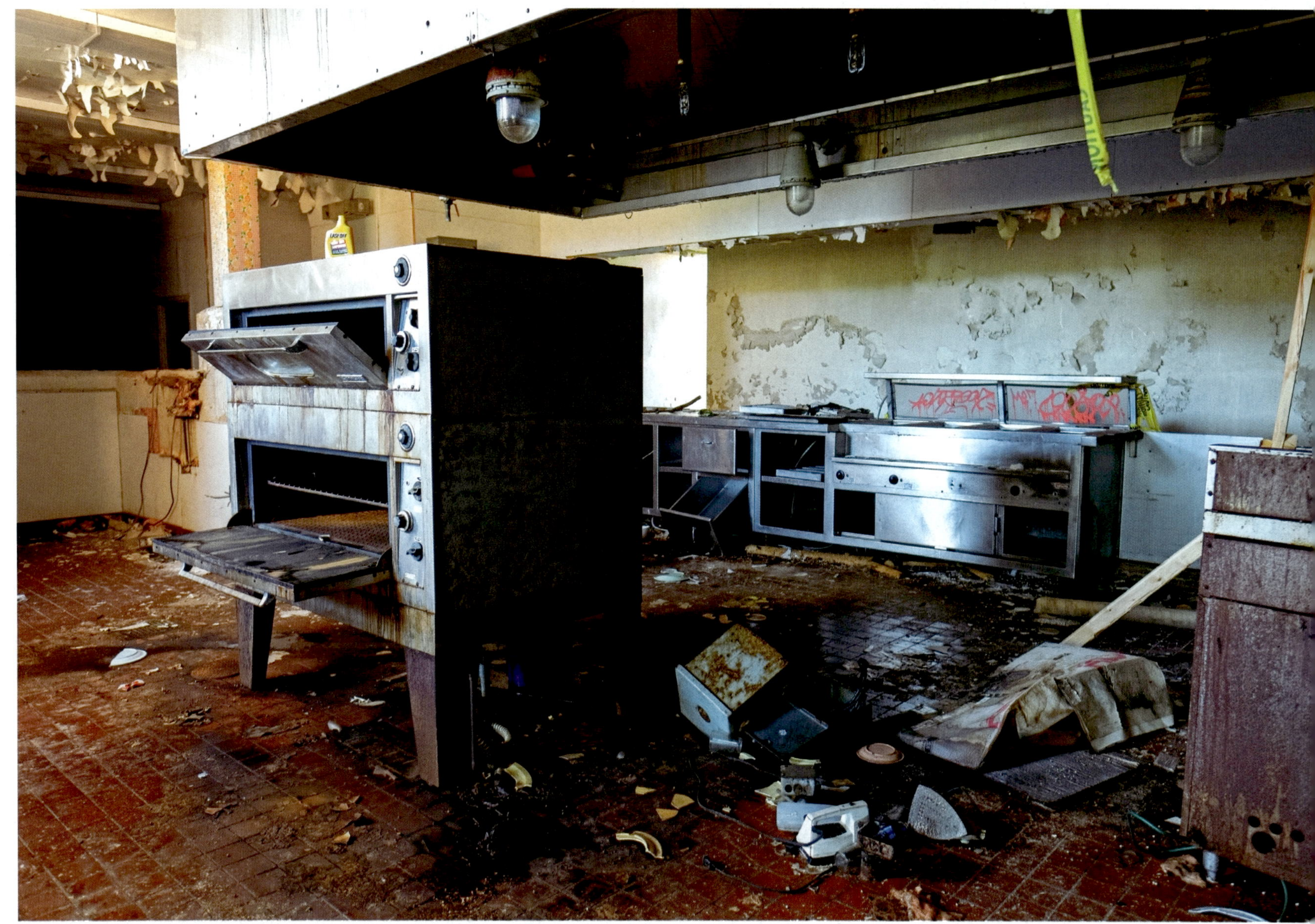

The kitchen area of the former Shelburne Youth Centre.

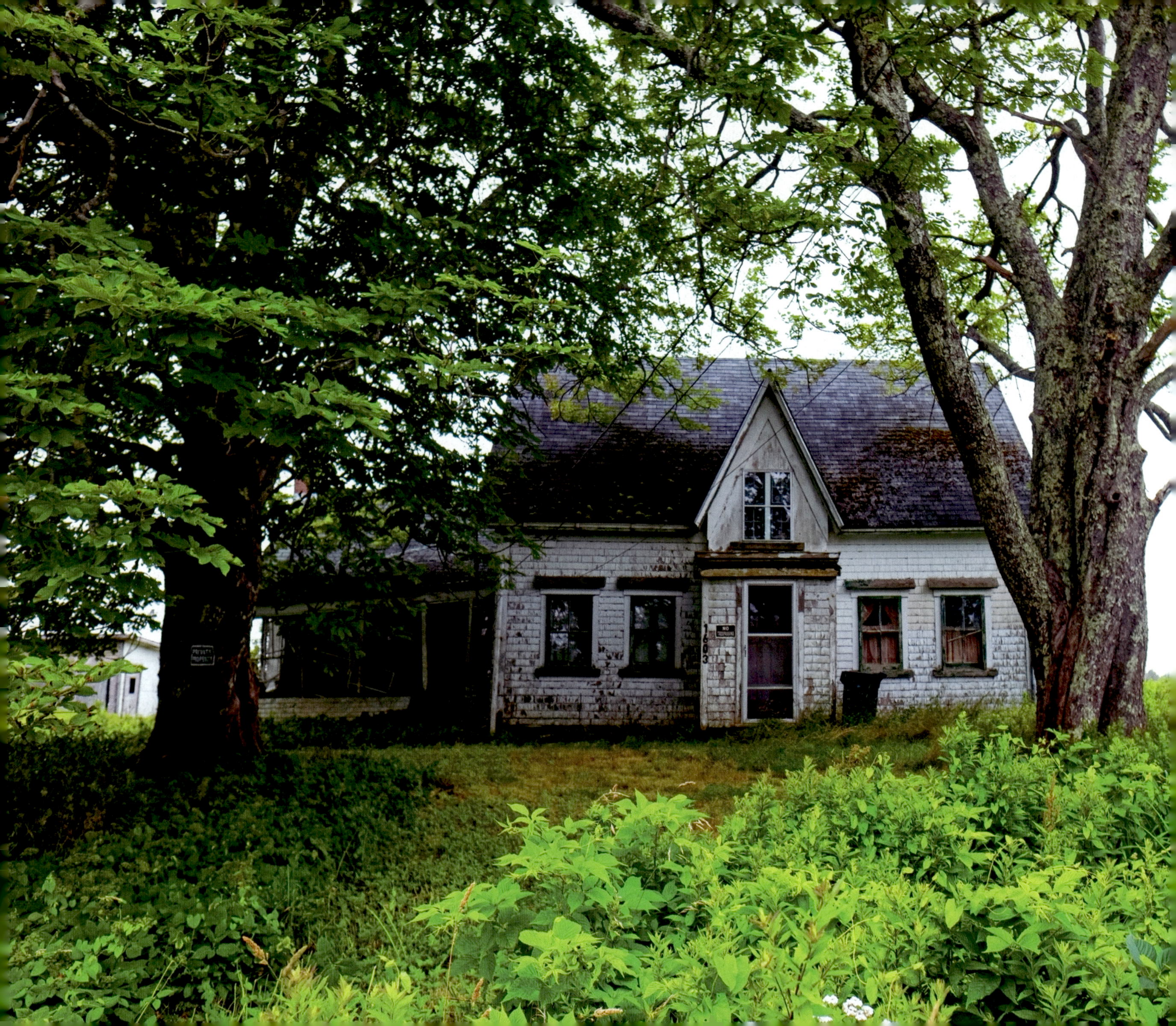
NO

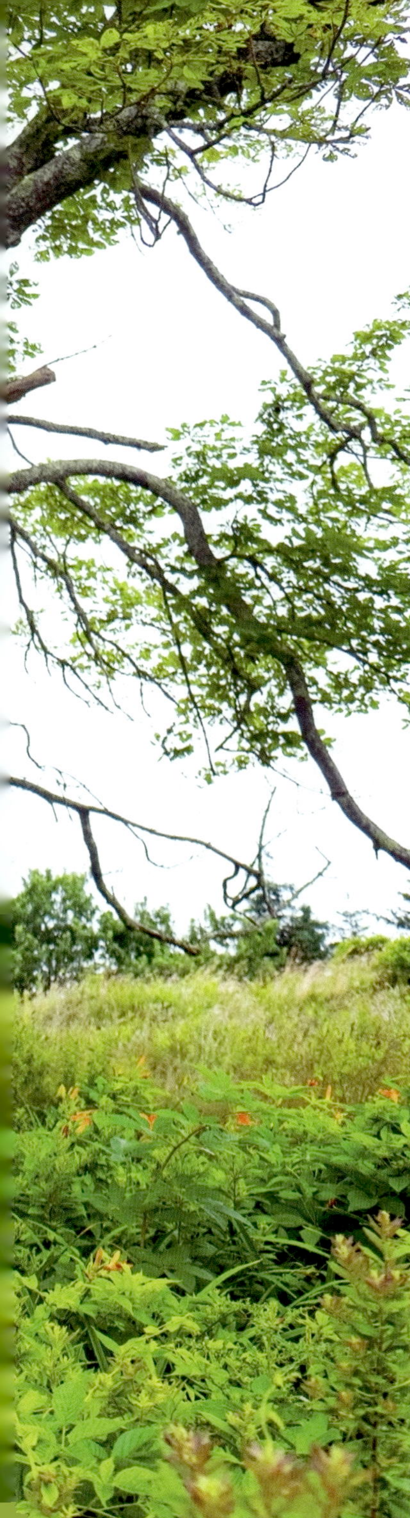

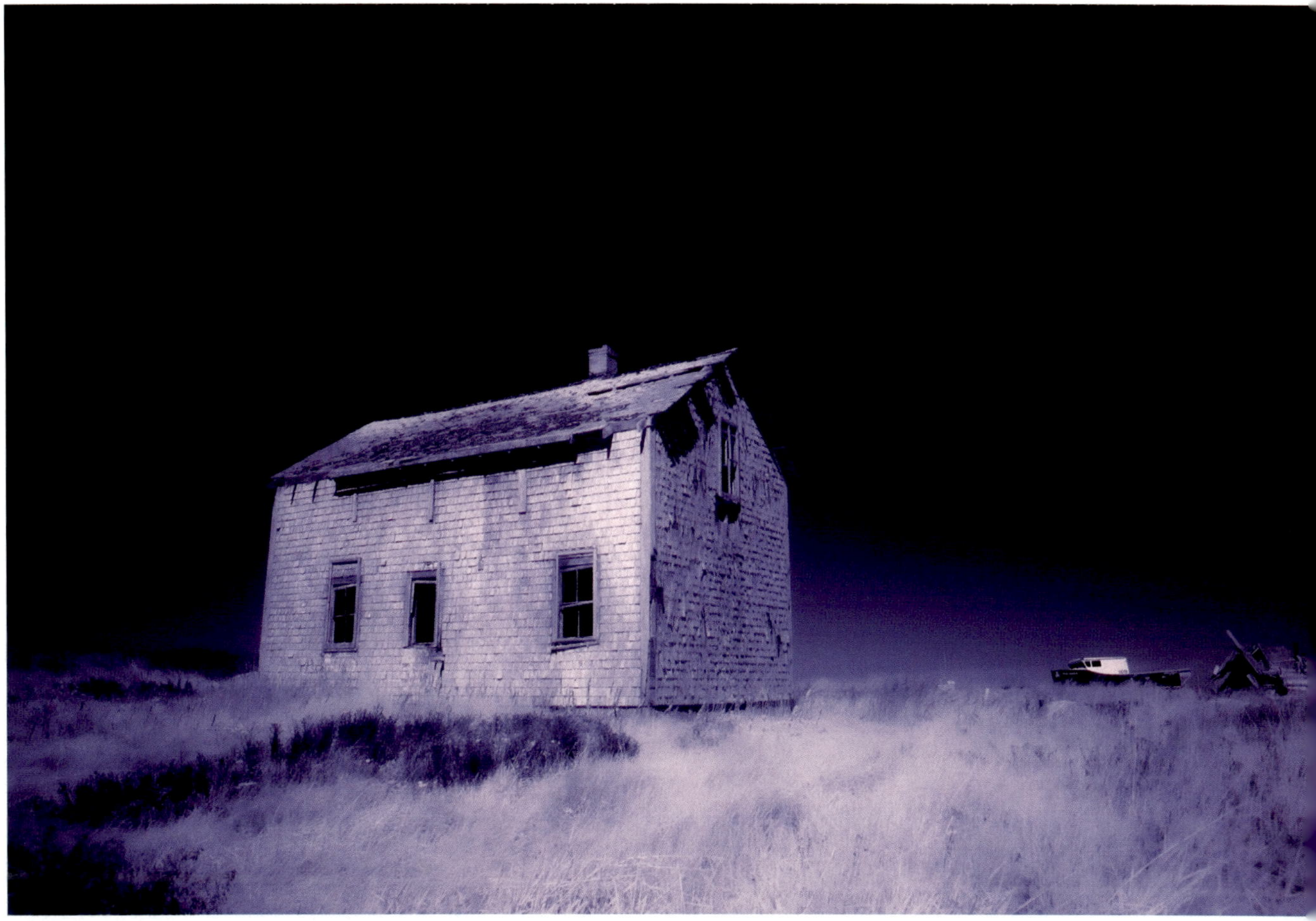

(Opposite) A Yarmouth County home near Wellington showing signs of neglect with the passage of time.

(Above) This weather-ravaged Flat Island home is on its last legs. After withstanding years of harsh storms and intense winds, it is only a matter of time before this structure too will fall.

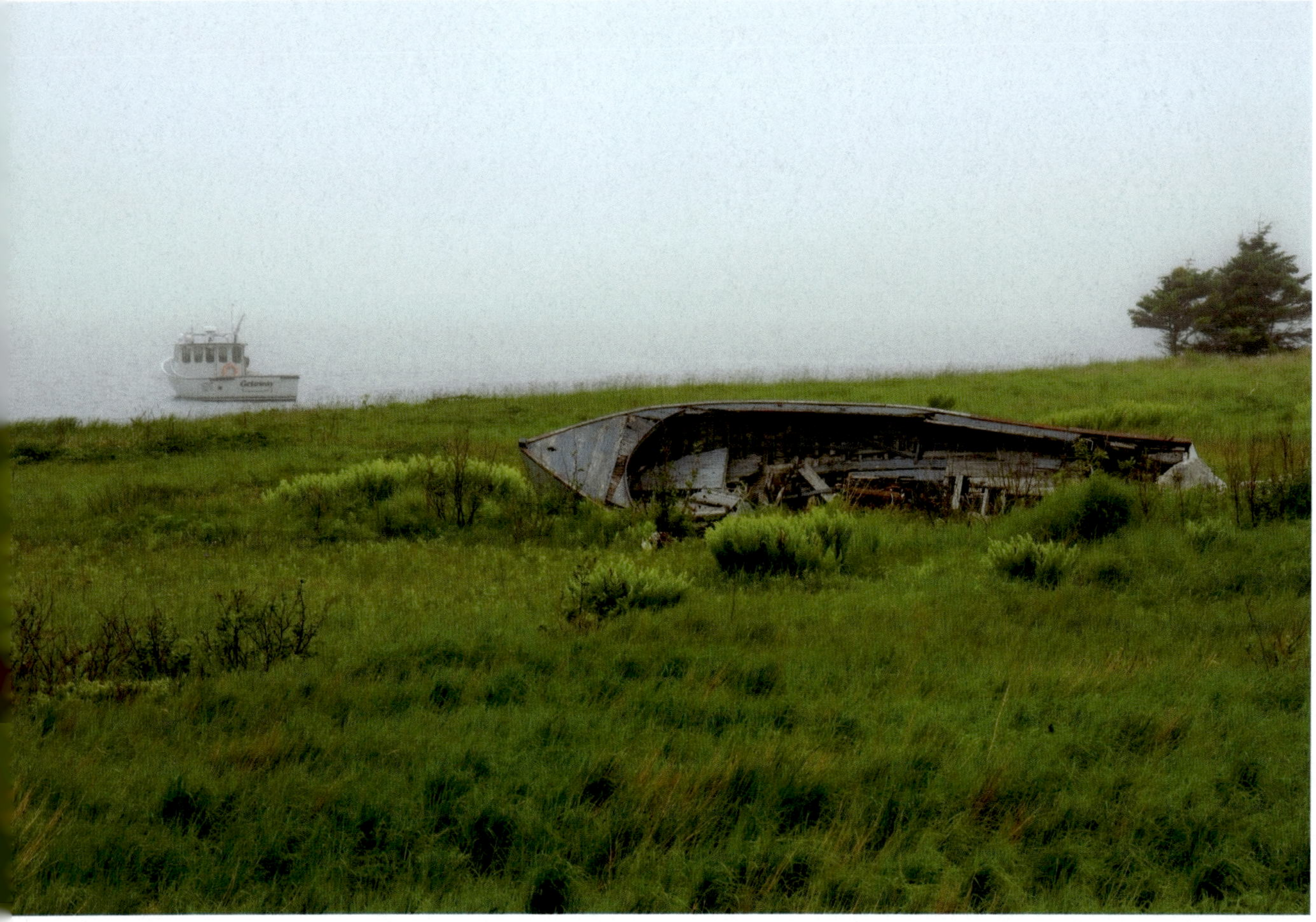

(Above) A small boat rests among grass and rocks near Port Felix. The main industry for the area since about 1797 was fishing, since the land was not fertile enough to accommodate farming.

(Opposite) In Guysborough County, a house appears to spill out onto the rocks near the shore in an area close to Port Felix. Early Acadian settlers named the community Molasses Harbour until about 1869 because a keg of molasses washed up on shore.

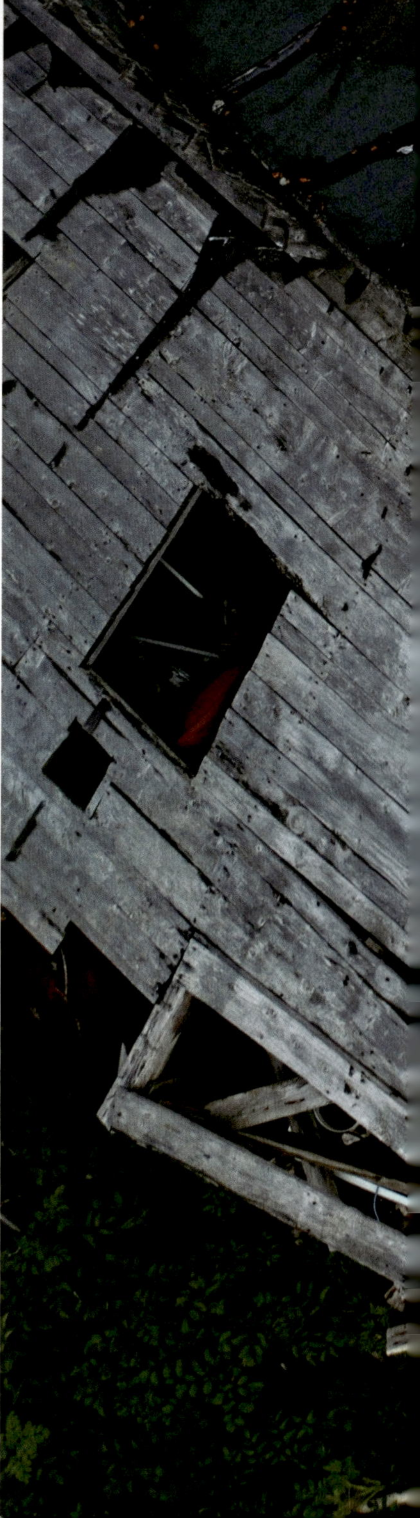

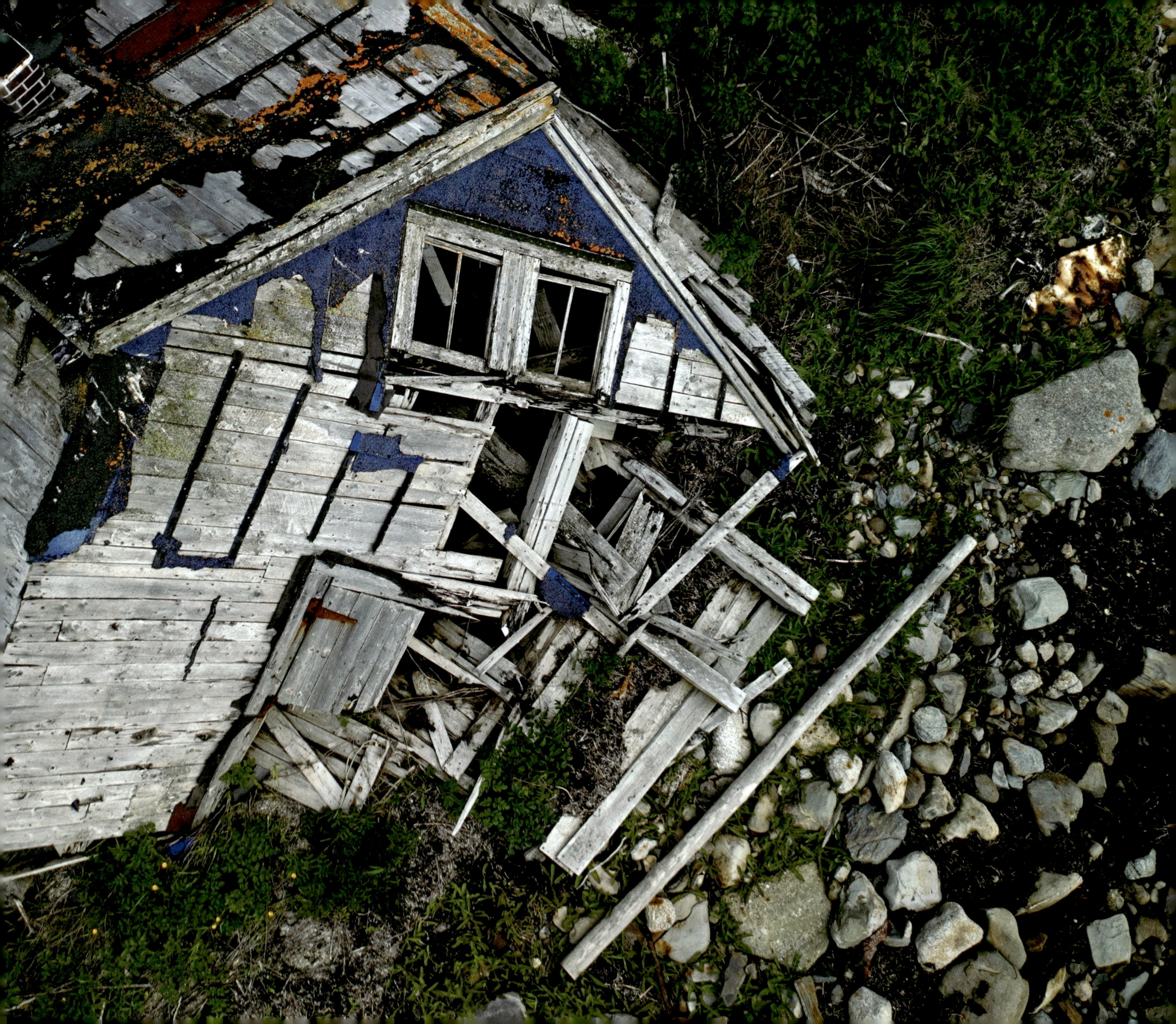

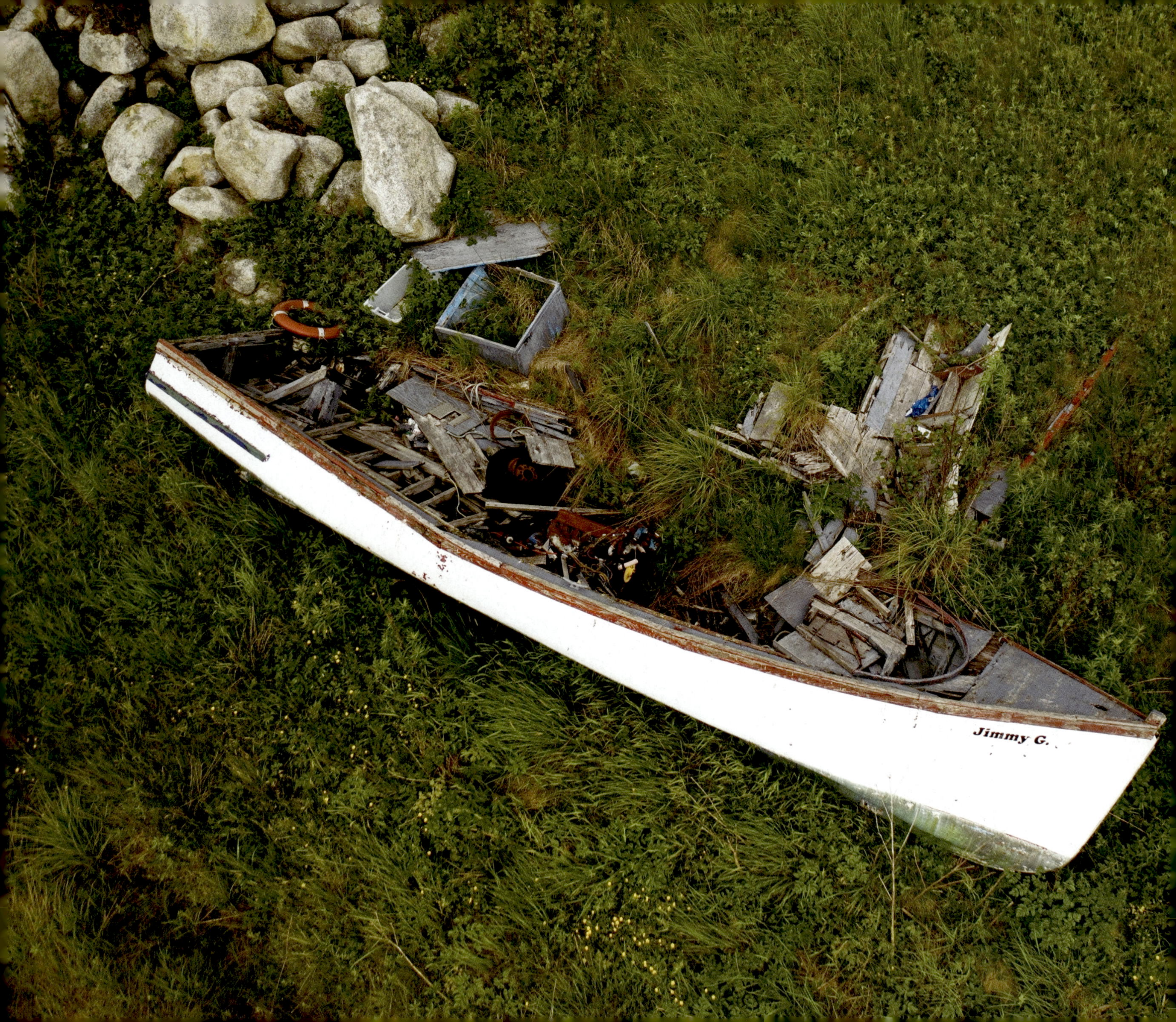
Jimmy G.

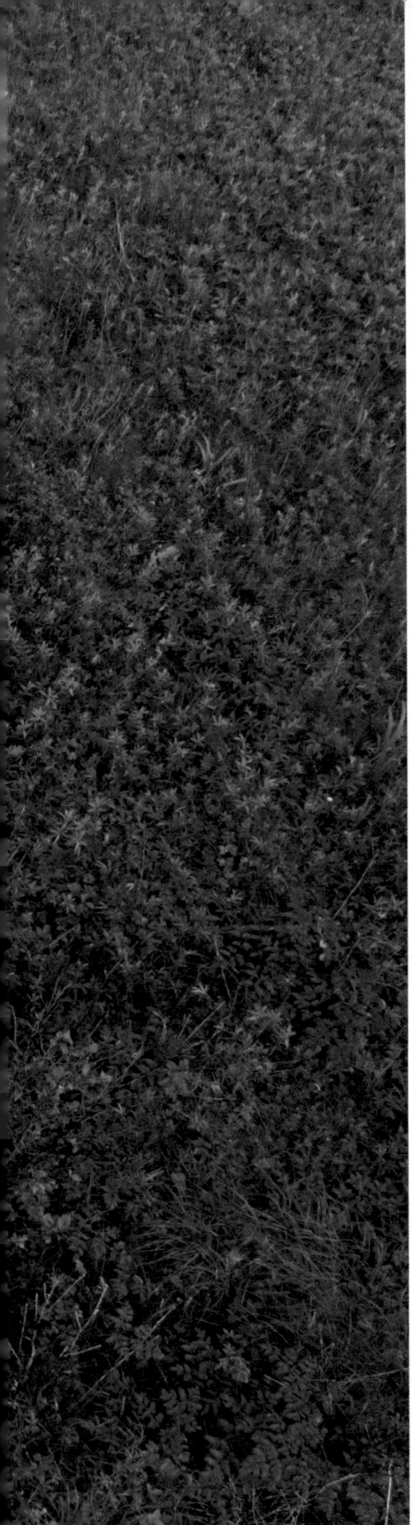

Ah, the smell of salt and sand. There is no elixir on this blessed earth like it.

— Joel Annesley, author

(Opposite) The hull of the *Jimmy G* lies grounded and exposed to the elements on the shores of Port Felix in Guysborough County.

Acknowledgements

We would like to thank MacIntyre Purcell Publishing Inc. for giving us the exciting opportunity to explore this rich subject matter with a great deal of personal and professional latitude. Special thanks to Vernon Oickle, Denis Cunningham, Rick Conrad, and the entire MacIntyre Purcell team for all the hard work in making *Forgotten Nova Scotia* come to life.

Ingrid Bulmer:

I would like to give special thanks to my wonderful parents, Jim and Inge, and sisters Sandra and Karen. Their support through the years for my photography, from constructive criticism to unequivocal approval, has been invaluable. Intentionally or intuitively, they consistently pushed me to try harder, and accept that some things in life are beyond our control but that we must never stop dreaming.

I extend gratitude beyond measure to Ted Pritchard as a partner on this book and as a special brother-in-law who made this project a fun adventure. Ted is not only an exceptional photographer but he was the main navigator of this team. Without Ted, I would probably still be trying to find my way out of some of the areas we explored.

I truly want to thank my son Axel. He was not always enthused about tagging along on the long road trips to look for abandoned places, but having overcome initial inhibitions he always enjoyed the ride and was happy to be part of this experience.

I would finally like to thank Frank Campbell for always being there for me and helping me better myself. He is a true friend whom I sincerely respect and appreciate.

Ted Pritchard:

I would like to express thanks and gratitude to my parents, Jack and Elaine, and sisters, Heather and Susan. My family has always been a great source of support and inspiration throughout my career, always teaching me to do what you love and to love what you do.

I would especially like to thank my book partner and sister-in-law, Ingrid Bulmer, who is a gifted and talented photographer. Working alongside her while co-creating *Forgotten Nova Scotia* has been a rewarding and fun adventure.

I would also like to say a special thanks to Paul Darrow. Bucky, you took a chance on me and introduced me to the world of photojournalism, and I will be forever grateful.